English Around the World

The global spread of English has had widespread linguistic, social, and cultural implications, affecting the lives of millions of people around the world. This textbook provides a lively and accessible introduction to world Englishes, describing varieties used in countries as broad-ranging as America, Jamaica, Australia, Africa, and Asia, and setting them within their historical and social contexts. Students are guided through the material with chapter previews and summaries, maps, timelines, lists of key terms, discussion questions and exercises, and a comprehensive glossary, helping them to understand, analyze, and compare different varieties of English, and apply descriptive terminology. The book is accompanied by a useful website, containing textual and audio examples of the varieties introduced in the text, and links to related sources of interest. Providing essential knowledge and skills for those embarking on the study of world Englishes, this is set to become the leading introduction to the subject.

EDGAR W. SCHNEIDER is Full Professor and Chair of English Linguistics in the Department of English and American Studies, and Dean of the Faculty for Linguistics, Literature and Cultural Studies, at the University of Regensburg, Germany.

Cambridge Introductions to the English Language

Cambridge Introductions to the English Language is a series of accessible undergraduate textbooks on the key topics encountered in the study of the English language. Tailored to suit the needs of individual taught course modules, each book is written by an author with extensive experience of teaching the topic to undergraduates. The books assume no prior subject knowledge, and present the basic facts in a clear and straightforward manner, making them ideal for beginners. They are designed to be maximally reader-friendly, with chapter summaries, glossaries, and suggestions for further reading. Extensive exercises and discussion questions are included, encouraging students to consolidate and develop their learning, and providing essential homework material. A website accompanies each book, featuring solutions to the exercises and useful additional resources. Set to become the leading introductions to the field, books in this series provide the essential knowledge and skills for those embarking on English Language Studies.

Books in the series

The Sound Structure of English Chris McCully

Old English Jeremy J. Smith

English Around the World Edgar W. Schneider

English Around the World

An Introduction

Edgar W. Schneider

CAMBRIDGE UNIVERSITY PRESS
Cambridge, New York, Melbourne, Madrid, Cape Town, Singapore,
São Paulo, Delhi, Mexico City

Cambridge University Press
The Edinburgh Building, Cambridge CB2 8RU, UK

Published in the United States of America by Cambridge University Press, New York

www.cambridge.org
Information on this title: www.cambridge.org/9780521716581

First published 2011
3rd printing 2012

Printed in the United Kingdom at the University Press, Cambridge

A catalogue record for this publication is available from the British Library

ISBN 978-0-521-88846-2 Hardback
ISBN 978-0-521-71658-1 Paperback

Additional resources for this publication at www.cambridge.org/schneider

Contents

Figures

Maps

Tables

Texts and audio samples

* ⬛ = audio file available on accompanying website

Acknowledgments

I am grateful to the following friends, colleagues, and institutions for providing me with texts and speech samples, for giving me permission to reproduce and use them in the book and on the accompanying website, or for answering questions of mine on them (in the order of apperarance of the samples in the book): Kevin Wilde (www.yorkshire-dialect.org) for permission to reproduce "T'Barber's Tale" from www.yorkshire-dialect.org/authors/dennis_rhodes_t_z.htm#T%E2%80%99Barber%E2%80%99s_Tale; Mrs. Wilann Powers (Lindale, GA) for permission to reproduce a selection from *Speakin' Suthern Like It Should Be Spoke*; Grove/Atlantic, Inc. for permission to use a selection from Michael Thelwell, *The Harder They Come* (copyright © 1980 Michael Thelwell); Allan Bell (Auckland) for improvements to the transcript of Australian English; Lucia Siebers (Regensburg) for two samples of South African Black English; Alfred Buregeya and Cedric Anjiji Voywa for providing Sheng and Engsh sample sentences; Dagmar Deuber (Freiburg) for permission to reproduce Nigerian Pidgin selections from Deuber (2005); Sebastian Hoffmann (Trier) and the anonymous author for permission to use the mixed-language letter from Malaysia; Azirah Hashim for advice on the Malaysian English samples; Lisa Lim for providing a sample from the Grammar of Spoken Singaporean English Corpus (GSSEC) and permission to use it; Peter Mühlhäusler for providing a Tok Pisin sample.

Thanks are also due to the following institutions for permission to reproduce graphs, tables, maps, and illustrations from previously published sources: Cambridge University Press for permission to reproduce the map "The division of the anglophone world by hemisphere," from Hickey (2004: 628, Map A3.2); the graph "Sources and processes leading to PCEs" from Schneider (2007a: 100); the table "The evolutionary cycle of New Englishes" from Schneider (2007a: 56); and the diagram "Kachru's Three Circles model," from Crystal (2003: 61); Pearson Education for permission to reproduce three selections from Schmied (1991), namely the map "The position of English in African nation-states," p. 44; selections from the table "Domains of English in East African states," p. 41; and the graph "Flow diagram of phases and factors in language policy," p. 188; Douglas Simonson and Bess Press, Inc., for permission to reproduce an entry from *Pidgin to da Max* (Simonson 1981); The Gleaner

Company Ltd., Kingston, for permission to reproduce a cartoon from the *Daily Gleaner*; Peter Trudgill and Wiley-Blackwell for permission to reproduce the maps "Traditional Dialects" and "Modern Dialects" and a sample sentence in various dialects from Trudgill (1990: 33, 63, 65–66); Taylor & Francis Books (UK) and Clive Upton for permission to use map "Ph50 butter" from the *Linguistic Atlas of England*; and John Benjamins Publishing Company, Amsterdam/Philadelphia (www.benjamins.com), for permission to reproduce a diagram from Mehrotra (1998: 115).

Every effort has been made to secure necessary permissions to reproduce copyright material in this work, though in some cases it has proved impossible to trace or contact copyright holders. If any omissions are brought to our notice, we will be happy to include appropriate acknowledgments on reprinting, or in any subsequent edition.

A big thank-you also goes to the people at Cambridge: above all, to Helen Barton for inspiring and continuously supporting this project; to Raihanah Begum from the textbook development department for advice; to the production editor, Christina Sarigiannidou; the cartographer, David Cox; and to the copy editor, Penny Wheeler.

Finally, there are so many who stand behind it all in many ways: friends and colleagues around the world who have told me about their countries and their areas of expertise (many of them at IAWE); institutions and universities which have invited me to all kinds of places or supported my travel experiences; students, colleagues, and team members at my home university; my friends who sing, play music, and jog, and do other pleasant things, with me; and, above all, my family. *Mahalo*!

A note on using this book

You are about to read and perhaps work with a book on the global spread of English. This is a topic with a number of different and interesting facets:

- the **reasons** why this has happened;
- the **processes** by which it has come about;
- the **results**, in terms of where around the globe you find English nowadays, and in which forms, with which functions;
- the **properties** which these forms of English have, as something like new dialects of the language; and
- the **consequences** of this process – what people think about these so-called "New Englishes" in many countries, how their presence affects their lives, how policy-makers have reacted and attempted to influence this process, and so on.

Personally, I find this a fascinating topic. It is a process which has come to be incredibly vibrant for the last few decades in particular, and it has transformed, or at least affected, many cultures and countries and the lives of many individuals all around the world, for better or for worse. And I hope I'll be able to share some of this excitement with you.

This **preface** is meant to highlight some of the specific features of this book, especially as a textbook – the features which I have consistently used to give you easier, and a more hands-on, access to the topic. Identifying these features beforehand should help you to use the book more effectively, and possibly to select those components which suit your needs and interests best. Take it as something like an instruction manual – I know many people avoid reading them, but using a gadget, or a book in this case, is easier and more effective if you do. And I promise it's short and not complicated.

Who is this book meant for? Well, it's not really restricted, but there is a most likely **target audience**. I suppose most of you reading this will be students, primarily but not exclusively undergraduates, and you may be enrolled in a class on "World Englishes," "Varieties of English," or such like. That's fine, and the exciting thing for me, writing this, is you are really likely to be sitting almost anywhere in this world, given the publisher's global outreach. (Drop me a line if you feel like it – I'd certainly be interested in learning who I can reach with this text.) It probably also means that your class is run and organized by a competent academic teacher who may give you further instructions, select materials, work with exercises or features of this text or the accompanying website, and so on – at this point I'll step back and leave you in the hands of your mentor.

The book is divided into nine **chapters**. Each of them covers a specific topic and is thus designed to serve as basic reading for one course **module** or course session. In fact, some chapters, notably the regional and the bigger ones (Chapters 4–8 in particular, I'd say) might actually be split up between several sessions, depending on how deeply your instructor and you wish to go into details, to look at individual samples, to work out the exercises, and so on.

Note, however, that none of the above applications are mandatory. I hope that the text as such is accessible and attractive to "the interested **lay reader**" outside of a class or even university context as well. It is certainly also possible to just read it cover-to-cover, or to pick select chapters in which for whatever reason you are particularly interested. There is no reason why you should not read this as a **standalone** text and work through all of this material on your own. I have done my best not to make it too technical (even if one purpose clearly is also to teach you some linguistic terms and concepts in passing).

The **contents** of this book, and its individual chapters, will be detailed further in the first chapter, the Introduction, but for a start, you should be prepared to deal with the following topics and components:

History, culture, society, in specific countries, regions, or continents: obviously, this constitutes the backbone and the necessary background of all the following discussions. Naturally, even if this is a book about varieties of English, language always and only works in social contexts, has been forged by them, and can be explained only in that perspective.

Linguistics: yes, sure – that's the discipline which describes and studies how language works, so we will need some of the terms and notions which linguists have developed for that purpose. I am not presupposing any substantial familiarity with linguistics and will do my best to introduce technical terms and concepts in an accessible fashion. I suppose you can sidestep this component if you are really not interested in it. But some technical knowledge and terminology simply gives you a much more solid grasp of the phenomena under discussion, and I suppose many of you will be expected to master some of this.

Text (audio) samples: I am convinced that talking about global forms of English makes sense and is fun only if you get some direct exposure to the object of discussion, i.e. to text and audio samples from the respective regions. In fact, this is one of the features that make this book quite different from many others on similar subjects, frequently with "World

Englishes" as part of their titles. Usually you get many general statements and a few short selected examples. Here I am providing authentic language samples representing a wide range of different regions, styles, and text types, to give you a hands-on feel for what we are talking about. Most of the samples you can also listen to – there are audio files (in mp3 format, mostly) of the texts transcribed in the book available on the website that accompanies it. And I am not only asking you to read or listen to these dialect samples – I will also be directing your attention to what is special about them, what to focus on in identifying regional characteristics. Each text is followed by extensive discussions of its noteworthy properties, usually looking at features of pronunciation, vocabulary, and grammar. Of course, this is also where some unavoidable linguistics sneaks in, because in these descriptive sections I will introduce and use some technical, descriptive terminology, customarily used in linguistic analyses. Don't worry if you do not understand each and every term. In the long run, however, such descriptions will build a network of connections, similarities between and comparisons with other texts. In principle, this is an open-ended activity – you can search and start analyzing further regional text samples, and some guidance to that is provided in some of the exercises at the end of each chapter.

A couple of **features** have been employed consistently to help you digest the material presented and to make this book more effective as a **textbook**. Features which you will find in each chapter include the following:

- a **chapter preview**, entitled "In this chapter ...," which is supposed to signpost the material coming up in the chapter, and thus to guide your attention;
- a listing of the chapter's **sections**, which structure the material by sub-topics;
- a **Chapter summary** which briefly revises what you have learned and puts things in perspective;
- an "**Exercises and activities**" section, meant to activate you – the best way of learning things! Some of the exercises are reflective in nature, asking you to think about or discuss some of the issues raised, and to bring in your own experiences and attitudes. Others are more practical and analytical, in several cases asking you to investigate further text samples, some of which are also provided on the website;
- "**Key terms** discussed in this chapter" at the end: the terms and notions which you should understand and be able to apply properly in your own discussions and analyses, especially if you are a language student;
- a "**Further reading**" section which guides you to additional sources on the chapter contents which I find recommendable, usually of an introductory or at least not overly technical nature, in case you are interested in pursuing this further.

In addition, some features are found in certain chapters only, depending on the nature of the material covered. In fact, you will find that there are essentially two slightly different **chapter types**:

- chapters focusing on general **subjects, concepts, and issues** (i.e., Chapters 2, 3, 7, and 8, in particular); and
- chapters focusing on **regions** and countries, and on their linguistic settings and regional varieties of English, respectively (i.e., Chapters 4–6).

Only the regional chapters provide you with materials which relate to specific areas, namely

- **maps** which, unless you know anyhow, show you the countries and locations under discussion, usually in a wider context;
- **timelines** which chronologically identify major events in the historical evolution of the region under discussion; and, of course,
- the **text samples** referred to above.

Finally, at the end of the book you'll find some sections which will also support your understanding of the text and your ability to access specific parts of it or to deepen your familiarity with the subject matter:

- an **appendix** which presents and illustrates the **phonological symbols** employed, for readers who have little or no familiarity with phonetic transcription;
- a second **appendix** summarizing guiding questions which can be asked on the status and properties of English in any region;
- a **glossary** which explains and illustrates technical terms in an understandable fashion (well, at least so I hope);
- the **references** list which provides the documentation which I owe to the colleagues and writers on whose work I have built, and which might guide you to further sources in case you are interested; and, finally,
- the **index** which should help you to spot pages where specific subjects are dealt with more extensively.

As has been implied above, however, that is not all. There is a website which accompanies this book; you find it at www.cambridge.org/edgarschneider. It provides

- the **audio files** for the text samples transcribed in the book, and further samples referred to in the exercises; and
- **links** to further interesting materials, especially other language-related websites.

So – (I hope you'll) enjoy!

CHAPTER 1

Introduction

In this chapter ...

This chapter introduces the topic of "World Englishes." It points out the present-day global spread of English and the variant roles of the language in different societies. It should also make you, the reader, aware of the fact that most likely you have already gained some familiarity with this fact. Nearly every speaker of English today has been exposed to different varieties of global English. For instance, in the media accents from all over the world are frequently heard – say, by watching an American sitcom, or by listening to an interview with an African politician. Many people have come across different varieties of English whilst travelling, or have met visitors from another country. By reading this book you will learn a lot more about where, when, why, and how such "new" forms of English have emerged.

It is not enough to remain on a purely theoretical level, however. Our topic comes alive only if we seek exposure to real-life language as produced in different regions, and so I suggest we begin by starting with a practical exercise right away. Just as an example of what we can look at and talk about when we encounter a slightly unfamiliar form of English, you will find a text reproduced, and I will comment on some of the properties of this speech form which I find noteworthy and illustrative. You can, and ought to, also listen to this sample by downloading it from the website which accompanies this book. I point out some of the features of this speech sample (i.e. words used, sounds employed, and constructions found in it), and comment on why these properties occur here, also considering the nature of the text itself. Linguists call this the "sociolinguistic conditions of text production." I hope to show that resulting from these conditions language use needs to be, and typically is, situationally appropriate. Thus, the individual forms used indirectly acquire something like a symbolic function.

Finally, a short preview of topics to be discussed in the book's chapters will give you a better idea of what to expect.

1.1 English, both globalizing and nativizing

Have you been abroad? Do you travel a lot? Then you know what I'm talking about. Wherever you go on this globe, you can get along with English. Either most people speak it anyhow, or there is at least somebody around who can communicate in this language. But then, you realize that mostly there's something you may find odd about the way English is used there. If you are abroad English is likely to be somewhat different from the way you speak it:

- people use strange **words**;
- it may take you a while to recognize familiar words because they are **pronounced** somehow differently; and
- sometimes people build their **sentences** in ways that will seem odd to you in the beginning.

Well, if you stay there, wherever that is, for a while, you'll get used to this. And if you stay there even longer, you may even pick up some of these features and begin to sound like the locals. What this example teaches us is: English is no longer just "one language"; it comes in many different shapes and sizes, as it were. It is quite different in the many countries and localities where it has been adopted. To grasp this phenomenon linguists have come to talk of different "Englishes."

No doubt English is truly the world's leading language today. It is used on all continents. In surprisingly many countries (more than 100, according to recent estimates) it has important internal functions as a "Second Language" in addition to one or more indigenous tongues, being used in politics, business, education, technology, the media, etc. It is almost always used as the mediator language (a so-called "lingua franca") by people who need to talk with each other but have different mother tongues, for instance, as suggested in Figure 1, in the classic shopping and bargaining encounters in tourism. All around the globe, English is learned by hundreds of millions of people in all countries simply because it is so useful. A recent estimate puts speaker numbers close to two billion (although this is extremely difficult to guess – it depends on how much you have to know to count as "a speaker"). One of the main reasons for all of this is that in many developing countries people from all walks of life perceive English as the primary gateway to better jobs and incomes, thus a better life. And the entire process has gained so much momentum that at the moment nothing seems to be able to stop it in the foreseeable future.

At the same time, however, English has become localized and indigenized in a great many different countries. It is not only viewed as a useful "international" language, as just described, but it fulfills important local functions. In doing so it has developed local forms and characteristics, so that not

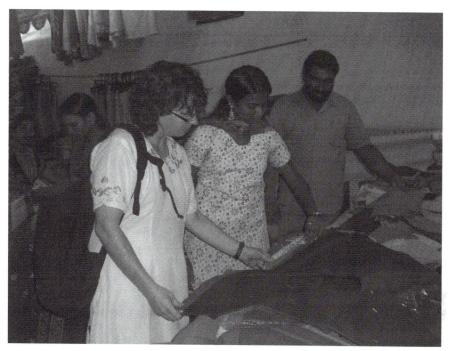

Figure 1 Shopping and bargaining with tourists – a classic situation which calls for English (here in India)

infrequently people enjoy using it in "their own" way. In many places local ways of speaking English have become a new home dialect which, like all local dialects, is used to express regional pride, a sense of belonging to a place which finds expression through local culture, including language forms. Furthermore, in many countries of Africa and Asia, where English was introduced just one or two centuries ago, there are now indigenous children who grow up speaking English as their first and/or most important, most frequently used, language. Some of them are not even able to speak the indigenous language of their parents and grandparents any longer. Come to think of it – isn't this an amazing phenomenon?

One really interesting aspect about all of this is that this indigenization and nativization process of English in many countries, frequently former colonies in the British Empire, is a product of the very recent past and not primarily of their colonial heritage of centuries ago. It is only for the last few decades, quite a while after independence in many cases, that English has made such inroads into local cultures. Again, this should come as a surprise to an outside observer. English was the language of the colonial power, the settlers and expatriate rulers, sometimes perceived as the oppressors. Once they were gone, wouldn't it have been natural for a newly independent country to breathe deeply and forget about the days of lack of freedom, to do away with all the colonial heritage, including their language? But interestingly enough, quite the contrary has happened. In many countries English has been embraced, appropriated, transformed, made "our own." And in fact, this issue of the "ownership" of English is very much a topic of current debate and has even hit headlines in international journalism. For example, on March 7, 2005, *Newsweek* had a cover page and story entitled "Who Owns English? Non-Native Speakers Are Transforming the Global Language." What has happened here?

This book describes this process of the global spread of English and its various facets, both from a general perspective (looking at sociohistorical circumstances, political issues involved, and linguists' explanations and categorizations) and in specific cases and regions. The core chapters (4–6) characterize the major world regions in terms of the reasons why English has been brought there, how and why it is used, and what its characteristic properties are. In each case, my strategy is that of "zooming in" from the general to the specific: I combine a general survey of characteristics of an entire region with a closer look at a case study from one select part of that region, allowing me to showcase a typical instantiation of English in use in a given context. Each case study will then include a model discussion of a select text from that locality. In fact, this text-centered, hands-on approach is one of the specific characteristics of this book as against others on the same subject, which may tell you something about English in specific regions as well, and may provide samples, but none will tell you exactly what to listen and pay attention to, which features characterize particular texts as samples of their respective varieties.

I assume no prior familiarity with any of these issues or regions, and very little, if any, with linguistics. Assuming that you, my readership, will comprise both some linguistics students and non-linguists just interested in this subject, I will employ a dual strategy. I offer some technical terms (which the linguists amongst you will know or may have to remember), but I will also do my best to introduce and explain them briefly. In case you find certain technical terms difficult, please have a look at the glossary, where you will find further definitions and explanations. The same applies to phonetic transcription, the conventional way of rendering pronunciation details on paper. Linguists employ some special symbols, "phonetic characters" as devised by the "International Phonetic Association," for that purpose. The ones I use are reproduced and briefly explained in Appendix 1. Many of you will be familiar with these IPA characters, and there is no other equally powerful and accurate way of providing information on pronunciation, so I will employ them too, using a broad phonological transcription set between slashes. In addition to that, however, I will do my best to indicate what you need to pay attention to, or what happens in articulating certain sounds, in non-technical terms as well.

If this sounds a little abstract and perhaps alien to you, different from your daily concerns and background – let me assure you it isn't, really. Whenever we communicate (and each of us talks much of the time), whenever we listen to somebody else talking, subconsciously this machinery works inside of us. We assess what we hear – not only the meaning, the message itself, but the way it is encoded. And the details of this encoding (one's "accent," for instance) actually signal quite a lot to us: who our interlocutor is in terms of background, status, age, etc., how friendly he or she wishes to be, what the situation is like, or what the hidden message is between the lines. I am not saying that we are all experts on global Englishes anyhow, and sure there may be hidden messages that we fail to understand, but yes, somehow we are all sociolinguists who constantly analyze how something is said, in addition to what is being stated. To each and every new communicative situation we are in we bring our accumulated, if incomplete, familiarity with different ways of talking, and our earlier exposure to all kinds of Englishes, local and global. And we not only listen explicitly but we also read between the lines, as it were. Frequently what we do as linguists (or students of linguistics) is no more than spelling out what on this basis somehow we "know" anyhow. Ultimately, however, this also means we need to develop methods, hypotheses, and "theories" to collect data objectively, to systematize our observations, to make our claims convincing to others (which is what we could call "proving our theory").

1.2 English, both global and local: a first example

That may sound grand, but I don't think it is; it begins with the very first steps. And to show you how this works, let us look at one sample text and see what, apart from the contents itself, it contains in terms of interesting, perhaps suggestive, indicative linguistic features as to its origins and implications.

Please read Text 1, "Knowledge," and, if you can, listen to it on the website accompanying this book. I have deliberately selected a sample which is not explicitly localized in its contents. There are no loan words from any indigenous languages and no local references (the text, you will find, is about the importance of acquiring knowledge). I will point out some properties which I find noteworthy, hoping you share that assessment. Of course, what you will hear and find interesting also depends on your individual background. But there are certainly a few observations which all of us will share and which, based upon your and my partial familiarity with other dialects of English (supported, possibly, by scholarly documentation in

TEXT 1: Knowledge

Okay. No, knowledge is not come from vacuum. You have to read, you have to meet with people, you have to have a discussion, and in fact, you have to appreciate the differences between your opinion and other opinion. Then, it start ... it create a thinking ... it create a thinking skill, it create ... it create ... something that will generate the ... the new things. Some people may be looking at how coconut falls from the tree. And when we ask them why coconut fall from a tree, maybe say, because it('s) is old enough and ripe enough and is fall. But if you ask a physicist, why falls ... why coconut fall from the tree, he will say, this is because due to gravity. So different person have different perception of falling object. Therefore, having a knowledge about falling object will create you some ideas how we can change, we can transform energy from one form to another form. Basically, knowledge is generator. So, if you want to build our nation, if we want to build ourself, if we want to improve ourself, there is no other thing other than knowledge. We have to ... we have ... we have to be very, very concerned about development and knowledge.

linguistics), can be stated objectively, independently of who we are. And this, after all, is the goal of linguistics, the scientific study of how language works.

The extralinguistic context is of course always important in the understanding of a speech selection, so I should state at the outset that this is a sample I recorded in the media, the concluding part of a TV speech, to be precise. Let us start with the obvious and move on to the more specific.

The speaker is a male adult, and clearly not a native speaker (he does not sound like someone from Britain, America, or the like). But we may assume he is educated – that is what the topic and the choice of words (formal and scientific vocabulary like *vacuum*, *physicist*, *gravity*, *perception*, or *transform*) imply. On the other hand, he hesitates repeatedly and sometimes struggles for words, coming up with a generic expression like *the new things*. Context and style are obviously formal, as suggested by the impersonal topic and the slow and careful mode of delivery, and of course also by what we know about the extralinguistic context.

What makes the speaker's pronunciation special, and how would we implicitly compare his accent to what we may know about other accents?

- Amongst his vowels, the most persistent phenomenon worth noting is that in words where British and American English (BrE, AmE) have a diphthong, a gliding movement from one tongue position to another as in *day* /eɪ/ or *show* /əʊ/, this speaker produces a monophthong, a pure

/e/ or /o/ sound (listen to the way he says *basically*, *nation*, *change*, or *no*). This is common if you know speakers from Scotland, the Caribbean, or many parts of Africa and Asia.

- In *gravity* he has a fairly open /a/, not an /æ/ where the tongue is more raised.

On a more general note, the speaker's accent, like standard BrE but unlike AmE, is "non-rhotic," i.e. he does not pronounce an /r/ after vowels, e.g. in *energy* or *form*. This is an indication that the sample may come from the domain of the former British Empire. Amongst consonants, the "th" sounds are largely as expected, though occasionally the friction that characterizes these sounds seems reduced down to a stop articulation /d-/ in *then*. The *p*'s in *people* sound very "weak," like /b/. The final fricatives in *ideas*, *improve*, and *knowledge* are articulated without voicing (vibration of the vocal cords in one's neck), as /-s/, /-f/, and /-ʃ/, respectively. What is more noteworthy is that final consonant clusters are consistently reduced. This means that whenever at the end of a word two consonants occur in a row, the second one is not realized at all. So in *fact*, *physicist*, *different*, or *object* the final -*t* is not there; in *build* or *concerned* -*d* is omitted, and the word *ask* is clearly articulated twice as *as'* without /k/. Speakers of British and American dialects do this as well in informal situations, but in language contact situations this reduction has been found to be especially widespread. Much less common globally, and an indicator of a possible Asian origin, is the omission of a single word-final consonant, to be found in this sample in *about*, pronounced without /-t/.

What gives this sample its distinctive sound most strongly, however, may be some rhythmic patterns which have to do with stress assignment.

- Certain words are stressed on unusual syllables, compared to more mainstream accents, and this also affects the respective vowels such that vowels which in standard English are an unstressed schwa /ə/ receive a full articulatory quality. Listen to *person*, stressed on the second syllable to yield /pə'sen/ (the apostrophe indicates stress on the following syllable), and to *transform* /'transfɔm/ and *concerned* /'kɔnsən/, with initial accents.
- Furthermore, in words like *different*, *physicist*, *perception*, *generate*, or *generator* the vowels in the unstressed syllables, which in ("stress-timed") BrE would probably disappear altogether or be strongly reduced, are articulated remarkably clearly and with some duration. This contributes to the impression of a "syllable-timed" accent (in which roughly each syllable takes equally long) which has been found to characterize many New Englishes.

The origin of the sample from one of these varieties can be deduced from many characteristic grammatical features as well. Note that in none of these observations I am passing any judgment on whether this is "right" or "wrong" – we will discuss such attitudes later, in Chapter 8; here we are just making and comparing some observations.

- In some cases there is a tendency to leave out grammatical endings, both on verbs (as in *it start* or *coconut fall*) and in nouns, when the plural is clearly contextually implied but not formally expressed by an *-s*, as in *other opinion, different person,* or *ourself.* Note that this is not as unusual as it may seem. In Norwich, England, the local dialect leaves out verbal *-s* frequently, and in America speakers may say something like *twenty-year-old* or *twenty mile away.*
- Article usage is variable sometimes, as it is known to be in some Asian (and other) varieties. We would expect an indefinite article *a* before *coconut*, introducing an object not mentioned so far in the discourse, and before *generator*, but on the other hand we might not say *a knowledge*, as this noun is commonly assumed to be "uncountable."
- Verbs also behave uniquely in some respects. The verb *create* allows a construction which it does not have in, say, BrE, namely complementation by an indirect object: *create you some ideas.*
- Questions do not require *do*-support or inversion in *why falls* and *why coconut fall.*
- Some constructions may be argued to increase the explicitness of marking and thus to contribute to securing the message. For example, in *because due to* the same idea is expressed twice in a row, as it were; and in *one form to another form* the noun is repeated where commonly the second occurrence might be left out.

Finally, note that some constructions cannot really be analyzed or explained, and possibly just understood, satisfactorily. Is the speaker saying *is … come*, and if so, why? Why *is fall*? Should *falling object* be understood as a plural without *-s* or as a singular lacking an indefinite article? Is the long /i/ audible in *maybe say* to be understood as a reduced *will*, which would make sense?

One's ability to precisely determine the local origin of this sample depends upon the individual backgrounds of us, the listeners, of course. All of us will know that this represents one of the New Englishes, and many will be able to trace it to Asia; and I suppose Asians will do better. On the other hand, if you happen to be from Malaysia I am sure you will not only recognize this as a voice from your home country but will also easily identify the speaker's ethnicity as Malay. In fact, closer familiarity with the cultural background helps to better contextualize the speaker's intentions. Muslims sometimes believe that a place in heaven is secured by performing praying rituals and religious duties only, and that the only knowledge required is that of Allah's word in the Quran. This speaker's statement is directed against such an opinion. He means to emphasize the importance of striving for worldly and scientific knowledge as well, also for the benefit of the process of nation building. In doing so he ties in with a call once made by the former Prime Minister Dr. Mahatir.

I hope you agree that this sample, even if it stems from a fairly formal context, actually tells us quite a lot about its origins and social embedding. Other samples would signal wildly different things to us and would display many other linguistic phenomena which, depending on our own individual linguistic backgrounds, we might think of as apparently odd – the more so the more we approach the informal end of linguistic production, the closer we get to "down-to-earth" speech forms. Some of this knowledge about speakers and varieties of English we possess intuitively, having accumulated it as competent speakers and through our own individual linguistic histories. Much more can be stated and taught, however. And all of this needs to be contextualized, to be connected with related knowledge about pertinent sociohistorical and political background information. Forms found in one particular text can be compared with properties and usage contexts of other varieties of English. And finally, all these observations need to be related to the issues and problems identified and the systematic frameworks and concepts developed by expert linguists.

1.3 Preview of the following chapters

The chapters of this book provide some of this factual background knowledge and will stimulate an increased awareness of problems, with the goal of enabling you to understand the globalization of English and to consciously interpret linguistic usage from all around the world in its proper contexts.

The following, second chapter spells out some fundamental observations which on second thoughts are likely to come quite naturally but which we have typically not been raised with when talking about language. Cases in point are the fact that all languages appear in different forms all the time; the fact that language contact and multilingualism are normal and not exceptional; and the fact that language largely depends upon external events and circumstances rather than being an independent entity in its own right. Furthermore, the chapter introduces models which have been proposed to categorize and conceptualize the varying types of global Englishes.

Chapter 3 lays the historical foundations. It discusses the history of European colonization, primarily with respect to the growth of the British Empire, and the more recent events that have promoted the further spread, modification, and predominance of English to the present day.

The next three chapters then look at the forms and functions of English in major world regions and individual countries.

Chapter 4 outlines its spread in what from the rest of the world is viewed as the "western culture," Europe and America. Ultimately, as elsewhere, even in the British Isles, English is the product of colonization and diffusion in contact with other languages, and it appears in a bewildering range of dialectal forms, as the case study of Northern English illustrates. From the "Old World" English was then transported to the "New World," North America, where it has been transformed in the conquest of a continent. At the same time, it has retained strong dialectal variants backed by regional pride and associated with a distinctive regional culture, as in the case of Southern English. In the Caribbean, exemplified by a closer look at Jamaica and Jamaican Creole, an agrarian plantation economy and the century-long mass importation of slaves from Africa have created uniquely blended languages and cultures.

It makes sense to distinguish northern from southern hemisphere colonies, settled in and after the seventeenth and the nineteenth centuries, respectively, and Map 1 illustrates this division. The Southern Hemisphere is the topic of Chapter 5, with closer attention paid to Australian English and Black South African English. Australia, New Zealand, and South Africa are products of later colonization. It will be shown that while different patterns of settlement

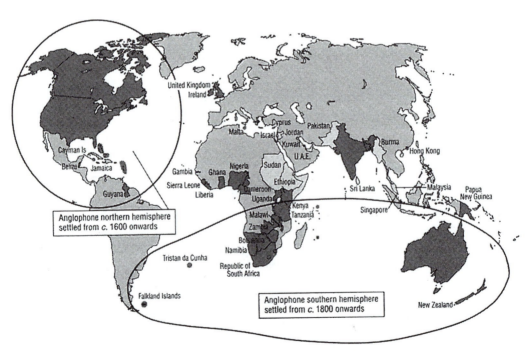

Map 1 The division of the anglophone world by hemisphere
(from Hickey 2004: 628; reproduced by permission)

and indigenous contacts have generated distinct societies and their own Englishes, similarities in the origins of the settler streams may explain some shared linguistic properties in these varieties.

Subsequently, Chapter 6 looks at the world regions and continents to which English has not been brought by large settler communities but by functional agents and where it has then been strongly adopted by indigenous populations as a second language: Sub-Saharan Africa, South and South-East Asia, and the Pacific region, respectively. In these regions, English is very important in the daily lives of large segments of indigenous populations. Case studies illustrate the language situations as well as the properties and uses of local adjustments of English in Nigeria, Singapore, and Papua New Guinea, respectively. Further, short text samples come from Kenya, Malaysia, and Vanuatu. The chapter concludes with a discussion of the spread of English as a foreign language in East Asia, notably in China – a process which may become extremely important for the future of the language.

Chapter 7 is intended primarily for those readers who are interested in understanding how language works. It asks for the linguistic processes which have produced these New Englishes, and surveys the structural outcomes of these processes (word, sound, and structure patterns) from a general perspective.

In contrast, Chapter 8 is concerned with the conflicting social evaluations of and reactions to the world's globalization under the banner of English, and a range of conflicting opinions and varying observations will be encountered. For example, the spread of English may have an elitist touch when the language is mainly diffused through the educational system and thus seems the property of affluent strata in a society, but it may also be the product of an almost uncontrolled spread "on the ground," by all kinds of speakers who just wish to use it somehow, under any circumstances. Some scholars have accused English of being a "killer language," while in fact the British colonial administrations had no intention of giving access to the language (and the power that came with it) to substantial proportions of indigenous populations. Related issues discussed in this chapter are

- the role of intelligibility and the putative emergence of an "International English,"
- the uses of localized language forms as symbols of indigenous identities,
- the ongoing growth of mixed language forms, signaling cultural hybridity,
- the discussions on which norms are to be accepted as correct in educational systems,
- the question of what (if anything) it means to be a "native speaker" under these circumstances, and

- how all of this translates into language policies and pedagogical strategies in the countries concerned.

The concluding chapter then evaluates this multi-faceted process, sometimes labeled the "glocalization" of English, and calls for linguistic tolerance (and social tolerance, for that matter).

Chapter summary

This chapter has argued that the global spread of English is a fascinating but also a complex process, with a number of possible, and sometimes conflicting, perspectives on and approaches to it. It has been argued that, based on their own linguistic backgrounds and more or less incidental cases of exposure to global varieties of English, proficient speakers of the language typically have intuitions on the sociosymbolic signaling functions of variant forms of English. Furthermore, I showed that a wide range of sociostylistic information can be culled from any individual text – as was illustrated in a discussion of a Malaysian speech on a scientific subject. Knowing more about these facts will enrich our ability to contextualize Englishes from all around the world – which is what this textbook sets out to do. In the next chapter, I'll start by introducing some basic concepts.

Exercises and activities

Exercise 1a   Sit back and relax for a moment, and consider your own background with respect to the situation discussed in this chapter. What kind of English is spoken in the area where you live? Do you think there is anything about this kind of English which speakers from other regions and countries would find peculiar, or difficult to understand?

Exercise 1b   Have you ever used English to communicate with somebody whose native language was not English? If so, did you find that useful, or difficult? Why?

Exercise 1c   Where have you traveled to? If you have been abroad, did you find English playing a special role in any of the countries you've been to? If so, for which purposes was it used? Was there anything that you found difficult to understand?

Exercise 1d   I am sure you can think of any public figure (say, a politician, an artist, or a sportsperson) who you heard speaking English on the media (in a speech or an interview) with an accent that you found different from yours. Try to remember, and possibly imitate, that person's usage. Work out for yourself which words, sounds, or possibly constructions in that person's speech you found noteworthy.

Key terms discussed in this chapter
consonant cluster
consonant cluster reduction
diphthong
Englishes
grammatical suffixes (endings)
international language
lingua franca
nativization
ownership of English
rhotic
second language
transcription
voicing
World Englishes

Further reading
The estimate that there are currently nearly two billion speakers of English can be found in Crystal (2008). Crystal (2003) is a light and easily readable discussion of the sociopolitical phenomena associated with the globalization of English. Other recommendable surveys of the subject include McArthur (1998, 2002), Melchers and Shaw (2003), and, with a special eye to teaching applications, Kirkpatrick (2007).

CHAPTER 2

Basic notions

In this chapter . . .

In this chapter we will have a closer look at a number of fundamental notions which will help us to understand how the varieties of English which have grown around the globe can be understood and conceptualized. This begins with challenging very deeply rooted ideas about the prevalence of "standard languages": I argue that it is more appropriate to think of "varieties" of a language, or "dialects" (of which a standard language is just one type), as systematic, communicatively effective entities with characteristic properties on various levels of language organization (sounds, words, grammatical rules). It is equally important to understand that languages are neither stable nor secluded – they always change in the course of time, and especially in the modern world they are continuously getting in contact with and influencing each other (so that, for instance, words of one language are picked up and used in another).

As the product of migration, variability, and borrowing, different kinds of English have emerged in different locations around the world. We will get to know some suggestions on how to get order into this bewildering range of dialects, on how to categorize varieties of English into different types, partly on the basis of how they have originated and how they are employed in a given society. In fact, it will be shown that what happens to a language in the course of time is not exclusively a linguistic process but that the social setting of language use is absolutely decisive for the properties which a language variety has. The evolution of a language depends very strongly upon external factors, the fates of its speakers.

2.1 **Language variation**

From their school days most speakers of English retain a rather monolithic concept of what English is. We are taught that there is a "proper English" or "Standard English" which is correct, "good," and more or less fixed, somewhat like mathematics. A grammar book informs us on how to build its sentences, and we look up the words of the language in a dictionary. These books, and our teachers, tell us what is "right" in language matters, and what we should strive for, and everything else, including, we suspect, some of our own performance, is somehow "wrong," deviant.

However, from the perspective of how language really works such a mindset is erroneous – as we may have suspected when we observe what people really do with language. People just talk differently, depending on who they are, where they come from, perhaps whether they are educated or not, and probably even how they feel in a given situation (whether they are at ease or wish to impress somebody). And despite these differences we usually understand each other well enough (and if not we can ask back). Speakers adjust their behavior to the needs of the situation, and manipulate it with considerable skill. What counts is only that the speaker and the hearer share knowledge, subconsciously, on how the message intended was encoded and is to be decoded. All speakers of English probably know what is referred to when somebody talks of a *dog*, an *island*, or a *thunderstorm* (i.e., utters the sounds /dɒg/, etc.). On the other hand, when somebody talks of a *stubby* or a *shivaree* British people might not know what these words (or merely sounds, actually, when they don't mean anything to you) refer to. Of course, fellow Australians or Southerners from the US will perfectly well understand and handle these words, which are just theirs (referring to a 'small beer bottle' and a 'noisy nightly wedding celebration', respectively, in case you are interested). Similarly, if the word *glass* is pronounced with a long /a:/ as in *father*, a short /a/, or the raised /æ/ vowel of words like *cat*, speakers from southern England, northern England, or the US, respectively, will just simply understand (because these pronunciations reflect their own pronunciation habits), while hearers from elsewhere may be facing difficulties. The same applies to syntactic constructions, as when in the midwestern US *a baby needs cuddled* or in Singapore *John kena scold*. There are equivalent ways of saying the same thing, and none of them is inherently superior to or worse than any other. It's just that they work for those who share the same speech habits or internalized knowledge, and they may cause difficulty to outsiders of a speech community. Speaking the same dialect means using the same coding system about how to get one's thoughts and meanings mapped onto sounds, and that needs to be done in a systematic, regular, predictable fashion shared by all other speakers of the same dialect – otherwise communication wouldn't work. And, as was illustrated above, this is a group-specific thing. There are words, pronunciation modes and structures which are known more or less exclusively to Yorkshiremen, African Americans, New Zealanders, Malaysian students, Igbo Nigerians, Indo-Trinidadians, and so on. Linguists nowadays emphasize the fact that **languages vary**, and they do so systematically, correlating with so-called "**sociolinguistic parameters**" like a speaker's regional origin, gender, age, or status, or the context of situation.

The neutral term that has come to be used normally for such group-specific language forms is "a **variety**." Any set of language habits that is shared by a certain group of speakers for use in certain contexts constitutes such a variety. The term is closely related to that of a "**dialect**," which also denotes a language form associated with a certain group of people but is usually associated with a given region (hence a "regional dialect") or a social class or group (a "social dialect"). Similarly, "**register**" refers to stylistically defined language varieties associated with certain channels (such as spoken or written) or situational contexts (e.g. letter writing, texting, or giving a political speech). The notion of "**accent**" relates to pronunciation only, but otherwise conforms largely to the reference of "dialect" – we can talk of a Welsh, Indian, or Otago accent (or dialect).

Finally, note that the above definitions also cover the language forms usually labeled "**standard**." "Standard British English," for instance, also describes a certain speech form shared by certain speakers for use in certain situations – probably educated ones from anywhere in the British Isles performing in formal or public contexts in this case. As a communicative system, however, standard English is not inherently superior to or "better" than any regional dialect. It just happens to be associated with situations and speakers more laden with official and public prestige. However, using a posh RP accent would be equally out of place and largely (certainly socially) ineffective in a Glaswegian pub or in a hospital in Kampala as would be speaking with a strong Scottish working-class accent in a London business meeting. In communication matters it is linguistic and situational appropriateness that counts, not some supposedly inherent notion of "correctness."

Dialect differences, and accent differences in particular, tend to be finely graded, and it's usually not any individual form but the overall composition of sets of variants which identifies any particular region. Table 1 provides a very nice example: Peter Trudgill's rendition (in conventional orthography) of the pronunciation characteristics of the main English dialect regions as applied to a single sample sentence. British people will probably feel tempted to compare their own speech habits to the data summarized here. Others may

Table 1 *Sixteen regional English dialect variants of the same sentence*

Regions	Sample sentence
Standard English	***Very few cars made it up the long hill***
North	
Northeast & Lower North	
Northeast	*Veree few cahs mehd it oop the long ill*
Central North	*Veri few cahs mehd it oop the long ill*
Central Lancashire	*Veri few carrs mehd it oop the longg ill*
Humberside	*Veree few cahs mehd it oop the long ill*
West & East Central	
Merseyside	*Veree few cahs mayd it oop the longg ill*
Northwest Midlands	*Veri few cahs mayd it oop the longg ill*
West Midlands	*Veree few cahs mayd it oop the longg ill*
Central Midlands	*Veri few cahs mayd it oop the long ill*
Northeast Midlands	*Veree few cahs mayd it oop the long ill*
East Midlands	*Veree foo cahs mayd it oop the long ill*
South	
Southwest	
Upper Southwest	*Veree few carrs mayd it up the long ill*
Central Southwest	*Veree few carrs mayd it up the long iooll*
Lower Southwest	*Veree few carrs mehd it up the long ill*
East	
South Midlands	*Veree foo cahs mayd it up the long iooll*
East Anglia	*Veree foo cahs mayd it up the long (h)ill*
Home Counties	*Veree few cahs mayd it up the long iooll*

(adapted from Trudgill 1990: 65–66; reproduced by permission)

still detect some aspect of their own usage represented. And I suppose every observer will take home the message of how subtly dialects vary and overlap in various ways. And of course that applies not only to British dialects but to varieties of English spoken anywhere on the globe.

Deciding whether any two language systems are dialects of the same language or different languages may seem trivial, but it is not at all. The usual criterion is mutual intelligibility: speakers of different dialects of the same language are assumed to understand each other, speakers of languages don't. But it's not that easy – understanding is not an all-or-nothing matter, and it is also a contextually dependent social activity, not a firm property of any language form. What if we roughly understand each other without really getting the details of what the other person is saying? If we are just able to identify what the topic of an utterance is but don't really get the message? If we just pick up one or the other word but little more, without overall comprehension of the intended meaning? Which of these versions counts as "understanding"? Besides, the assumption that speakers of different dialects of the same language understand each other is also clearly open to challenge – I very much doubt whether an elderly Scottish fisherman from the coast near Aberdeen and a London adolescent speaking the city's current mix of left-over Cockney and Caribbean-inspired youth slang get along with each other linguistically when each of them just speaks in their own vernacular. Linguists have come to recognize that the distinction between languages and dialects is essentially a political one (epitomized in the widely quoted phrase that "a language is a dialect with an army and a navy," coined by the Yiddish linguist Max Weinreich). Language forms spoken in different nation states are commonly considered languages, like Danish, Swedish, or Norwegian – even if they are very similar and mutually largely intelligible. Language forms spoken in one nation are usually labeled "dialects" – like Cantonese, Hokkien, and Mandarin in China, even if they are far from mutually intelligible.

So, to sum this up: a language is not a monolithic entity; in reality, it comes in many shadings, in varieties and dialects. And such varieties are all linguistic systems which in their respective contexts are communicatively fully efficient, regular, and "grammatical." Grammar, in this sense, is knowledge of speech habits, of how to do things linguistically, how to encode and decode the thought–sound relationship that makes up communication. It is knowledge acquired and held subconsciously, and shared by all members of a speech community. Language varieties include standard languages and national varieties, but also regional, social and ethnic dialects, group-specific language forms, contextually and stylistically defined expressions, and so on, for use in their respective cultural contexts.

2.2 Levels of language (variation)

People tend to believe that a language is a rather simple thing, if only because every healthy human being speaks one, and thus we believe we know everything that needs to be known. But this is only true if we accept "knowing" to mean subconscious, internalized knowledge – as soon as we try to spell out the rules that we apply without thinking we run into all kinds of problems (if this weren't the case engineers would have developed The Perfect Speech Computer decades ago, a machine allowing us to translate anything into any other language without loss of information). Just an example: English allows the structures *believe in a miracle* and *hand in a paper*, and they look very similar (verb + *in* + *a* + noun). Why, then, can you say *believe in it* but not *hand in it* (note that the preceding asterisk by convention marks a structure which is not permitted under the subconscious rules of a language), and *hand it in* but not **believe it in*? You are more likely to know an answer if you are a second-language speaker of English who has learned such a rule at some point, and less so if as a native speaker you just apply any rule perfectly well (and in that sense of course you "know" it perfectly well, subconsciously) but could not spell it out explicitly.

So, to sum up our insights so far: there are rules in language, but these rules have to be understood as shared habits in a speech community and as subconscious knowledge on how to encode and decode information with sound sequences; and these regularities are not of the quasi-mathematical, one-to-one kind (such that one "thought" would allow exactly one form of expression, and no more) but are rather fuzzy, permitting choices. There are always many different ways of saying the same thing, and the choice of any individual form of expression depends upon a speaker's background, the context of situation, or subtle nuances in the message intended. This is "**language variation,**" and it is ubiquitous. To be able to grasp (i.e. describe and analyze) this bewildering variability, linguists usually focus upon smaller, more manageable units. They break down "speech behavior" into its small(est) constituent units (or "**features**") of a "language variety" and attempt to work out and explain how these behave and are employed in their respective contexts. Fundamentally, these features are ordered into three main "**levels of language** variation": sounds (described in the discipline of phonetics and phonology), words (the units of lexis, or vocabulary), and structures (we may also call these "patterns" and describe them by "rules", i.e. deal with the grammar, or syntax, of a language variety). Let me briefly have a look at each of these levels in turn. I point out some principles of how they work and are usually described, and I illustrate some of the variants we will be encountering when looking at Englishes around the world.

Speaking first and foremost means producing **sounds** with one's articulatory organs in the oral cavity. Hence, **phonetics** describes how the air stream coming from the lungs is modulated and given its meaningful shape by the lips, the teeth, the tongue, the nose, etc. Some of these movements are minute, and produce the finely graded sound distinctions which we associate with "an accent" – but these differences can be described and systematized. Take the /t/ sound, for instance (note that by convention the slashes "/.../" around a sound symbol mark a **phoneme**, a sound which systematically exists in a language, while, if we wish to be precise, square brackets "[...]" are taken to express phonetic details, i.e. slight variations of the articulation of any given sound). It may or may not come with strong aspiration, an audible /h/-like breathing sound, following – strongly with Welsh speakers, hardly at all with Maoris, for instance (and of course variably, depending on context, also in standard English pronunciations – hold the palm of your hand directly in front of your mouth and feel the difference in intensity of air stream which hits it when articulating the "t" in *tip* and *stick*, respectively!). Indian speakers produce a characteristic /t/ sound: not aspirated, and frequently "retroflex," i.e. with the tongue touching the roof of the mouth further back than usual ("postalveolar") and slightly curled back. Americans typically produce their *t*'s between vowels with voicing (i.e. with the vocal cords vibrating) and as something like "weak" *d*'s, with much less muscular tension – think of a typically American pronunciation of *city* or *writer* (which sounds like *rider*). Young urban British people (and many others – in Malaysia or Australia, for instance) increasingly articulate a /t/ in *but* or *butter* as a so-called "glottal stop," a sudden ("plosive") opening of the vocal folds in the larynx (or "voicebox" in one's neck), often indicated by *uh-oh*. Notice that all of these variants are typically associated not only with a certain region but also with a certain position in a word: of the above variants, the Indian form of /t/ occurs at the beginning of words, the American one in the middle between vowels, and the British one at the end (or also word-centrally). Quite a lot of variability for a single, seemingly plain sound, isn't it? (Not that this is all that could be pointed out about it . . .) So, phonetic description can be quite detailed and complex.

Abstracting from such minimal distinctions, all languages use a limited set of sounds which can be identified and which they use systematically in building their words, the "phonemes," the units of **phonology**, the second way of looking at pronunciation differences. Phonetics deals with all possible human sounds and their articulation, including minimal distinctions; phonology investigates language-specific sound systems. Different languages just "have" certain sounds, which do not exist in others – and the same applies to language varieties; and in fact the relationships can then, again, get fairly complex. English varieties commonly have sounds which do not exist in standard English, for instance. French has nasalized vowels (and so do Texans); German has a voiceless fricative in the back of the mouth, spelled *ch* (and so does Scots, as in *loch*); and Zulu languages of southern African have those famous "click" sounds which everybody elsewhere finds almost unpronounceable (and which you can hear at the beginning of the word *Xhosa* pronounced by a South African). These are cases where certain varieties of English seem to be richer in their phonemic inventories, i.e. seem to have more sounds, than others. Conversely, sounds and sound distinctions may also "disappear" in dialects. The difference between the vowels of *bit* (commonly transcribed as /ɪ/) and *beat* (symbolized by /iː/), for instance, is not made ("neutralized," we may say) in many varieties of English in Africa (e.g. in Kenya) or Asia (e.g. in the Philippines) – so these varieties may have fewer sounds, a different **phoneme system**, from others.

Incidentally – you have certainly noticed that **spelling** does not reflect sound properly. For example, on the basis of writing alone no one would guess that "gh" in *laugh* signals /f/ or how "ea" is to be pronounced (compare *sea*, *head*, and *break*!). So linguists have developed a better, unique **transcription** system in which precisely one character signals one sound – the International Phonetic Alphabet (**IPA**). For talking about sound variation this is most useful, almost indispensable if we do not want to clumsily describe articulatory movements all the time. So, in line with the dual presentation strategy mentioned in Chapter 1, in this book I use and quote IPA characters (see Appendix 1, in case you are not certain about them) but frequently supplement them by brief (and necessarily reduced) descriptions of articulatory movements.

Lexical variation, word choice, and usage, needs little discussion, I suppose – everybody knows that people from different dialectal regions or countries have words of their own, like the *stubby* or *shivaree* quoted earlier. The list could be carried on almost endlessly: Hawaiians say *mahalo* for 'thank you'; South Africans have the word *veld* for what may be compared to the *outback* in Australia; Hong Kong people give *red packets* and eat *dim sum*; Fijians live in a *bure* ('traditional house') and Malays in a *kampong* ('village'); US Southerners use *skeeter hawk* (or *mosquito hawk*) for a flying insect which elsewhere is called *darning needle*, *snake doctor*, or *dragonfly*; Indians wear a *dhoti* (pictured in Figure 2, though here worn by the author); Nigerians use *oga* and Cameroonians *fon* for certain high-status leaders; Maori New Zealanders may prepare their food in a *hangi* ('earth oven'); and so on. Caucasians (white European-descendants) were formerly politely addressed as *Sahib* by Indians and are today *Palangi* for Pasifika people, *Pakehas* all across New Zealand, *whitefellas* for Aboriginal Australians, *haoles* to Hawaiians (visible in Figure 15 in Chapter 6), *palefaces* to Native Americans, *buckra* in the Caribbean; and so on. While this may sound like a fairly chaotic (and unproductive) listing, it is in fact possible to systematize words along certain criteria; I postpone this to Chapter 7.

The set of lexical items available to speakers of any language or dialect does not consist of individual words only, however. Complex expressions, that is, local phrases and idioms, make up an important part of the vocabulary, and one, it seems, which is liberally coined or transferred by "calquing," word-by-word translations from one language to another. So, local **phraseology** is characteristic of many young World Englishes. An important type in this domain are **idioms**, i.e. word groups which only together have a specific meaning, so knowing their parts, the words individually, does not help at all. The cartoon in Figure 3 shows how this works in Indian English, for example. All of the three speakers use nothing but English words, but unless you happen to be Indian yourself you are probably not able to understand

Figure 2 A *dhoti*, the common Indian garment for males

what they mean – they use phrases and expressions which are unique to India. Both "What is your good name?" and "What goes of my father?" literally translate phrases from Hindi – the first is a polite inquiry for one's name, the second one a colloquial expression meaning something like 'How does it affect me and my family (economically)?' A *lift*, in this variety, may indicate a permission to come closer and to build a friendly relation.

Variation is least conspicuous on the level of **syntax** (or "**grammar**"), the way we combine words to form constructions and sentences, though it is there as well. Which words or constituents in a language or variety may or may not follow each other, and with which effect, is a much more complicated matter than we may think, and the rules as to how to do what with which words vary more or less subtly. Actually, the Indian English cartoon just discussed illustrates this as well. The use of *only*, in the third speaker's statement, is regionally characteristic in subtle ways, in terms of its position and meaning: it highlights the words left of it (not, as frequently elsewhere, those to the right), and it just adds this thought somewhat incidentally, rather

Figure 3 Indian English phraseology
(from Mehrotra 1998: 115; reproduced by permission)

than, as we might expect, emphasizing its exclusive status. Some of this syntactic variation may almost go unnoticed because it is purely quantitative in nature, such that some varieties use certain structures much more frequently than others. For instance, it has been shown that Indians tend to say *pelt something at someone* rather than *pelt someone with something*. Some patterns which we observe with speakers from elsewhere may seem a little odd – like the article-omission tendency noted in Text 1 (*knowledge is generator*), question formation patterns in unusual contexts (e.g. *I asked where did he go* in India and elsewhere), or when New Zealanders say *a TV show screens* or Singaporeans *discuss about* something. But of course there are also pattern formation habits which are really difficult to grasp for speakers from other regions – as cases in point, take two patterns from Singapore (both of which will be illustrated in a text sample in Chapter 6): the *kena*-passive mentioned above (*John kena scold*), or the use of *one* as something like a relative clause marker (e.g. *That boy pinch my sister one* '... who pinched . . .'). Again, further examples and a more systematic survey of such phenomena are to follow later.

For the more linguistically minded readers: distinguishing pronunciation, lexis, and grammar offers a convenient grasp on the core language levels (and their variability) but does not exhaust this topic. A possible level worth mentioning is **morphology**, the study of the internal make-up of complex words. It is implied in the above categorization, however, in that it is usually divided into two halves which align themselves with lexis and grammar,

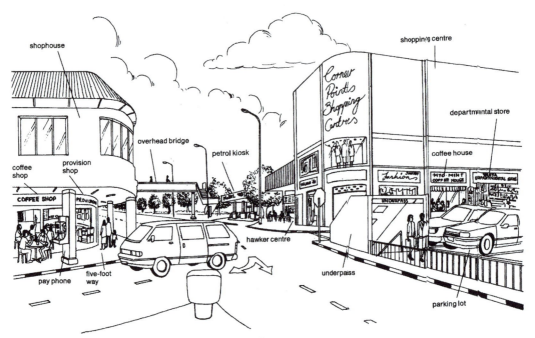

Figure 4 A Singaporean–Malaysian street scene, including a *petrol kiosk*
(from *Times-Chambers Essential English Dictionary*, Singapore 1997: 987)

respectively: word formation and inflection. Both, of course, also contribute systematically to inter-variety language variability.

- **Word formation** describes how simple items combine to form new and complex lexical entities. There are variety-specific compounds and derivatives, e.g. *sheep station* (New Zealand), *careers master* (Kenya), *senatoriable* (Philippines), *democrator* (India). Figure 4 shows, amongst other local expressions, a characteristically Singaporean compound noun, *petrol kiosk*, for what, for example, Americans call a *gas station*. In addition, certain dialects may develop characteristic formative preferences. Indian English, for instance, has many compounds with *wallah*, e.g. *rickshaw wallah*, *fruit wallah*, *plastic wallah*, or *chai wallah* (used at one point as the reference to the hero in Hollywood's 2009 blockbuster movie *Slumdog Millionaire*) 'person in charge of bringing tea', or shows a preference for *lady* to denote female professionals, e.g. *lady doctor*.

- **Inflection**, the use of endings to express grammatical categories, represents the grammatical side of morphology, and again it may be the source of lots of variability, both subtractive (as when East Anglian traditional dialects or Caribbean speakers of English omit their verbal *-s* endings, as in *he go*) and additive (e.g. when in many New Englishes mass nouns take a plural ending, e.g. *informations*, *alphabets*).

Phonology, lexis, and grammar constitute core levels of language organization and variation – but there are further, more marginal possibilities as well. A related and wide open field, though understudied, are differences in **pragmatics**, conventions on how to behave, also verbally, in specific contexts – e.g. the use of honorifics or expressions of politeness. For example, American-style first-naming each other after only brief contact in professional encounters may be perceived as rude by status-conscious Asians. Such conventions may vary widely. For example, it is known that Caribbean cultures or African American English employ ritual insults, frequently of a sexual nature – but these are to be understood more as a verbal game and a training ground for linguistic creativity and are not meant to be taken seriously or offensively. In cross-cultural encounters, however, such behavior might certainly cause tensions . . .

Other areas of differences may be even more subtle, and perhaps even marginal to language (though not to communication). One possibility concerns **conceptualization**: different cultures may categorize things differently. When talking about large numbers, for instance, Americans think in hundreds and Europeans in thousands (so 2500 is "twenty-five hundred" and "two-and-a-half thousand", respectively), while for Indians the central entity is the lakh, 100.000 (so 250.000 is "2.5 lakhs"). Even **gestures** vary: Indians signal "yes" not by nodding but by a mild sideways shaking of the head (which resembles and may be mistaken for what means "no" elsewhere!); Filipinos may greet each other by raising the eyebrows and tilting the head upwards.

2.3 Language change and language contact

Why, then, all this variability – wouldn't life be easier if we all just spoke the same way? For an answer we might be tempted into the philosophical sphere. Biological diversity, as we all know, sustains life by enabling mixtures of gene pools and processes of selection and environmental adjustment. In a similar vein, we might speculate that linguistic diversity allows us to manipulate our human relationships of bonding and disagreeing on all levels – national, local, personal – in very subtle ways by signaling inclusion and exclusion and symbolizing proximity and distance through speech – apart from the very mundane condition of having to make the best of our breathing, chewing, and eating organs for the purpose of symbolic communication. Note that the biological imagery can be extrapolated – it is believed that varieties emerge via a process of selection from a feature pool to which all available variants are brought (Mufwene 2001, Schneider 2007; see Chapter 7).

But let us stick to solid ground, the basics which linguists have studied and documented thoroughly. All languages always change, and practically all languages are in contact with other languages and are modified thereby. Language change and language contact constitute essential causes of differences between varieties.

Languages **change** all the time, whether we like it or not, and irrespective of whether we are aware of this or not. We may notice lexical innovations – fashionable words and "word-of-the-year" choices, for instance, or the fact that all the computer and internet terminology which we use all the time now did not exist some twenty-plus years ago, simply because a *browser* and *downloading* did not yet exist in people's lives, and a *mouse* meant a totally different kind of thing, a small grey animal and not a pointing and clicking device. But we are usually not aware of changes in pronunciation and grammar. They do proceed nevertheless, however, as we notice when the time gap becomes wider: read Shakespeare, Chaucer, and (if you can) Beowulf – and you'll know, and see the amount of differences (and difficulties!) increasing. Closer to home, perhaps the most vigorous ongoing change in the English-speaking world in recent decades has been the spread of "new quotatives," especially the form *be like* to introduce direct speech. In contexts where just three decades ago people used to render a conversation by words of saying such as *I said "...," and then she said "...,"* nowadays young people, with females in the lead, use *I was like "...," and then she's like "..."* This new usage was first documented in the late 1980s in the US, and since then it has spread all around the globe, and with the users of this "speech habit" growing older and still retaining this pattern it can now be found in the speech of the forty-year-old age bracket (but it is practically never heard among speakers in their fifties or older). Have you noticed?

Linguists have studied principles of language change for a long time, and many of these mechanisms are understood well. This is not the place to discuss them in detail, but we should recognize that in the emergence of new varieties of English around the globe these principles are also effective, some more strongly than others. Social causes of change (prestige alignments; group solidarity and its symbolization by language forms; negotiating shared and thus more effective language forms; manipulating identity expressions; etc.) play an important role, and the same applies to language-internal causes (such as making optimal use of the available articulatory space; increasing transparency through analogical formation and regularization; giving distinct formal expression to distinct meanings; etc.). A language-learning component may play a specially strong role in this, given that many of the new World Englishes are ultimately products of individual and group second-language acquisition and sometimes language shift. You'll learn more about this in Chapter 7.

While most nations have a national language and every speech community has a distinctive language or dialect of its own, in most parts of the world other languages can be heard as well. In fact in many regions **bilingualism** and **multilingualism,** the ability to speak two or more languages (more or less well) are extremely widespread or even the norm. So in many contexts, and certainly so in those which have produced new varieties of English, it is normal for a language to exist side by side with one or more other languages – in the region, or in the minds of multilingual individuals. Such languages are said to be in **contact** with each other, and, quite naturally, they influence each other in many ways. Similarly to language change, language contact is an intensely studied problem area in linguistics, the importance of which has been recognized forcefully in recent decades.

One of the main consequences of contact is **borrowing,** or **transfer**: words, sounds, and also structures (pattern-forming habits in the minds of speakers) are taken over from one language context into another, and many of them become firmly integrated in a newly emerging linguistic system. As is well known, standard English itself in some ways is a mixed language, of Germanic origins but with strong contact influences from French, Latin, Scandinavian, and loan words from many other languages. The same applies to the "New Englishes" of Africa and Asia, which tend to have been shaped to some extent by contact with the indigenous tongues of the region, which are also normally the home languages of their respective speakers or their ancestors. Many of the linguistic forms and examples pointed out above and also later in this book can be accounted for as being contact-induced. You may think this is confusing, but in fact it enriches the expressive potential of English, like that of any other language. New sounds or newly adopted patterns allow for further means of expression in the recipient language. And newly borrowed words in many cases mean much more than any existing, semantically similar word could express; they provide added value. For example, Singaporeans are said (and expected) to be *kiasu*, but this is much more than being 'competitive' – the word implies a positive determination to succeed, to persist despite difficulties, to make the best of one's potential, in line with the nation's self-definition. Similarly, to a Maori New Zealander *mana* is much more than 'standing' or 'respect' (the word's conventional dictionary translations). Such words come with a whole lot of cultural baggage – or potential, depending on how one wishes to see it – attached and transferred.

Language contact comes in different degrees of intensity, and this cline of contact intensity correlates with specific linguistic effects. Light, superficial contact, let's say of one culture admiring and being influenced by another, results in lexical borrowing. More intense forms, for instance when a minority population lives in a majority's territory, produces structural interferences, some changes in morphology and syntax. Very intense contact, with two peoples living together very closely, frequently in unequal power

Figure 5 A West African market

relationships, may end up in the birth of new language systems – truly mixed languages, or **pidgins** and **creoles**. In the course of the last few centuries many English-based pidgins and creoles have emerged, mostly in tropical regions in association with colonial plantation cultures, in the Caribbean, in West Africa, Australia, and the Pacific region. Usually they have a vocabulary which is largely derived from English (though many words have been phonologically modified, sometimes to the point that they can hardly be recognized). Their grammar, however, tends to encompass structures which have been produced either by indigenous transfer or by fundamental cognitive principles of language formation. Pidgins are defined as reduced second-language forms which are not anybody's mother tongue but used only in interethnic contacts where there is no other shared language. They are typically restricted to certain situations and locations, such as the West African market depicted in Figure 5.

Creoles, in contrast, are fully fledged but newly emerged languages, with all the potential functions of any human language and with novel and frequently complex grammatical properties. The distinction between the two has come to be increasingly blurred, because many pidgins, spoken for centuries in a region, have expanded their ranges of use and become native languages, thus, strictly speaking, creoles. These are interesting processes and language forms – but the question is whether they are varieties of English (and thus parts of the topic of this book). The question is disputed. Early creolist theory vigorously held that creoles are new languages, independent of (and some creolists said even unrelated to) their European "lexifier" languages, the vocabulary donors. But this view has come under fire in recent years, given that most of the words of an English creole text can be identified by an English speaker, and to some extent these varieties are mutually intelligible. (The argument is more complex, and has to do with the fact that there are no linguistic forms which uniquely identify creoles as a language type – but this is not our concern here.) In the present context I adopt this modern view, with Mufwene (2001) and others, and consider English-related pidgins and creoles as related to English and, in a wider sense, varieties of English themselves, not central to but also included in the global range of varieties considered here. This is a grey zone, and in my view it is wiser to be inclusive – otherwise the absurd conclusion would be that, say, a Jamaican Creole text like the one discussed in Chapter 4 would not be "English" at all.

2.4 Categorizing World Englishes

A range of different labels has come to refer to "English(es) around the world." (Note that it has become customary to use the plural *Englishes* nowadays, meaning 'kinds of English'.) To some extent this is characteristic of a young field of study; in part terms may be used just indiscriminately; and at times some labels may imply subtle differences of meaning. Some scholars use "new varieties of English," or also "indigenized" or "extraterritorial" varieties, and will also use some such paraphrases, including the terms dialect and variety, for stylistic purposes. The following three terms, however, have more precise implications:

- "**World Englishes**" is the most encompassing of all, denoting all or any of the varieties spoken around the world, including British English, and, of course, forms such as Nigerian, Malaysian, or New Zealand English. When using this term the perspective is usually a national one; regional dialects would probably qualify only indirectly. The term goes back to Braj Kachru, a Kashmiri–American scholar who on an international scale counts as the founding father of the discipline, and his school, and in many contexts it may imply notions conventionally associated with this paradigm (like the "Three Circles" model discussed below, and the special importance of the Outer Circle). With the recent growth of the discipline, however, it has emerged as the most neutral and most widely used term.

- **"New Englishes,"** coined by Platt, Weber, and Ho (1984), is explicitly restricted to the newly grown second-language varieties especially of Africa and Asia, like Tanzanian or Indian English.
- **"Postcolonial Englishes,"** used predominantly in Schneider (2007), unites all the varieties which have shared origins in (mostly) British colonization activities, emphasizing this historical origin and the processes which have resulted from it. So it excludes British English but includes American or Australian English, the "New Englishes," and English-related creoles.

Obviously, all these varieties are similar in some respects and different in others. It makes sense to categorize them, based on shared properties. Several classification schemes have been proposed (see McArthur 1998). There are three models which have received wider currency (two more, emphasizing historical circumstances and sociolinguistic settings, will be introduced in the next chapter).

The first one categorizes countries in which English is spoken into three types:

- "English as a Native Language" (**ENL**), in which the language is spoken and handed down as the mother tongue of the majority of the population (as in the UK, the USA, Australia, or New Zealand);
- "English as a Second Language" (**ESL**), in which English has been strongly rooted for historical reasons and assumes important internal functions (often alongside indigenous languages), e.g. in politics (sometimes as an official or co-official language), education, the media, business life, the legal system, etc. Thus, many speakers, especially educated ones, use it frequently in their daily lives. Typically, these are postcolonial countries, e.g. India, Malaysia, Nigeria, or Uganda.
- "English as a Foreign Language" (**EFL**), in which English is widely taught in the education system, and people strive to acquire it for its international usefulness, but it does not really have any internal functions (except for things like its attractiveness in advertising or the occasional English-language newspaper with an international readership in mind).

This classification goes back to a proposal made by Barbara Strang, then a well-known historical linguist, in the 1970s. Subsequently it was adopted and developed further by other scholars, including Lord Randolph Quirk and his co-authors of the most monumental grammar of English (1985, with a 1972 precursor version) and the influential German scholar Manfred Görlach in several books in the 1990s.

As an example, Map 2 illustrates the application of this scheme to one major world region, the African continent. In this scheme "International"

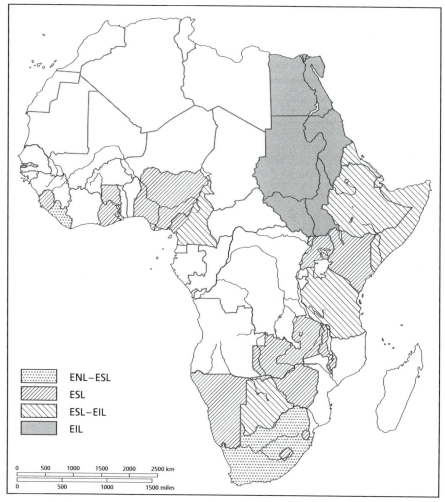

Map 2 The status of English in African nation states
(after Schmied 1991: 44; reproduced by permission)

and, correspondingly, "EIL" are used as roughly corresponding to "Foreign" and "EFL." Note that a few countries are also marked as standing between an ESL to an EIL status – some of these have decided to adopt an "endoglossic" language policy of promoting an indigenous rather than the former colonial language.

In several articles of the 1980s Braj Kachru developed his **"Three Circles"** model, which then received programmatic support in his 1992 edited volume *The Other Tongue.* In this framework, illustrated graphically in Figure 6, varieties of English (or countries in which it is used) are typically represented as three overlapping or concentric circles. In terms of membership and definition, they largely correlate with the earlier scheme, with ENL appearing as the **"Inner Circle,"** ESL being conceptualized as the **"Outer Circle,"** and EFL being the **"Expanding Circle."** There is more going on than just relabeling,

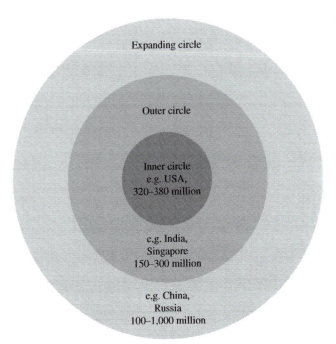

Figure 6 Graphic representation of Kachru's "Three Circles" model (from Crystal 2003: 61; reproduced by permission)

Expanding circle

Outer circle

Inner circle
e.g. USA,
320–380 million

e.g. India,
Singapore
150–300 million

e.g. China,
Russia
100–1,000 million

however. The ENL/ESL/EFL scheme may be conceptually clear-cut, but it is probably a bit dry and unappealing. Kachru's line of thinking adds a sociopolitical and developmental component (note that being "in" or "out" aren't just neutral terms, and "expanding" implies a process of growth!), and a whole new agenda for research and generating awareness of issues. Kachru and his followers challenge the implicit predominance of the Inner Circle and emphasize the independence and practical importance of the Outer Circle (and also the Expanding Circle). They argue that English belongs to all those who use it (so there is no need to slavishly strive for a British model of usage and pronunciation), and view the Outer Circle countries as developing norms of their own. This model has thus instilled increasing self-confidence in localized varieties of English and strongly influenced language teaching and applied linguistics in countries of Asia and Africa in particular.

Nevertheless, both of these classification schemes are also a bit problematic in that they abstract from complex realities, and perhaps both may be a bit dated by now and fail to reflect the vigorous spread of English and changes of its status in many regions over the last few decades. For instance – how about multilingual countries such as Canada or South Africa? Based on the presence of a majority or at least a strong cohort of ancestral native speakers of British descent they are usually classified as ENL/Inner Circle, but this clearly disregards the presence and importance of groups such as French Canadians or Bantu- or Afrikaans-speaking South Africans. Of course, even seemingly homogeneous Inner Circle countries are not "ENL only," strictly speaking: millions of Americans speak forms of Spanish, Native languages, or other immigrant languages as their mother tongues; in Britain one can hear Welsh, Gaelic, and of course several Asian languages in immigrant communities; in Australia, we find Aboriginal languages and in New Zealand, Maori retained; etc. – and all of these speaker groups are excluded, in a sense, by a plain ENL classification. Furthermore, things have been changing massively in the recent past. Take Singapore, where roughly a third of all children today grow up with English as their first language (and similar situations, though on a more restricted scale, apply in parts of Africa). This seems more than "ESL" – so is the country on its way into the Inner Circle?

A more recent approach which attempts to take such processes into consideration is the "**Dynamic Model**" of the evolution of Postcolonial Englishes, proposed by Schneider (2003, 2007a). It builds upon earlier developmental schemes and argues that emerging varieties of English in postcolonial contexts have typically followed an underlying, fundamentally uniform evolutionary process caused by the social dynamics between the two parties involved in a colonization process. The model suggests that in the long run characteristic processes of group identity formation and accommodation will decrease the social separation of these parties involved, and will cause the growth of new dialects as symbolic reflections of these social realignments and re-negotiations of social distance or proximity. In colonization, settlers move into a territory inhabited by people with different cultural roots and a different linguistic background. In the beginning both groups perceive each other as distinct and separate, but in the course of time these boundaries get increasingly blurred. Typically, after having shared the same territory for many decades or even centuries both parties recognize that they will be forced to co-exist for good, and they move more closely towards each other, both socially and linguistically. Frequently this happens after political independence from the erstwhile mother country (in our case mostly Great Britain), and it also typically involves a stage of nation-building intended to diminish ethnic boundaries and to develop a pan-ethnic feeling of nationhood. Postcolonial Englishes grow and are increasingly accepted as symbols of belonging in such young nations.

The model assumes five developmental stages, and on each of them a unilateral implication of four social and linguistic sets of conditions:

- the political history of a country is reflected in
- the identity re-writings of the groups involved in these processes, which, in turn, determine

Table 2 *Phases and constituent conditions of the "Dynamic Model"*

Stage	History and politics	Identity construction	Sociolinguistics of contact / use / attitudes	Linguistic developments / structural effects
1: Foundation	STL: colonial expansion: trade, military outposts, missionary activities, emigration / settlement; IDG: occupation, loss / sharing of territory, trade	STL: part of original nation; IDG: indigenous	STL: cross-dialectal contact, limited exposure to local languages; IDG: minority bilingualism (acquisition of English)	STL: koinéization; toponymic borrowing; incipient pidginization (in trade colonies)
2: Exonormative stabilization	Stable colonial status; English established as language of administration, law, (higher) education, …	STL: outpost of original nation, "English-plus-local"; IDG: individually "local-plus-English"	STL: acceptance of original norm; expanding contact; IDG: spreading (elite) bilingualism	Lexical borrowing (esp. fauna and flora, cultural terms); "-isms"; Pidginization / creolization (in trade / plantation colonies)
3: Nativization	Weakening ties; often political independence but remaining cultural association	STL: permanent resident of English origin; IDG: permanent resident of indigenous origin	Widespread and regular contacts, accommodation; IDG: common bilingualism, toward language shift, L1 speakers of local English; STL: sociolinguistic cleavage between innovative speakers (adopting IDG forms) and conservative speakers (upholding external norm; 'complaint tradition')	Heavy lexical borrowing; IDG: phonological innovations ("accent," possibly due to transfer); Structural nativization, spreading from IDG to STL: innovations at lexis–grammar interface (verb complementation, prepositional usage, constructions with certain words / word classes); lexical productivity (compounds, derivation, phrases, semantic shifts); code-mixing (as identity carrier)
4: Endonormative stabilization	Post-independence, self-dependence (possibly after "Event X")	(Member of) new nation, territory-based, increasingly pan-ethnic	Acceptance of local norm (as identity carrier), positive attitude to it; (residual conservatism); literary creativity in new variety	Stabilization of new variety, emphasis on homogeneity, codification: dictionary writing, grammatical description
5: Differentiation	Stable young nation, internal socio-political differentiation	Group-specific (as part of overarching new national identity)	Network construction (increasingly dense group-internal interactions)	Dialect birth: group-specific (ethnic, regional, social) varieties emerge (as L1 or L2)

(from Schneider 2007a: 56; reprinted by permission of Cambridge University Press)

- the sociolinguistic conditions of language contact, linguistic usage and language attitudes; and these affect
- the linguistic developments and structural changes in the varieties evolving.

Table 2 spells out some specific processes which are considered typical of each of these levels at each stage. In a nutshell, the development in each of five phases is as follows:

- "Foundation": English is brought to a new territory, which leads to incipient bilingualism, the borrowing of toponyms, and other minor processes.
- "Exonormative stabilization": during a stable colonial situation, the politically dominant "mother country" determines the norms of linguistic behavior, and elite bilingualism spreads amongst some representatives of the indigenous population, with lexical borrowing continuing.
- "Nativization" is the most vibrant and interesting of all the phases. With ties with the settlers' country of origin weakening, and interethnic contacts increasing, bilingual speakers forge a new variety of English, shaped strongly by phonological and structural transfer – though conservative speakers resent such innovative usage.
- "Endonormative stabilization" implies that, after independence and inspired by the need for nation-building, a new linguistic norm is increasingly recognized (and commonly perceived as remarkably homogeneous), is beginning to be codified and to be accepted in society, and is employed culturally in literary representations.
- "Differentiation" may follow in the end, i.e. in a stable young nation, internal social group identities become more important and get reflected in the growth of dialectal differences.

Of course, like any model, this description abstracts from realities which in individual cases are more complex (for example, subsequent phases typically overlap, and not all constituent phenomena can be observed), but the basic pattern is well established, based upon observations drawn from a wide range of different countries. Since its publication this model has met with a lot of attention and approval. Many scholars have tested and adopted it and have applied it to further contexts and countries, and some have suggested modifications, additions, and improvements, but the basic idea seems sound and widely accepted.

2.5 Ecology comes first

A final point in this survey of basic terms, concepts, and frameworks relevant in our discussion of global English concerns the relationship between intralinguistic and extralinguistic factors. Linguists typically distinguish these two perspectives when discussing principles underlying change and evolution. Conditions purely internal to language have to do with speech production, perception, and processing, beginning with

- the nature of the vocal tract and our articulatory organs (which determine which sounds we can produce and how these can be kept distinct, thus circumscribing the framework for the encoding of thoughts by sounds) via
- the conditions of perception (how we hear and analyze the sound stream, for instance) to
- the cognitive foundations of language (weighing principles such as analogy, regularity, simplicity, frequency effects, and the cognitive "entrenchment" of speech forms, optimal encoding conditions, etc.). Frequently they also deal with
- the interaction between language levels (such as how sound changes may affect the encoding of morphological categories and, in turn, the expression of syntactic relationships).

Conversely, extralinguistic conditions have to do with language use in historical and sociolinguistic settings:

- the fact that people talk differently in different nations, regions, social classes, groups, styles, and situations, including, quite simply,
- demographic relationships, i.e. which speaker groups participate in which numbers in any communicative situation, and
- the fact that choosing which language and linguistic form to use has also something to do with power and solidarity in a community. We may attempt to choose forms which have "prestige," typically because their regular users are viewed as prestigious, or we attempt to accommodate to someone else's speech because we wish to decrease the social distance to that person and to express solidarity.

It is widely believed that language use and development is determined by inherent linguistic qualities of a language – that French sounds beautiful and Latin is expressively rich, for instance, and that English is so successful because it is considered easy to learn (because it has few inflectional complications and a historically mixed vocabulary which allows speakers of many language backgrounds to grasp glimpses of it). From all we know, however, such assumptions are erroneous. Of course, it is difficult to weigh these various effects, and in any individual case of language contact and change we are faced with a hugely complex interplay of all kinds of factors which may be more or less influential. At the end of the day, however, it seems clear that language-external, social and historical conditions are more decisive for what happens to a language than its internal structure and quality. Thomason and Kaufman (1988), in a book on creoles, were the first to vigorously present this argument, showing that, for instance, subdued peoples are likely to undergo language shift, or at least a strong impact of a dominant language is likely to affect their usage, sometimes leading to creolization or the birth of truly mixed languages. Mufwene (2001) also made this point very strongly and convincingly, arguing that "ecology rolls the dice."

That is not to say that it is the only cause of developments, of course – many properties of new varieties of English can be accounted for by purely language-internal processes and principles. It appears that language-internal (cognitive, perceptual, articulatory, etc.) conditions establish a framework for possible structural options and evolutionary trajectories, but which of these is then realized depends first and foremost upon extralinguistic conditions. It is primarily the historical and sociolinguistic background – the communicative conditions, the fates of peoples, and things like linguistic and social attitudes, in short the "ecology" of the setting of a variety – which determines its fate and evolution.

The same applies to English and its history, including its global diffusion and adjustments. It has become the world's leading language not for its beauty or its simplicity, but simply, as Crystal (2003) put it, because the language happened to be "at the right place at the right time" – three times in a row, in fact.

- English was spread around the globe as the language of the British Empire.
- It was the language of the industrial revolution and of technological innovation and has been sought as a window to the sciences, western technology, etc.
- And in the twentieth century it was strengthened further as the language of the world's remaining superpower and the leading force in globalization, the United States.

Let us have a closer look at these historical circumstances and their effect upon language development in the next chapter.

Chapter summary

In this chapter we have learned a number of basic facts about how languages work, and these have then been applied to the evolution of English in its global context. A few basic notions were introduced and defined – including dialect, accent, and variety, and widespread prejudices as to language "correctness" were compared to the notion of communicative adequacy in given contexts. We found that all languages vary, i.e. there are different ways of saying the same thing, and there is typically a choice between alternative realizations of some linguistic entities. These units (or "features") can be described best on various language levels:

- pronunciation (phonetics and phonology),
- vocabulary (lexis, including morphology), and
- grammar (syntax).

Global varieties of English show variation on each of these levels, and this variation has been caused and can be explained by processes and principles of

- language change in the course of time and
- language contact between speakers of different languages who communicate with each other and transfer forms from one language to another in bilingual or multilingual minds, as it were.

Conceptualizations and categorization frameworks for the new varieties of English around the globe were introduced, including two well-known tripartite classifications,

- ENL-ESL-EFL, and
- Kachru's "Three Circles"; and the newer
- "Dynamic Model" which suggests five subsequent developmental stages which newly emerging postcolonial varieties typically go through.

Finally, the point was made that while language-internal and language-external conditions always interact in complex ways, ultimately the extra-linguistic, ecological factors are more decisive for what happens to a language and how it develops in the course of time.

In the next chapter this historical perspective will be pursued in greater detail, when we look at the colonial and postcolonial contexts and patterns which have brought English to all corners of the earth.

Exercises and activities

Exercise 2a   Reflect on and discuss your own speech behavior. Do you think you speak a kind of English which is somehow "dialectal," or "with an accent"? Are you aware of speaking differently in different situations? If you move from your home 100 miles in any direction – do people speak noticeably differently there? Use linguistic terminology to describe and pin down some of your own or somebody else's distinctive linguistic features.

Exercise 2b	Think of some dialect (probably in a neighboring region) which you and your friends find "strange." Identify some words, sounds, or patterns of that dialect which you would not use yourself.
Exercise 2c	Think of some words in English which may have been borrowed into the language at some point in time. Try *bishop, parliament, stanza, bronco, orang-utan, verandah, kangaroo,* or *taboo,* for a start. Which language were they borrowed from? Can you speculate on when and why this may have happened?
Exercise 2d	Here is a short selection from the best-known poem by Geoffrey Chaucer, *The Canterbury Tales,* from the late fourteenth century:

Thanne longen folk to goon on pilgrimages
And palmeres for to seken straunge strondes
To ferne halwes, kowthe in sondry londes
And specially from every shires ende
Of Engelond, to Caunterbury they wende,
The hooly blisful martir for to seke
That hem hath holpen, whan that they were seeke.

Does this give you a feel for how the language has changed in the intervening centuries? Try to replace each word by its modern corresponding form! Can you recognize things you wouldn't say like this (i.e. patterns/structures which obviously have changed)? Which word forms are different from today's? Can you find words which seem used in odd ways, i.e. whose meaning may have changed? How, do you think, does all of this relate to today's "New Englishes"?

Exercise 2e	Have you heard the form *be like* to introduce a report of direct speech? Do you use it yourself? Have you been aware of the fact that this is a fairly new and spreading kind of usage? Do you have intuitions as to who would (or would not) say something like *and then I'm like bla bla . . .?*
Exercise 2f	Reflect on and discuss the amount of bilingualism and multilingualism in your environment. How many languages do you speak? How about your parents, other members of your family, your friends? Do you have friends or acquaintances whose family background includes a history of migration, and who therefore command an ancestral language which is not the language of the area where they live? In any of these contexts, have second or further languages been acquired in school, or just naturally, by trying to communicate with speakers of these languages?

Key terms discussed in this chapter

accent
aspiration
bilingualism
borrowing
calquing
change (i.e. language change)
conceptualization
contact (i.e. language contact)
creoles
dialect
Dynamic Model
ecology
endonormative
exonormative
English as a Foreign Language (EFL)
English as a Native Language (ENL)
English as a Second Language (ESL)
Expanding Circle
features (of a language or language variety)
glottal stop
grammar
idioms
Inner Circle
International Phonetic Alphabet
language versus dialect
levels of language organization / variation
lexifier
lexis
morphology
multilingualism
New Englishes
neutralization (of sound distinctions)
Outer Circle
parameters of variation
phoneme
phoneme system
phonetics
phonology
phraseology
pidgins
Postcolonial Englishes
pragmatics
quotatives

rules of language organization
sociolinguistics
sounds
spelling
standard
syntax
transfer
variation
variety
word formation

Further reading

In this chapter I have touched upon a wide range of topics and sub-disciplines of linguistics, and for almost all of these an equally wide range of scholarly studies, including many introductory textbooks, are available. The following list, therefore, represents a personal choice of books which I find particularly informative, accessible, and recommendable.

In case you wish to improve your familiarity with phonetics and phonology, McCully (2009) is an excellent textbook which not only introduces the basic concepts but also pays a lot of attention to differences between varieties of English.

Basic notions concerning language variation and dialects of English are accessibly introduced in Chambers and Trudgill (1998). One of the best and most readable introductions to sociolinguistics and parameters underlying social variation is Chambers (2003). For anybody interested specifically in principles of language change, excellent textbooks include Aitchison (2001) and McMahon (1994). The current standard surveys for the field of language contact are Thomason (2001) and Winford (2003). In the field of World Englishes, McArthur (1998, 2002) provides lots of interesting material and food for thought; recommendable textbooks include Crystal (2003) and Melchers and Shaw (2003). Kirkpatrick (2007) has an applied perspective and teaching issues in mind, and Mesthrie and Bhatt (2008) skillfully survey structural properties of World Englishes. The Dynamic Model is presented in greater detail and applied to seventeen different countries in Schneider (2007a). The ecological perspective is worked out in Mufwene's influential (2001) book. Kachru, Kachru, and Nelson (2006) is a voluminous handbook surveying many aspects of the field, and for those interested in more specific scholarly writings, mainly from a Kachruvian perspective, Bolton and Kachru (2006), a six-volume collection, provides access to reprints of many classic articles and texts.

CHAPTER 3

Historical background

In this chapter ...

World Englishes are mostly products of colonialism, so in this chapter we will get familiarized with the history of European colonization and, in a brief survey, the expansion of the British Empire and the role of the United States in the globalization of English. In particular, we'll look at the social conditions and the linguistic consequences generated by specific types of colonies, the outcomes of varying motives for colonial expansion. We'll learn that, surprisingly, the global growth of English gained even more momentum after the end of the colonial period. To confirm this point, we will get exposed to some numbers, of users of English and of countries where it is in use, and some typologies of kinds of Englishes produced by these historical conditions will be introduced.

3.1 European colonization: a few introductory observations

At the dawn of the modern age, late in the fifteenth century, European powers set out to conquer the world. From the early explorers of that time to the Berlin Conference of 1884, they entered the race for colonies, for various motives, but essentially to increase their economic and political strength and power. Several reasons combined to drive this development:

- social ones, like the decline of the feudal system and the nobility (so that some landowners were forced to seek their fortune in adventures abroad) and a population surplus in some countries;
- technological ones, like new shipbuilding and navigation techniques, which made longer overseas journeys possible;
- economic ones, like the growth of capitalism and desire for profit;
- political ones, like the increasing competition between European powers; and
- cultural ones, like a zeal for missionary activity accompanied by an unquestioned belief in the white man's and the Christian faith's superiority, which did not leave room for moral concerns even with respect to the conquest and enslavement of foreign peoples.

The early motive of improving trading conditions especially with Asia soon gave way to other causes for colonization – the exploitation of indigenous resources to the advantage of one's own nation, the satisfaction of land needs for settlement, the imperialist expansion of one's political and economic power, and finally quite simply the internal competition between the European powers, with balances changing in the course of time. Britain entered this race at a relatively late point in time but turned out to be highly successful in the long run (more on this below).

The first agents in this expansionist strategy were Portuguese explorers, who in the fifteenth century ventured down the West African coast, establishing fortified outposts, and ultimately found a naval route to India, thus opening radically new perspectives to the lucrative oriental trade. Spanish support of Columbus' voyages was motivated by the jealousy of the Portuguese success, and his (re)discovery of America in 1492 opened Central and South America (with the exception of Brazil, which became Portuguese) to settlement and exploitation, with horrible consequences for the indigenous peoples and cultures. The Spanish were driven by a curious mixture of greed for gold, land, and power combined with missionary zeal, legitimized by the Pope. The colonial powers which came later, in the seventeenth century, were more interested in trade, wealth, and also the possession of land for settlement. The Dutch established a colony in South Africa and expanded into Asia, where, for example, they founded Melaka (in today's Malaysia) and held Indonesia for centuries. The French competed with the British in North and Central America, and later in Africa. Colonies were frequently objects of negotiations between European powers, and not infrequently changed hands as a consequence of some war fought or treaty signed in far-away Europe. Take South Africa as a case in point, which became British after the Napoleonic Wars and in the Congress of Vienna of 1815, even in the absence of a notable settlement there up to that point.

The last of these fierce series of competitions was what came to be known as the "scramble for Africa" in the later nineteenth century. By then most of the world had been divided up between the European colonial powers into possessions, colonies, and spheres of influence. The exception was Africa, just explored and made familiar by the expeditions of Livingstone, Stanley, and others. So on this continent, which promised new resources, markets, and wealth, and seemed to be still "available," the European powers struggled to build and expand their footholds. Many of these strategic conflicts were settled in the "Berlin Conference" of 1884–85, in which rules of conduct in the setting-up of new colonies in Africa were agreed upon. The decisions made there resulted in nominal and frequently artificial borders, drawn without considering the ethnic composition or regional homogeneity of newly formed colonies. Most of today's nation states of Africa, together with their ethnic and linguistic heterogeneity and all the problems resulting from this, can be traced back to that period. Indirectly, however, these origin conditions are also responsible for the strong second-language role of English in many of these states. The composition of the state of Nigeria, for instance, founded as a protectorate and then turned into a colony early in the twentieth century, can be traced back to the recognition of a British sphere of influence at Berlin, and subsequently the foundation of the Royal Niger Company in 1886. The strong role of English in today's Nigeria is clearly caused by its ethnic neutrality in a highly multiethnic polity.

History tends to be written from the perspective of those in power, but we must be careful to avoid sharing a "triumphant" perspective. Colonialism meant huge amounts of violence, suffering, and cruelty to indigenous populations. Most notoriously, it brought about the infamous institution of slavery and the enslavement of millions of Africans. More generally, it entailed the loss of liberty and of developmental perspectives for indigenous cultures, in some cases even their eradication. It is hard to see how people who perceived themselves as faithful Christians could act so relentlessly. The moral justification for colonial conquests derived from the desire to convert pagan peoples and thus to "save their souls," sanctioned and supported by the Roman Catholic church, and, more generally, by the colonizers' firm belief in their cultural superiority over "uncivilized" indigenous peoples and their obligation to "develop" them; it was epitomized in Rudyard Kipling's well-known poem about "the white man's burden." Missionary activities in particular, which in many cases have probably been more influential "on the ground," for the average human individual, than political decisions, have to be viewed as a double-edged sword. On the one hand they have improved many people's lives, bringing healthcare, learning, and a message of love and humanitarianism; but on the other hand they have failed to pay respect to indigenous cultures, and have contributed to their weakening and eradication in too many cases.

3.2 Colonization types: motives and consequences for communicative patterns

Colonization, as we have just seen, was far from a uniform process. In particular, varying motivations for colonizing certain world regions at different points in time resulted in varying colonization types, and these, in turn, have produced specific communicative settings. There tends to be a strong connection, therefore, between colonization patterns on the one hand and linguistic ecologies which have resulted from them on the other. A useful classification goes back to Mufwene (2001). In a slightly modified form (for Mufwene, the fourth group is a subtype of the third one) it considers four main types.

In the early phase of European expansion **trade colonies** predominated, i.e. seafarers and merchants traveled to new lands primarily with the intention of exchanging goods with the locals. In the late Middle Ages, for instance, the oriental trade in spices and other luxury goods was highly profitable because of the huge demand for these commodities in Europe; and slaves were also viewed as no more than an object of commerce. Trading contacts are relatively short-lived. Both parties tend not to speak the other group's language, so in order to communicate they develop a pidgin, a reduced limited-purpose lingua franca. In many cases trading posts were established, for instance along the West African coast and in many Asian ports. In such contexts contacts became more permanent, and pidgins may have stabilized, expanded, and in fact come to exist for long periods of time as distinct language forms. Some trading colonies tended to develop into exploitation colonies in later developmental stages.

Exploitation colonies were typically set up later, during the heyday of colonialism in the eighteenth and nineteenth centuries, with the intention of gaining political influence and control and of exploiting indigenous resources for the benefit of the "mother country." The Empire was represented by administrators, servicemen, commercial agents, etc. – a relatively small but powerful stratum. The British strategy was to educate and train an indigenous elite to serve their interests and to participate in governing a colony. Education in these contexts meant teaching English, and admitting the sons of local rulers to prestigious schools. Thus, English was mainly introduced through formal education (though the impact of the presence of lower-status military and agents should not be underestimated), and its use came to be associated with status and authority, also and especially among the indigenous higher ranks.

Notice that access to English was controlled as an instrument of power. The language was made available to those sandwiched co-ruling classes, who thus became associated with the Empire's power, and became culturally Anglicized to a certain extent. It was largely withheld from the masses, however (Brutt-Griffler 2002). It is interesting to observe how education and language learning interacted with acculturation. For the indigenous elites, learning English also meant exposure to westernized culture and some degree of association with the colonizers. Their motivation to acquire English in exploitation colonies may have been purely instrumental, but it seems unavoidable that an integrative effect results from the very process.

The English found in exploitation colonies thus tended to be an elitist class marker, formal and influenced by written styles to the point of being "bookish." Most likely this was not the only form of English – underneath the surface less educated soldiers, traders, and so on brought nonstandard forms of English as well, influenced lower-rank indigenous speakers through daily contact, and got influenced linguistically by them as well. For example, we have reports of "white babus" in India speaking a decidedly Indianized form of English, and forms like "Butler English" are widely documented.

However, the policy of distributing English only in slices and to the powerful continued until after World War II. In the middle of the twentieth century, after the independence of India in 1947, it became clear that all colonies would be lost in the long run, and Britain's language policy changed quite radically. Now, and for the last few decades of colonialism only, English was taught widely and made freely available, with the intention of creating broader bonds to last beyond a country's release into independence.

The third major colony type, **settlement colonies**, was characterized by large-scale population relocation and the establishment of permanent extra-territorial pockets of English-ancestry people resident in foreign lands – as suggested in Figure 7, from Cape Breton, Canada.

In general, population growth and a surplus of labor in England were a permanent cause for emigration. Individually, however, motives to leave the homeland varied greatly. There were

- religious dissenters, such as the Pilgrim Fathers who sailed to Massachusetts in 1620,
- petty criminals sentenced to deportation (think of Australia's First Fleet and long-lasting convict colony status),

Figure 7 A settler woman in a historic village, Cape Breton, Canada

- debtors and deportees obliged to serve as "indentured laborers" in a colony for several (typically seven) years (who then stayed – as in many parts of the Caribbean),
- individual and family settlers hungry for land and in search of new opportunities, and also
- commercially organized large-scale settling activities like the one run by the "New Zealand Company" of the 1840s.

In a strictly linguistic perspective, two types of processes tend to characterize settler communication. Group-internally, the fact that the settlers typically spoke different dialects caused them to develop a compromise variety, omitting rare and communicatively unsuccessful forms and increasing the use of useful ones – a process commonly called koinéization. Externally, indigenous groups were faced with the presence of a dominant group of invading strangers, which frequently had devastating effects for them and their culture, and ultimately caused them to become bilingual or even to undergo language shift towards English. In the long run, typically this constellation triggered the process of nativization, which via contact phenomena such as indigenous-language transfer has ultimately produced new varieties of English.

Finally, **plantation colonies** had substantial numbers of English settlers as well, but developed in more specific settings. They were set up to facilitate the large-scale cultivation of agricultural products, typically in the tropics and most effectively for the growth of sugar cane, which from the mid-seventeenth century promised enormous profits. The European settlers' status ranged from aristocratic owners via overseers and craftsmen to poor "white trash," frequently indentured servants and their descendants. The majority of manual laborers on plantations was brought in in large numbers from elsewhere, however. Between the seventeenth and the early nineteenth century the demand for labor was met by forcing Africans into slavery and transporting them primarily to the Caribbean and the Americas, with the result frequently being the emergence of creole languages. In the second half of the nineteenth century, India provided large numbers of migrant laborers on indentured contracts, and usually many of these workers and their descendants stayed – so today we find substantial population groups of Indian extraction most notably in Trinidad, Guyana, Fiji, and South Africa. At other times other groups jumped in – Hawaii, for instance, towards the end of the nineteenth century, drew much of its labor force from southern China, Japan, Portugal, and the Philippines, and consequently has come out as one of the most multiethnic places on earth today, with a distinctive local creole. Thus, in plantation colonies this juxtaposition of a numerically small ruling class and a majority of workers who had to adjust linguistically provided for distinctive social and linguistic settings and strong language contact effects.

3.3 A short survey of British colonization: from the Empire to the Commonwealth of Nations

The colonial expansion of Britain began during the so-called Elizabethan Age and thereafter, first trailing the Spanish and Portuguese lead, competing with the Dutch in Asia and the French in the Americas for a while, and ultimately, in the nineteenth and early twentieth centuries, building an Empire that spanned the globe. Different parts of the world were targets of expansionist moves at different periods. Map 3 broadly summarizes some of the major moves and migrations of British colonizers and settlers and of some later disseminators of the language, roughly identifying target locations and periods.

Except for a claim to Newfoundland and Raleigh's failed settlement attempt on Roanoke Island in North America, it all began in the seventeenth century. Originally trade was the most immediate goal, especially when in 1600 the East India Company was granted a charter for the Far Eastern trade. Settlement and exploitation followed soon, first in North America

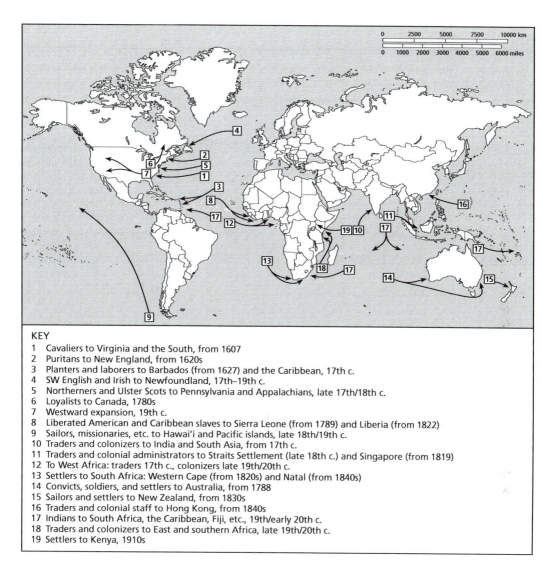

Map 3 English speakers on the move: global migration streams

KEY
1 Cavaliers to Virginia and the South, from 1607
2 Puritans to New England, from 1620s
3 Planters and laborers to Barbados (from 1627) and the Caribbean, 17th c.
4 SW English and Irish to Newfoundland, 17th–19th c.
5 Northerners and Ulster Scots to Pennsylvania and Appalachians, late 17th/18th c.
6 Loyalists to Canada, 1780s
7 Westward expansion, 19th c.
8 Liberated American and Caribbean slaves to Sierra Leone (from 1789) and Liberia (from 1822)
9 Sailors, missionaries, etc. to Hawai'i and Pacific islands, late 18th/19th c.
10 Traders and colonizers to India and South Asia, from 17th c.
11 Traders and colonial administrators to Straits Settlement (late 18th c.) and Singapore (from 1819)
12 To West Africa: traders 17th c., colonizers late 19th/20th c.
13 Settlers to South Africa: Western Cape (from 1820s) and Natal (from 1840s)
14 Convicts, soldiers, and settlers to Australia, from 1788
15 Sailors and settlers to New Zealand, from 1830s
16 Traders and colonial staff to Hong Kong, from 1840s
17 Indians to South Africa, the Caribbean, Fiji, etc., 19th/early 20th c.
18 Traders and colonizers to East and southern Africa, late 19th/20th c.
19 Settlers to Kenya, 1910s

(with well-known landmark dates being the foundation of Jamestown, Virginia, in 1607 and the Pilgrim Father's landfall in Massachusetts in 1620), then in the Caribbean (most notably, 1627 Barbados, 1655 Jamaica). The seventeenth century saw continued settlement in North America and expansion in the Caribbean, a growing economic involvement in India, and the establishment of the earliest trading forts along the West African coast.

In the second half of the eighteenth century, several events redirected the British attention. In the New World, the American colonies declared and gained independence, but the influx of loyalists and the victory over France established and secured authority in Canada. The late eighteenth and early nineteenth centuries saw a rather quick series of events that practically built the core of the Empire. The East India Company gained an increasing hold over South Asia, and the Battle of Plassey in 1757 brought with it firm authority in India, later the "jewel" of the Empire. In South-East Asia, competition with the Dutch resulted in gradual expansion into Malaysia, beginning with Penang in 1786.

Cook's explorations opened up the Pacific. The decision to solve the domestic problem of overspilling prisons by declaring far-away Australia a penal colony introduced the settlement of Australia, beginning with the "First Fleet" of convicts to Botany Bay in 1788. Early in the nineteenth century, after an earlier but short-lived occupation of the Cape Province, formal authority over the region was given to the British in the Congress of Vienna, and it was filled with life by major settlement waves which came to the Cape in the 1820s and to Natal in the 1840s. In 1819, at the southern-most tip of the Malay Peninsula, Sir Stamford Raffles founded Singapore, soon to become a thriving colony and now a nation which owes its existence as a political entity to British colonial activity. The treaty of Waitangi of 1840 stabilized and greatly expanded the influx of British people to New Zealand; and the Opium Wars of the 1840s led to authority over Hong Kong. Later on, the British expansion and involvement in all these regions, and in most cases also the geographical range of possessions, kept growing, and finally the Empire also gained authority in parts of Africa, with colonies established, for instance, in Lagos in 1861, in Uganda in 1893, in Kenya (after a substantial influx of English settlers) in 1920, and so on. As Map 4

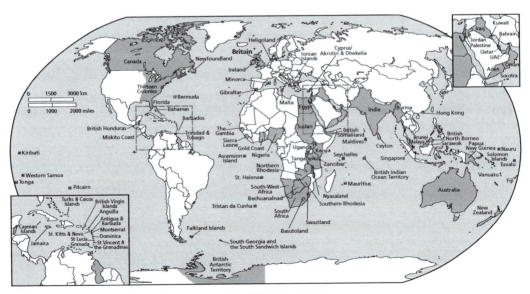

Map 4 The British Empire at its greatest extent

shows, at its greatest extent, after World War I and the Treaty of Versailles, the British Empire truly spanned the entire globe.

Settlement colonies were the first to be released into independence via various intermediate stages such as a dominion status. This process began with Canada in the late nineteenth and Australia in the early twentieth century. Elsewhere, however, the Empire's colonial grip remained tight, typically practicing the principle of "indirect rule," with formal authority being assigned to (English-speaking and English-educated) indigenous leaders who were induced to be loyal to the Crown. The turning point was World War II, however, with all kinds of disruptions loosening the affiliation of many colonies with Britain. India's independence, gained in 1947 after Gandhi's nonviolent persistence, became a model for many others. As stated above, this caused Britain to change her strategy. Colonies were now deliberately and explicitly "developed," which included support for mass education in English, so that in the long run ties with the former colonial power would be maintained. In the course of the following decades most of the British colonies were ultimately released into independence. Many have retained special symbolic, political, and economic relations, however, through the nominal role of the Queen as the sovereign and through membership in the Commonwealth of Nations.

3.4 America jumps in: the growth and impact of a superpower

The British Empire spread and established English as a global language, but in the twentieth century this role was secured and expanded by the rise of Britain's former colony, the United States of America, to the status of a global superpower – the only one left, in fact, by the end of the century.

Throughout the nineteenth century the then young nation of the United States was occupied with herself. The USA consolidated her independence in the British–American War of 1812, extended her territory through westward expansion and the Indian Wars, and strengthened her unity in the Civil War of 1861–65 after the secession of the South as the Confederate States of America. By the end of the century, however, the nation was stable enough to turn her attention outward. With the Spanish–American War of 1898, the USA entered the world scene. As the outcome of that war, Americans received authority over Puerto Rico (still a dependent territory), Guam, and, most importantly in the present context, the Philippines, ceded by Spain. With this step America became a colonial power herself, and the intention was to turn the Philippines into a model colony. America acted with strength and determination, sending large numbers of teachers, for instance. It is highly questionable whether their cultural goal was achieved in the long run, but the rapid and thorough spread of English in the Philippines is unprecedented.

The United States entered both World Wars of the twentieth century after some years of conflict, and decided them victoriously; and by the end of the century, after decades of "Cold War," the breakdown of the Soviet Union left the US as the world's only remaining military and political superpower. Alongside that, America's economy became the world's largest one and the dollar the leading currency of all international business – developments which together clearly gave a fresh boost to the English language on the global scene. Globalization, perhaps the most important cultural development of the last part of the century, in many respects also means westernization, and Americanization in particular. American-based transnational companies have been leading in this process, and have built global supply structures in mass market conditions. American cultural dominance operates on many levels, including the world's economy (sometimes also called "McDonaldization"), in the media (with Hollywood movies and American TV serials to be found almost everywhere), politically, and so on. Reactions to this trend vary, obviously. Whether it should be welcomed as "development" and an increase of opportunities or deplored as a loss of cultural (and linguistic) diversity is hotly debated but ultimately immaterial, somehow – the process as such seems to be progressing irrespective of what we think of it. And of course this has serious implications for the global role and spread of English. For many developing nations the USA is a desirable business partner, so the acquisition and competent and regular use of English are goals worth striving for for both many nations and millions of individuals almost everywhere. In many countries knowledge of English is perceived as the gateway to a better life.

Interestingly enough, these processes also have immediate consequences for the forms of English to be heard around the globe (even outside of the movies, CNN, and so on, of course). As former British colonies, in practically all Postcolonial Englishes (except for the Philippines, obviously) the input source and the model for language pedagogy used to be and still is British English, and all of these varieties have ultimately been derived from and still show strong similarities with this lead variety. Increasingly, however, it has been reported that in many countries (such as Australia, New Zealand, South Africa, Singapore, and elsewhere) significant traces of the Americanization of World Englishes can be heard, with American expressions, words, and pronunciation habits (such as rhoticity) creeping in, especially among the young. There is little solid documentation of this available, but all the incidental evidence taken together is strong. And usually attitudes to this development are critical. Nobody, it seems, wants to be dominated by the

Americans – but obviously American English is imbued with a whole lot of covert prestige.

3.5 Internationalization and localization: post-independence developments

None of these developments, however, are sufficient to explain what has been happening with English on a global scale over the last few decades and what is going on today. The British Empire is certainly not sufficient as an explanation. After independence, one could have expected the English language to have been removed in former colonies, as an undesirable piece of colonial heritage and reminder of days without national sovereignty. In reality, however, only very few nations (notably, Tanzania and to some extent Malaysia) did try to replace it with an indigenous language. In contrast, in most nations English has remained highly desirable and strong.

And most likely this is also not the case because everybody nowadays wants to speak like an American or with Americans. In fact, Britain and America are no longer the only "epicenters" of the language – Australian and New Zealand English are largely linguistically independent and endonormatively oriented these days, i.e. they accept language norms of their own. And they are internationally influential especially in Asian countries, for obvious geographical reasons and because of many economic and academic connections. English has become a pluricentric language.

The internationalization of English is clearly a major trend. It is disputed, however, whether this process correlates with the emergence of a specific form of English for such contexts, an "International English." There is certainly a common core of vocabulary items, grammar rules, and also pronunciation conventions which is shared everywhere. Such homogeneity seems primarily restricted to writing, however, and it fades away on the level of pronunciation. One major reason for the international appeal of English is certainly its usefulness, its association with prestige and power, and its role as a primary tool for socioeconomic advancement, all of which require a "standard" form of speech production. But that is clearly not the whole story.

The alternative process which has strengthened English in many localities, and a most interesting one for linguists to observe and study, is its localization, indigenization, and nativization. English has grown local roots in many countries and cultures. It has become nativized, i.e. it has developed indigenous forms, and these local ways of speaking English have been adopted by many speakers as symbols of regional identities. Just like Yorkshiremen and American Southerners, English speakers from Singapore or Lagos speak English in a distinctive fashion, recognize each other by their accents, and view their ways of speaking English as immediate expressions of their personalities and their respective cultural settings. It is the growth of such indigenous roots that gives English much of its current vitality.

Furthermore, many communities on all continents have undergone language shift, and English, spoken in local ways, is now the main or even the only language of several indigenous ethnic groups. In some countries in Africa and Asia, English is increasingly chosen as a first and family language, most commonly so in Singapore, and amongst educated couples in African cities. The children born into these families grow up as native speakers of English, even if this seems to conflict with the traditional definition of "native speaker." One interesting question is whether or to what extent these children have an internalized language knowledge, a linguistic competence which is different from that of British or American speakers. Studying the new native speakers of these new varieties of English should be an interesting topic for future research.

3.6 Variety types on historical grounds

All of these historical processes and contact conditions have produced a range of varieties of English resultant from and suitable for their respective settings, characterized by specific formal properties. Consequently, let us return to the previous chapter's attempts at working out similarities and differences between Englishes, this time specifically in the light of how varieties can be classified as output types, produced by their historical origins. Two categorizations are particularly useful in such a perspective.

The first one was proposed by Gupta (1997). She considers the number of languages spoken in a given ecology and the pattern of transmission and acquisition of English (with three options: ancestral transmission from parents to children in their infancy, informal language learning in contact situations, and formal language teaching in schools). On that basis she distinguishes five kinds of settings of English (though, again, in some cases this implies abstractions):

- "Monolingual ancestral English": This describes the classic settlers' community, as found, e.g., in Australia;
- "Monolingual contact variety": Here, in addition to regular transmission, the informal emergence and acquisition of nonstandard language forms under contact conditions has produced creoles, as in Jamaica;

- "Multilingual scholastic English": This describes multilingual countries like India, in which English was introduced by formal education, and individual competence in it correlates with the amount of schooling an individual has received;
- "Multilingual contact variety" countries, such as Singapore, Ghana, or Papua New Guinea, combine the multilingual ecological setting with some degree of informal transmission and acquisition, leading to strong contact effects; and
- "Multilingual ancestral English," a situation which like the first one is marked by direct transmission in a strong group of English settlers who co-exist, however, with other language groups, e.g. in South Africa or Canada.

A much more detailed list of historically based entries in what they call the "English Language Complex" is offered by Mesthrie and Bhatt (2008), who distinguish the following:

- metropolitan standards, recognizing only two such "mother-state" norms, i.e. British and American English;
- Colonial standards, the formal, increasingly accepted speech norms of extraterritorial settler countries, including Australia, New Zealand, Canada, South Africa, and, in their view, also former Rhodesia;
- regional dialects, esp. in England and America, and less prominently in Australia, etc.;
- social dialects, comprising class and ethnicity-based varieties such as Britain's RP, Australia's "Broad," or South Africa's "Respectable";
- Pidgin Englishes, e.g. in West Africa;
- Creole Englishes, e.g. in the Caribbean;
- ESL, the formal usage of, say, Nigeria or Sri Lanka;
- EFL, as used in China, Europe, Brazil, etc.;
- Immigrant Englishes, spoken by migrants coming to an English-dominant country, e.g. Chicanos in the US;
- Language-shift Englishes, where English has (largely) replaced an erstwhile indigenous language, as in Ireland;
- Jargon Englishes – rudimentary and unstable forms, less systematic than even a pidgin, e.g. South Seas Jargon;
- Hybrid Englishes, the thriving mixed codes like "Hinglish" in India or Taglish in the Philippines.

Such a listing may be helpful, although, as the authors admit, it also raises questions, e.g. as to which varieties belong where (or even whether they should be included in a listing of "Englishes" at all), possible overlaps, and status distinctions.

3.7 **The spread of global English: some numbers**

One of the first and most obvious questions which anybody talking about World Englishes will be faced with is the one for numbers: How many speakers of English and how many global varieties are there? Understandably enough, though next to impossible to answer with any precision or reliability, given all the uncertainties involved. What does it mean to "speak English" for instance? Would a learner who has acquired dozens of words but can barely communicate fluently count? Also, I pointed out earlier that dialects (and even languages) are next to impossible to delimit from each other, and thus to count, and it is equally difficult to determine how much English there needs to be in a community or region to be accepted here. So, all of these figures involve a high degree of uncertainty – it is possible to make educated (hopefully!) guesses, but little more. Note that varying estimates on big countries may make a huge difference. The population of India exceeds one billion today, and English is strong as a second language there – but no one can tell whether the proportion of "speakers" is 3 percent (a conservative estimate frequently given a few decades ago but most likely much too low today) or 30 or more percent – and obviously that results in huge numerical differences. Similarly for China – millions, probably hundreds of millions are struggling to learn English there, but there is no way of telling how many are really able to speak it.

So, with all these reservations, what might speaker numbers be like? For "native speakers," add up first-language speaker numbers from the leading L1-countries (note that even in the UK and the US millions of people do not speak English as their first language!): very roughly 250-plus million in the US, 60 million in the UK, 20 million in Australia and New Zealand, 5 million in the Caribbean, 3 million in Ireland – we are likely to end up somewhere between 350 and 380 million. Competent second-language users certainly exceed that number – take some 40–50 million in the US, up to 30 million in South Africa, somewhere between 60 and 120 million in Nigeria, and possibly 300 million or more in India – up to 600 million people seems not an exaggerated figure. Learners, with more or less fluency – well, see my points above, with respect to China alone; and even in a country like Germany, with a population of more than 80 million most of whom would have had some schooling in English at some point earlier in their lives – how many people could really hold a simple conversation?? Global learner estimates vary somewhere between 500 million and 1500 million; and most recently Crystal (2008) estimated that the number of "speakers" of English globally might be somewhere in the region of 2 billion by today.

Actually, Crystal also makes a few additional, more fundamental, and less contestable points which may be considered quite stunning. Native speakers of English are outnumbered by second- or foreign-language users by a ratio of about one to three or four today; and over just the last quarter-century the proportion of users of English on a global scale has risen dramatically from roughly one fifth to about a third of the world's population!

For varieties and countries, we are on slightly safer ground. McArthur (1998) has put together some extensive listings and counts on the basis of reasonable assumptions, facilitated also by the fact that the status of a language in a nation tends to be more stable. He lists 36 ENL territories (many of them very minor, and in six of them other strong languages co-exist), 57 ESL territories, and 139 EFL territories. Again, individual cases may be discussed and possibly disregarded, but the overall magnitudes seem sound. McArthur (2002: xvi–xvii) identifies and locates 104 territories in which "English is a significant language." Similar lists and representations can be found in Crystal (1988: 5–9), Melchers and Shaw (2003: 146, 161), and Crystal (2003: 57–60). Map 5, which digests input from all of these sources, shows those countries around the globe in which English has some sort of a special status. Note that I am being deliberately fuzzy here, and not making a distinction between ENL, ESL, and so on. Any such classification would be inaccurate in some respects, and unfair to some speaker groups.

3.8 Global spread, regional contexts, local issues

So – present-day English around the world is a multi-faceted topic, and we have learned that it is better not to talk about just "one language" but about many different varieties. Each of these has its distinct set of properties on various language levels, even if these features are typically not assigned to any specific language variety in an exclusive fashion. It is the mix of features that causes the distinct identity of varieties of the language, not any single, uniquely recognizable form. And each of these varieties also operates in its own, characteristic circumstances and social settings. Interestingly enough, the reference range of these settings varies widely, from the global (for International, common core English) via the national or regional sphere (in the form of national norms or more encompassing regional dialects) to the local or group-specific domain (for dialects and dialectal forms which are directly tied to local identities or group membership).

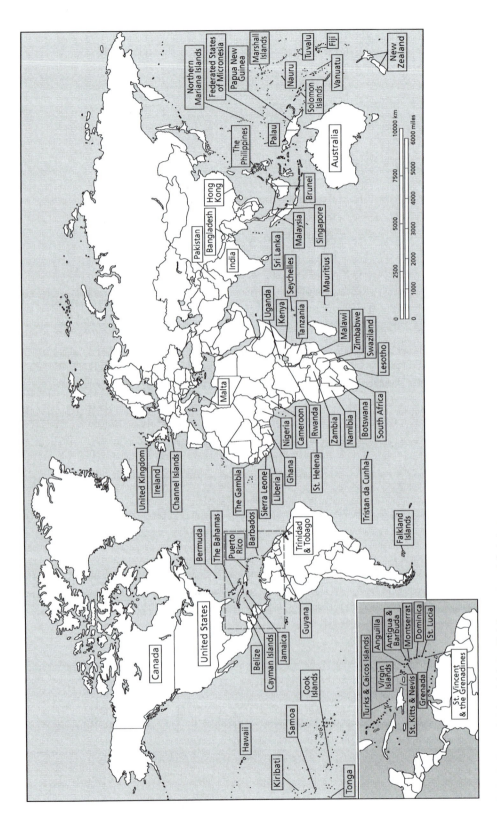

Map 5 Countries in which English has a special status

In the last two chapters we have done our homework and covered the basic ground – we have been familiarized with basic terms and notions, categories, and approaches, and also historical background facts and their specific linguistic consequences. It is now time to fill this framework with life, by looking at specific varieties of English in their respective contexts. This is what we'll be doing in the following three chapters, in which English in specific parts of the world will be presented. Given that this is a textbook, there is no point in providing lots and lots of details, so my tactics will be a combination of the general with the specific and exemplary. In each case, the broader regional context (the historical background, motives for using English, typical forms and sociolinguistic settings of the language in a region or country) will be surveyed first. Subsequently, I will zoom in on one country or variety from this region which is to be characterized and discussed in somewhat greater detail, as a "prototypical" model case of the respective region.

I don't think it is enough to remain aloof, on an abstract level, however. The real fun in this topic is getting exposure to Englishes as spoken on the ground, as it were. Therefore, as a prominent part of these case studies I provide brief text samples illustrative of the respective variety, typically in the form of a transcript or a sample text, and in many cases you'll be able to listen to the real-life speech which underlies the transcripts on the website accompanying this book. You'll certainly realize that these samples are distinctive and characteristic of their respective origins. Depending on where you live yourself you might find them odd, interesting, or difficult to understand, somewhat generically. It may be more difficult, however, to pin down what is really distinctive and noteworthy about them in purely linguistic terms, and I suppose it is better to provide guidance in that respect. Therefore, each of these samples will be followed by a commentary, i.e. an exemplary listing and discussion of select linguistic features which give the respective sample and variety its distinctive flair, the features that you might want to pay special attention to. And actually in a few cases I'll ask you to pay that special attention to some additional samples as well which I'll refer to in the Exercises sections.

We'll start by looking at some traditional, baseline dialects of the "Old World," i.e. in Britain, and at its expansion into the "New" one, American dialects and Caribbean varieties and creoles. Next, we'll note similarities between forms of English found in the Southern Hemisphere – Australia, New Zealand, and South Africa. And finally, we'll be paying attention to the myriad of "New Englishes" and contact varieties which have been mushrooming in the "Outer Circle" – in Sub-Saharan Africa, South and South-East Asia, and the Pacific region, down to the "Expanding Circle," the emerging learner varieties of East Asia, notably China.

Chapter summary

This chapter surveyed a number of topics which have to do with the historical background of the global spread of English and its linguistic consequences:

- European colonialism and colonization types;
- the growth and decline of the British Empire;
- the contribution of the United States to the globalization of English;
- the tension between the internationalization and the localization of English;
- consequently, the range of variety types which have grown in specific circumstances; and
- an assessment of the numbers of varieties and speakers involved.

The constant leitmotif in all of this is probably the relationship between the language-external and the internal, the direct functional relationship between historical events and constellations, the communicative patterns caused by these, and, consequently, their effects upon the development of linguistic forms and varieties. This relationship will continue to be explored and illustrated.

Exercises and activities

Exercise 3a   Situate yourself and your own variety of English in the listings of variety types provided in this chapter: What kind of a variety do you speak yourself, and in which kind of historical context do you operate? Of the other variety types listed, which ones are familiar to you, and which aren't?

Exercise 3b   Pick three of the expansionist stages of the British Empire (to a specific region at a specific point in time) referred to in this chapter and imagine being a typical participant in this migration or event. Where would you possibly come from, how would you feel, how would you speak? How would you react to the fact that others around you speak differently?

Exercise 3c   Which other varieties that you can think of (and possibly have been exposed to) could be classified as "Immigrant Englishes" in the above sense?

Key terms discussed in this chapter
Berlin Conference of 1884–85
British Empire

colonization
colonization types
exploitation colonies
globalization
indentured laborers
indirect rule
international English
koinéization
language shift
plantation colonies
scramble for Africa
settlers, settler colonies
trade colonies

Further reading

McArthur (1998) and (2002) provide lots of material on global varieties of English in
their respective historical perspectives. Hickey (2004) focuses specifically upon
the conditions of the transmission of the English language from Britain to all other
world regions, and on possible continuities and discontinuities in this process. The
perspective of the colonial and postcolonial history of varieties of English in a
number of specific countries and in all world regions, connecting historical facts
and linguistic properties, is also at the heart of the approach and discussion by
Schneider (2007a). From a purely historical perspective, disregarding language
for a moment, I have found Dalziel (2006) a most attractive guide to the history of
the British Empire, with lots of beautiful maps and illustrations.

CHAPTER 4

Language crossing an ocean: Old World and New World

In this chapter ...

In this chapter we will learn about the earliest and most deeply rooted processes of colonization which have shaped the English language, in what used to be known as the "Old World" and the "New World." English itself is shown to be a product of colonization, namely of the settlement of the British Isles by Germanic tribes more than 1,500 years ago, similar to the effect on language of colonial expansion in the modern age. British English was influenced and shaped by contact with an indigenous language (Celtic) and with later "adstrates" (Scandinavian and French, mostly). We then look at the initial stages of the colonial diffusion of English in the seventeenth century, to North America (ultimately producing American English as we know it today) and to the Caribbean (with the forms of English found there being largely products of a major restructuring process, creolization). In each of these cases I will survey the general sociohistorical context and will then zoom in to a closer, exemplary discussion (including a text sample) of one characteristic regional variety of English found there.

4.1 Roots and early expansion: the British Isles

4.1.1 The growth and spread of British English

In the last chapter you read about colonization as a historical activity of European powers and about how this process of expansion, diffusion, and dominance came to an end in the twentieth century (but has left substantial traces to the present day). Certainly this was a distinctive phase in human history, and perhaps in its global extension it was a unique one. On the other hand, migration, and all the social consequences and conflicts that it entails, has always been a part of human experience, and it may help to assess the status of English to consider that the language itself is a product of migration, colonization, settlement processes, and contact settings. In this section we look at the beginnings and at the earliest steps of expansion, and you may find more hybridity than expected.

Languages do not suddenly emerge "out of thin air," as it were – they are transmitted from one generation to another (and possibly modified in that process). This transmission process can be traced back through time to the point where we have no more written records, and presumably it went on further back in time in much the same way. The same applies to English. It is customary to date its beginnings to the middle of the fifth century AD, when Germanic tribes conquered England, bringing their own West Germanic dialects with them, but these very same tribes were descendants of speakers of Proto-Germanic and ultimately Indo-European somewhere in eastern and central Europe earlier on. We know something but increasingly less about these peoples the further back we go in time, but we can be certain that they, in turn, had contacts with tribes and peoples of other genetic and cultural origins. They certainly exchanged not only goods but also words and probably other linguistic bits and pieces with them.

The Germanic tribes on the continent, for instance, took over words from Latin for things and concepts they did not have or know and which therefore for them meant cultural innovation and progress: technologies like *street*, measurements like *mile* and *pound*, or pleasures like *wine*. Exchange and contact also on the level of language and communication occur whenever humans of different origins come together and interact. Until fairly recently traditional philological scholarship tended to downplay or ignore this fact, perhaps because of a nationalistic attitude that prevailed in the nineteenth century when the earliest influential descriptions of the history of English were crafted ("discursively constructed," our literary colleagues might say) by scholars who tended to emphasize the "purity" of the Germanic ancestry of English.

So, by conventional wisdom it all began in 449, when a few West Germanic tribes, known as Angles, Saxons, and Jutes, crossed over to England. "Timeline A" begins with that date, and then lines up major events in the history of British English to the present day, described below.

The earliest Germanic invaders were followed by many more settlement waves, who subdued the indigenous population. In the course of the next few

Timeline A: The British Isles	
449	Germanic tribes begin to conquer the British island
597	Pope Gregory sends out St. Augustine to christianize England
878	King Alfred and Guthrum sign the Treaty of Wedmore, which grants residence rights to Scandinavian settlers in the so-called "Danelaw"
1066	The Norman Conquest starts centuries of diglossia and French dominance in England
1204	King John loses England's possessions on the continent
1400	Death of Chaucer
1476	Caxton introduces the printing press to England, thus greatly contributing to the evolution of a standard language form
1536	Formal unification Statutes of England and Wales
1558–1603	Reign of Queen Elizabeth I
1616	Shakespeare's death
1707	Union of England and Scotland as Great Britain
1755	Publication of Dr. Johnson's *Dictionary*
1801	Act of Union with Ireland
1845–49	Great famine in Ireland
1837–1901	Reign of Queen Victoria
1914–18	World War I
1922	Secession of southern Irish Free State from United Kingdom
1939–45	World War II
1973	Britain joins the European Union (then the European Economic Community)

centuries they established various regional kingdoms, which were later united in the ninth and tenth centuries under King Alfred and his successors. On the island they encountered Celts, another Indo-European but non-Germanic tribe, who had lived there for several centuries. The Celts had themselves been influenced culturally (and probably linguistically, but we have no records to reliably tell us) by other early contacts. Romans had held Britain as a province for about three centuries. In the north reportedly "wild" tribes known as the Picts and Scots were perceived as a threat. Actually, even further back in time there must have been other ethnicities living on the British Isles of whom we know next to nothing (the builders of Stonehenge, for instance).

When the Celts were conquered by the Anglo-Saxons, many of them were pushed back to the co-called "Celtic fringe" in the west and the north (Celtic languages can still be heard today in Wales, the northwest of Scotland, and Ireland, and existed until fairly recently also in Cornwall and on the Isle of Man). Most likely, however, some of them also stayed and were culturally and linguistically assimilated. Whether this early instance of colonization and hybridization influenced and modified the Anglo-Saxon language (later called Old English) is a matter of some debate today. Traditional, purist scholarship proclaimed that except for a few place names the Celtic contact has not left any traces on the English language. In recent years, however, some scholars have suggested that, similar to current contact processes, the assimilation of Celtic people and the Anglo-Saxon contact with their language must have left traces in English, possibly even in some of its core grammatical properties – an early case of "structural nativization" in a contact setting, as it were.

From its heyday, in the eighth and ninth centuries, we have reliable and respectable documents of Old English, but nothing would be more mistaken than assuming it was a pure, honorable, and stable Germanic language, preserved in epic poems and biblical texts and untouched by external influences. First of all, assuming a homogeneous "Old English language" is a simplifying myth anyhow, supported by the fact that most of our records happen to have been preserved from one dialect (West Saxon). In reality, there was a myriad of dialects of which we know little because they were spoken by peasants, hard-working women, and warriors – people whose utterances left no written traces. Secondly, there were important external influences which influenced and hybridized the language substantially, certainly not that dissimilar from the evolution of postcolonial dialects discussed in other chapters of this book.

Christianization was a case in point, spreading from the very late sixth century, both from the south in a missionary move organized by Rome and from the north through the zeal of Scottish and Irish monks spreading their faith. This meant heavy lexical borrowing from Latin, the church language, into early English, and also transformations of old language habits (for instance, words which had long been in use like *God*, *heaven*, or *sin* acquired radically new meanings shaped by the new cultural context).

In the eighth and ninth centuries Danes and Vikings first raided and then invaded the island, and ultimately were given permission to settle and preserve some of their lifestyle in part of the country (in the so-called Treaty of Wedmore of 878). They spoke Old Norse, a language distantly related to Old English (being North, not West, Germanic in origin), and the intimate contact between the two peoples after the Scandinavians settled for good triggered a new wave of language contact and external influences upon English. This results in heavy lexical borrowing (including everyday words like *call*, *cast*, *egg*, or *take*) and even some important grammatical influences. Most notably (and indicative of the strength of contact), Old English adopted function words like the pronoun *they*. Furthermore, it seems likely that Old English speakers dropped some word endings when they talked to Scandinavians, because the inflection endings of both languages differed from each other and were thus difficult to handle, while many word stems themselves were probably similar and mutually recognizable, and thus communicatively more helpful.

In 1066, England was conquered by invaders from Normandy, who spoke a northern French dialect. It is noteworthy that this dialect itself was also a product of hybridity and language shift (and most likely substrate transfer). As the name suggests, the invaders were descended from "Norse-men" who had resided in France for only about 150 years but had assimilated completely (well, almost so – it's not a surprise that they spoke a funny kind of French). Anyway – within a short period of time they occupied all the powerful positions in society, and for a few centuries their "Anglo-Norman" dialect was spoken widely in England as the language of the ruling class, often their only one. Perhaps it is ironic that during these centuries the English language largely underwent the same situation that it caused (if we believe that a language, and not its speakers, may cause anything) to so many indigenous languages centuries later, during colonization. In any case, it largely experienced the same process of mixture, although for external, political reasons ultimately it resurfaced as *the* language of England.

It did so in a substantially transformed shape, however. The English vocabulary was enormously expanded and influenced by French, so much so that the word stock of modern English counts as half Germanic and half Romance in character (and most of these loan words, like *saint*, *royal*, *profound*, or *pleasure* are no longer felt to be foreign at all). Note that the French impact did not only affect the lexical level, however. Similar to the process of "structural nativization" in the colonial period we can observe influences on the pronunciation level. For example, the middle consonant in the word *pleasure*, /ʒ/, a sound which had characterized French but had not existed in English, became a new phoneme of English. In English grammar there are also some patterns which have been suggested to follow French structural models. They include

- the comparison of adjectives by means of a separate word *more/most*, similar to French *plus*;
- the use of the erstwhile plural pronoun *you* to address individuals, similar to French *vous*; and
- the spreading habit of using interrogative pronouns like *who* or *which* also in relative clauses, similar to French *qui*.

The gradual integration of the French vocabulary component into Middle English also had the indirect effect of increasing the receptiveness of the English-speaking language community to foreign borrowings in general. In addition to select borrowings from other European languages, at the end of the Middle Ages this primarily meant borrowing words from Latin, because through the cultural wave called the Renaissance, classical texts and concepts became highly fashionable, and the words denoting such concepts entered English directly through translations of ancient texts. Again, many of these words (take *expect*, *habitual*, *dedicate*, *disrespect*, or *illustrate* as examples) have been thoroughly integrated without appearing foreign any longer, while many others have remained rare in English. And finally, the colonial expansion enriched not only the "New Englishes" which are one central topic of this book with indigenous words but also "mainstream" English back home and everywhere. Words like *barbecue*, *moccasin*, *bungalow*, *taboo*, or *boomerang* are unquestionably fully integrated into the international core of the English vocabulary, even if many of them remain semantically attached to their original cultural contexts.

The idea of colonization being central to the character of British English itself, developed in this section so far, can be made fruitful to an understanding of the non-English varieties of the English language in the British Isles as well. Scotland had been and remained essentially a Celtic-speaking territory throughout the Middle Ages (and still has pockets of Gaelic spoken in remote locations), even if English, in the form of northern dialects, had infiltrated southeastern Scotland as early as in the Old English period, and spread further later. In the sixteenth century, Scots was a distinct language with a rich literary tradition, but after the Union with England in 1707 it gradually gave way to English, though Scottish has remained a highly distinct dialect. Similarly, in Wales and in Ireland English was introduced slowly and in waves, replacing the native Celtic languages Welsh and Irish, respectively, only gradually, and to varying extents in different regions. To the present day this replacement has not been completed. Some scholars today claim that there are distinctive "Celtic Englishes," dialects which emerged in these early steps of colonial expansion and have been influenced by Celtic substrate effects.

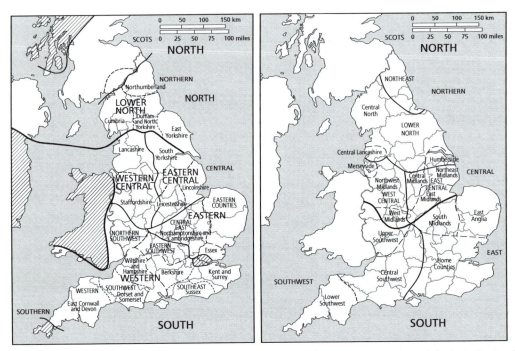

Map 6 Regional distribution of traditional dialects versus modern dialects in England
(from Trudgill 1990: 33, 63; reproduced by permission)

In England itself, the language displays a substantial amount of regional variation. England is commonly divided into dialect regions which roughly continue Anglo-Saxon tribal settlement patterns, with the major regions being South-West, South-East, West and East Central, and the North (Trudgill 1990). Reflecting demographic and sociopolitical changes of the twentieth century, England's linguistic landscape has changed considerably over the last few generations. An older generation of rural people, whose dialects were studied in the *Survey of English Dialects* of the middle of the twentieth century (Orton *et al.* 1962–1971), spoke so-called "traditional dialects," which are now strongly recessive. But new regional distinctions have emerged, and so-called "modern dialects" still show regional speech divisions. Map 6 shows how the dividing lines between traditional and modern dialects have moved.

Urban conglomerates have produced distinct and well-known stereotyped dialects, like Scouse in Liverpool or Geordie in Newcastle; and the big cities are still the centers of linguistic variation and innovation (see Folkes and Docherty 1999). Large numbers of immigrants from former colonies, notably from South Asia and from the Caribbean, have chosen Britain as their home, and their linguistic integration has produced new varieties of English in the mother country itself, for example "British Black English." And of course this changing situation has strongly affected long-standing English ways of speaking as well. Cockney, the traditional dialect of London's city, is reported to be vanishing today, or rather, to be replaced, at least among urban adolescents, by a mixture of traditional Cockney elements with young immigrants' speech forms. (If you don't know what I am talking about watch some Ali G clips, for instance on YouTube – certainly an artificial speech form, but suggestive of and playing with ongoing linguistic innovation processes.)

Higher up in the social continuum, in middle-class and upper-class speech forms, there is also something going on. Regional speech models are nowadays accepted in many public contexts, like in the media (which was not the case just a few decades ago). "Estuary English," a mixture of RP and some Cockney and southeastern dialect features, is said to be gradually replacing RP, certainly its conservative variant, as the commonly preferred prestige form.

4.1.2 Case study: Northern English

We have seen so far that even British English, which in a global perspective is so often viewed as an ideal model variety to strive for, is far from pure, and has emerged as a product of colonization and various kinds of cultural adaptation and hybridization in itself. It is also far from homogeneous. The differences between its regional and social dialects are enormous, and many local dialects are clearly far from easily intelligible to an outsider. Let me illustrate that by looking more closely at a single dialect, that spoken in northern England. Map 7 identifies the region, showing both the traditional county structure which is still strongly alive in cultural documents on the region, and the new county structure introduced in 1974.

"The North" in England is a cultural notion in the first place, and its dialectal speech contributes significantly to the region's distinctiveness. The notion itself is also far from homogeneous. At its core there is the rural component: "North" associates farming, pastures, and beautiful landscape in the Lake District or in the Yorkshire Moors, and prototypical northerners from earlier days would have been Lancashire peasants or Whitby fishermen. Far from being merely idyllic, however, the North has also been marked by its harsh side. It has been a region characterized by mining and the demanding conditions of life that came with it, by early industrialization and consequently urbanization, hard labor, and poverty. Somehow the regional culture combines strong historical roots and regional pride with a sense of marginalization from the perspective of the center of political power, London. And this very same sense of ambiguity characterizes the region's speech as well. Like many distinctive dialects, attitudes towards northern English vary. From the outside it is strongly stigmatized, and has always tended to appear, as Wales (2006: 4) puts it, "provincial," "working class,"

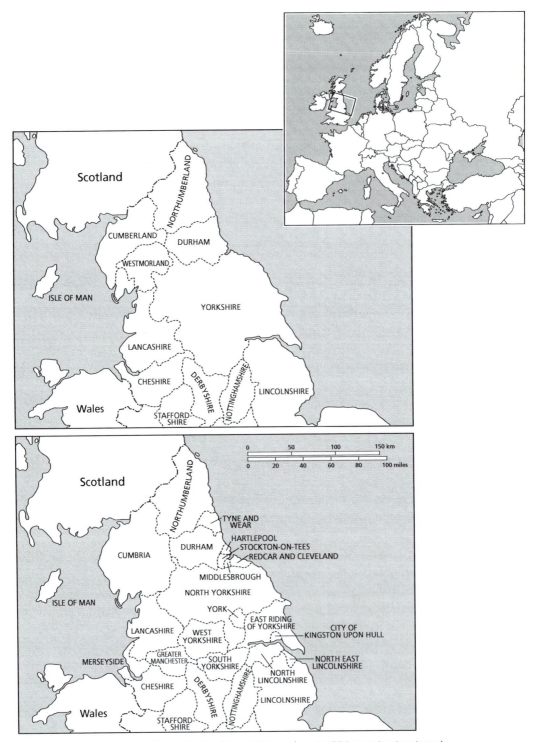

Map 7 Northern England (pre-1974 and post-1974 county structures)

and "uncouth." To its speakers, however, it is a source of pride, enjoying strong covert prestige (as sociolinguists have called such a situation).

Like many culturally defined regions, the North is not clearly delimited. It extends from the Scottish border southward to include Lancashire and Yorkshire, but whether Cheshire, Nottinghamshire, or Lincolnshire count as northern or "Midland" depends on one's purpose and on varying criteria. There is also no clear linguistic demarcation line. Interestingly enough, despite their overt low-prestige associations some characteristically northern pronunciation features have been moving further to the south in the course of the last century. For example, the comparison between "traditional" and "modern" dialects, drawn by Trudgill (1990) and represented in Map 6 above (see p. 68), shows this quite nicely. In the modern but not the traditional pattern the central region aligns itself with the North, not with the South.

Historically, the region's unity goes back to the Anglo-Saxon kingdom of Northumbria. As was implied in my earlier historical survey, the linguistic distinctiveness of the northern dialect can also be traced back to a major instance of our central topic of colonization and the mixture resulting from it: this is the area where Scandinavian settlers, and whatever linguistic influences they brought with them, were strongest. In addition to East Anglia, the "Danelaw," the region where according to the 878 agreement the Scandinavians were permitted to settle and practice their (Danish) legal system, encompassed the entire region, north of Watling Street, an ancient connection roughly from London to Chester. Consequently, place names and loan words of Scandinavian origin are almost exclusively concentrated in this region, and north of that line. Thousands of such words, regional survivals of early Viking borrowings, have been identified, including, to quote just a few examples, *garth* 'yard', *laik* 'play', *by* 'farmstead', and *aye* 'yes' (Wales 2006: 55).

We know that, similar to other cases of intensive social contact across language boundaries, the Scandinavian impact was even more profound and affected also select grammatical features, as stated earlier. The third person plural pronoun *they*, and also its derivatives *them* and *their*, started here and gradually replaced the corresponding Old English forms *hie* and *hem*, spreading to southern English throughout the Middle English period. It is fascinating to see that actually many characteristic properties of modern English originated in the North. Features like the loss of grammatical gender or of case endings in nouns or the use of the verbal ending *-s* can be originally found in this region and can be observed diffusing from here to the South. The social process which probably accomplished this change was another large-scale migration at the end of the Middle Ages, namely that of northerners to the South to supply the demand for labor there, caused by depopulation in the Black Death and other sociopolitical processes. Research has focused on the southern English standard, so these processes and their causes

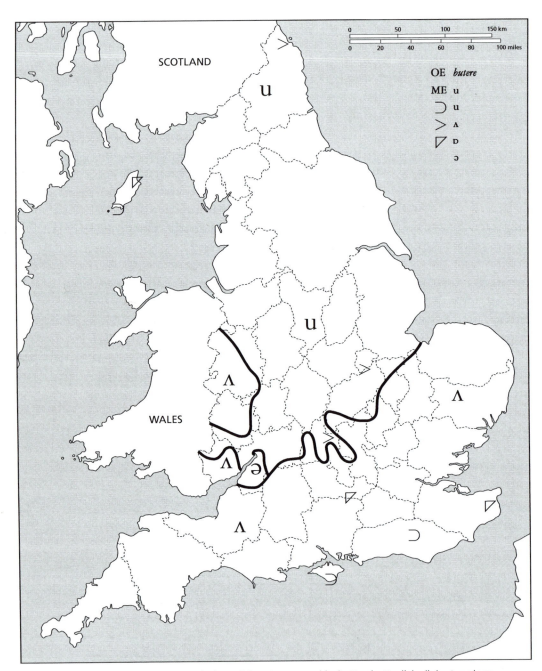

Map 8 The pronunciation of the stem vowel in *butter* in English dialect regions
(adapted from Orton, Sanderson, and Widdowson 1978: Ph50; reproduced by permission)

are insufficiently understood and tend to be downplayed in conventional
language histories. Somehow, however, we can detect a relationship here
which is not that dissimilar from the emergence of New Englishes: a low-
prestige substrate, as it were, has infiltrated the emerging shape of a new

language. Ironically in this case, the newly emerging, "polluted" dialect happens to be southern standard English.

In other respects, northern English is also fairly conservative. For instance, some monophthongal long vowel pronunciations, in words such as *mouse* (rhyming with modern *shoes*), *time* (which sounded like today's *team*), *goat* and *face*, represent Middle English pronunciations which in the south (and hence, in Standard English) were changed in the Early Modern English "Great Vowel Shift." Another characteristically northern form which has been retained from Middle English days is short /ʊ/ in words which in the south have /ʌ/, for example *blood* or *but*, which in the north rhyme with *foot* or *put*. Map 8, taken from the *Linguistic Atlas of England*, which in turn is derived from the large-scale *Survey of English Dialects*, shows the clear north–south divide of this pronunciation pattern in the word *butter*.

Text 2 is supposed to give you an idea of what northern English may look and sound like. It is taken from a highly recommendable website which Yorkshire dialect lovers have put together, thus continuing a long-standing tradition of local poetry and cultural performance.

As you see, the text is densely packed with dialect features. Of the ones listed below, the first four (article reduction, /ʊ/ in *but*, short /a/ in *bath*, and monophthongs in *goat* or *face*) are highly characteristic of northern English, and most others are also widespread in the region but either found in some parts of it only or, conversely, occur elsewhere as well.

* One of the most frequent and noticeable features stands at the border between lexis, grammar, and phonology, namely article reduction. It is highly typical of northern speech that the definite article *the* is reduced to a plain stop *t'*, as in *t'chair, t'shop, t'dooar*, and many more times in this text.

Pronunciation details are clearly most conspicuous:

* The characteristic northern /ʊ/ for /ʌ/ can be heard in *cut, shut, cum* 'come', *sumbdy* 'somebody', etc.
* The /a:/ sound which elsewhere tends to be long is short in the north: *passed* /a/, *fast*.
* Diphthongs are usually monophthongized: the vowels /oː/ in *goa* 'go', *noasy, groan*, /eː/ in *face, cem* 'came', and /iː/ in *freetnin* 'frightening' have no audible offglide.
* Conversely, we also hear standard monophthongs diphthongized, e.g. *leean* 'lean' and *feeat* 'feet', which clearly have a gliding sound /ɪə/, also a characteristically northern conservative feature. Interestingly enough, the same applies to the word *head*, which was shortened in standard English but originally had the same long sound as *lean*, with the length

TEXT 2: "T'Barber's Tale" by Dennis Rhodes

[…] Well, one afternooin, Freddie wor sat i' t'chair evvin 'is 'air cut an ther wor nob'dy else i' t'shop when little Jimmy Fulbright shoved 'is 'eead rahnd t'dooar an sez ter mi: "Mi grandad's passed on an mi Mam wants ter knaw if tha can cum an tidy 'im up fer t'undertekker."

Wi'd bin expectin owd Charlie Fulbright ter goa fer sum time soa it wernt no surprise, poor owd devil ed bin ailin fer years. Soa Ah sez "Aye, Ah'll just get finished wi Freddie an then Ah'll shut t'shop an cum ter see ter 'im. Ther'll bi nob'dy else cummin 'ere terday."

Nah Ah wor a bit capped when Freddie assed if 'e cud cum rahnd wi mi cos fer all 'is blether 'e wor 'ardly t'soart ter bi 'angin rahnd a corpse. Still, Ah sed it'd bi awreyt, it'd bi gerrin dahk i' Fulbright's back bedroom an Ah cud do wi sumbdy ter od t'cannle while Ah shaved owd Charlie.

Soa wi gets rahnd theear but Freddie wernt long as 'e wor wishin 'e edn't bin ser noasy. 'e wor oddin t'cannle bur 'is 'and wor shekkin that much Ah cudn't see reyt wor Ah wor doin. After a bit Ah took t'cannle off 'im an stuck it i' owd Charlie's mahth. That wor awreyt till Ah wor reychin ower ter shave tuther side on 'is face an Ah 'appened ter leean on 'is chest.

Well, t'bit ov air left i' t'body cem aht wi a groan an blew t'cannle aht.

Ah've nivver seen owt move ser fast i' my life. Ah'll sweear Freddie's feeat dint touch a step as 'e went dahn t'stairs an 'e wor aht o' t'front dooar like a dog ahten t'trap.

Ah wudn't a sed owt like but nex mornin, when Ah'd a shopful, 'is missis cam rahnd an sez "Oh Sweeny, whativver did ta do ter my Freddie when 'e cem fer 'is 'air cut yestdy. 'e walked in 'ooam, white as a sheet, supped ayf a bottle o' whiskey an wudn't say a word."

Soa, Ah'd ter tell 'er wor ad 'appened an o' cooarse, all t'lads i' t'shop cracked aht laffin.

Then shi sez "Ah'm capped at thee Sweeny, tekkin 'im wi thi on a job like that. The knaws as weall as ennybody at 'e's all wind an watter. Fancy freetnin 'im like that." An off shi flahnced.

Word sooin went rahnd t'village an Freddie dint ayf tek sum stick till it all blew ovver but yer knaw 'e nivver assed ter goa wi mi ageean.

Source: www.yorkshire-dialect.org; reproduced by permission of Kevin Wilde (abbreviated; reprinted sample begins after 2:31 minutes of recording; full text and audio track on website)

retained here. The /aʊ/ diphthong is realized by this speaker as a long low monophthong, as in *aht* 'out', *mahth* 'mouth', or *rahnd* 'round', which is reported to characterize South Yorkshire; elsewhere in the north a long /u:/ is also common in these words.

Amongst the dialect pronunciations which are to be found both in this sample and also more widely in England are the following:

- In words like *granddad* or *back*, the vowel is a low /a/, not a raised /æ/.
- Word-initial *h-* is commonly dropped, so *'is* means *his*, *'air* represents *hair*, and so on with *'ere*, *'ardly*, etc. In the North this pronunciation characterizes working-class males and some sub-regions.
- Postvocalic /l/ is vocalized, as in *owd* 'old', *od* 'hold'.
- As in many dialects, a word-final velar nasal /ŋ/, represented in writing as *-ng*, is pronounced at the alveolar position directly behind the teeth ridge, as /n/: *evvin* 'having', *expectin*, *cummin*, etc.
- Final consonants are readily omitted, as in *i'* 'in', *wi* 'with'. Word-internally, consonant clusters may be reduced, as in *assed* 'asked' or *cannle* 'candle'.
- Notice that this speaker is non-rhotic, i.e. he does not pronounce an *r* in words like *wor*, *chair*, *hair*, etc. Some parts of the region, notably those close to the Scottish border in the far north as well as parts of Lancashire and Northumbria are rhotic, others are not.

The sample also illustrates some phenomena of dialect grammar:

- The verbal suffix *-s*, which is restricted to the third person singular in standard English, occurs freely in other grammatical persons as well: *Ah sez* 'I say', *wi gets*, *the knaws* 'you know'. Both in a historical and in a regional perspective this is a characteristically northern feature.
- The copular form *were*, positive as well as negative, occurs where *was* might be expected: *Freddie wor sat*, *it wernt*, *Ah wor*, *'e wor*.
- The old second person singular pronoun *thou/thee*, replaced in the standard by the plural form *you*, has been preserved: *tha/ta*, *thee/thi*. This marks the dialect employed as rather traditional.
- The possessive form of *my* is *mi*, as in *mi Mam*.
- As in so many colloquial forms of English, double negatives can be found: *it wernt no surprise*.

Finally, there are also a few characteristic dialect words in the sample, including *lads* 'men, boys', *aye* 'yes', *owt* 'anyone', *capped* 'surprised', and *outen* 'out (of)'.

In general, let us take note of a fact which characterizes all language varieties: a dialect consists of all kinds of elements and influences, with varying degrees of conspicuousness. There are usually a small number of character-istics which are salient, known to observers and perhaps adduced to identify a speaker's origin – as in this case the pronunciations of *cum* and *pass*. But beyond that there are many features which are perhaps more or less closely associated with the dialect in question but not really distinctive, shared with many other dialects (as, for instance, the pronunciations of *face* or *o(l)d*, double negation, or possessive *mi*) or, for that matter, of course, also with standard English (including, just as an example, an irrealis subjunctive in *wishin 'e edn't bin* 'wishing he hadn't been ...' and most syntactic structures, like *Freddie asked if he could come round ...*). It's a mixed bag.

4.2 Building a New World? North America

4.2.1 A short history of American English

Even if by now it is conventionally perceived as an established reference variety, American English is the first and oldest of all colonial settler vari-eties. Important dates in the history of North America and the emergence of this variety are put together in Timeline B.

Beginning with the Puritans, Cavaliers, and other settlers of the early seventeenth century, the continent has been swamped by wave after wave of immigrants, first from various parts of the British Isles, later from all over Europe, and finally from almost anywhere in the world. All of these migrants brought along and contributed their distinctive speech forms. American cultural mythology has forged the "melting pot" metaphor for this process, where all immigrant groups contribute something to but also are ultimately assimilated to a fairly homogeneous culture. And the same line of thinking certainly can be applied to the growth of the American "language" (as Mencken and others have called it). American English is undisputedly a product of a mixing process. First, this concerns the mixing of many dialects, a process which linguists call koinéization, characterized by the loss of extreme dialect forms (because they tend to be communicatively unsuccessful in many cases) and the emergence of a "middle-of-the-road" dialect, as it were. Secondly, the same applies to the integration of immigrants whose ancestral language was not English. Typically, the second generation tended to be bilingual and the third one Americanized also linguistically. Some linguistic heritage of their original languages was usually left in a number of loan words and possibly, less visibly, in transfer phenomena on the sound or structure levels. Sadly enough, in comparison with other, later colonial societies the impact of the indigenous population of Native Americans and their languages has remained highly restricted, largely to place names, because the amount of friendly social interaction was low for a long time.

Timeline B: North America

1497	John Cabot claims Newfoundland for the British Crown
1607	Settlement of Jamestown, Virginia
1620	The Pilgrim Fathers land at Plymouth Rock
1763	Britain gains French North America (amongst other regions) in the Peace of Paris
1773	Boston Tea Party
1776	Declaration of Independence of the United States of America
1783	End of American War of Independence
1803	Louisiana Purchase, giving the US legal authority over much of the West
1812–14	British–American "War of 1812"
19th century	Westward expansion of United States territory
1848	Gold rush in California begins
1861–65	Civil War in the US
1867	Dominion of Canada created
1898	Spanish–American War
1941	US enters World War II
1959	Admission of Hawaii and Alaska to the Union as the last states so far
1960s	Civil Rights Movement
1991	Collapse of Soviet Union ends the Cold War and leaves the US the only superpower
2009	Barack Obama becomes first African-American President

It has been disputed how conservative American English is. For example, dialect geographers have attempted (more or less successfully) to trace back linguistic forms of American English to British dialectal roots. The notion of "colonial lag" was coined, suggesting that colonial societies tend to be conservative in their retention of old, cherished forms of behavior. Correspondingly, for some American dialects (notably those in the South and in the Appalachian Mountains) we frequently encounter the popular myth that they represent pure "Elizabethan" or "Shakespearean English."

There may be some truth in this idea, even if, strictly speaking, it is at the very least hugely exaggerated. For example, the American pronunciation feature which is probably most audible in comparison with British RP, rhoticity (the explicit articulation of a postvocalic /r/), is regional and characteristic of an earlier stage of the language in Britain. American English (or large parts of it, for that matter) did not participate in the loss of postvocalic /r/, a pronunciation change which in British English became fashionable in the eighteenth century.

On the other hand, this is clearly only half of the story (or less!). The new colonial environment required new terms for newly encountered things and, in general, triggered many linguistic adaptations and changes, so many features of American English are clearly innovative in character. Actually, the relationship between both major varieties, the amount of similarities or differences, is also fairly difficult to assess. In older textbooks we tend to come across simple-looking lists of British versus American forms on the levels of vocabulary, pronunciation, and grammar, e.g. *petrol – gas, lorry – truck, pavement – sidewalk*; a low /ɑː/ vs. a higher /æː/ vowel in words like *dance* or *can't*; and *Do you have ...* vs. *Have you gotten ...* But in reality, things are much more complex. For example, the supposedly American word *fall* (for *autumn*) occurs in Britain as well but is regional there; and both rhotic and non-rhotic pronunciations can be heard on both sides of the Atlantic, just with different regional and social distributions and evaluations (as to which choice is considered "standard," for instance). More recent research shows that the difference lies not in clear choices of one variety using one form and the other another one, but in a host of highly subtle preferences in word and construction choices: many words and expressions can be used next to anywhere, but they are very strongly preferred in certain varieties over other options.

Beginning with the settlement of Jamestown, Virginia, in 1607 and the Pilgrim Fathers coming to Plymouth in 1620, American English branched off of British English. It thus had its roots in an Early Modern English form of the language – and a rather cultivated one, for that matter, because these earliest settlers came not because of poverty but as religious dissenters. It was the Puritans and some Cavalier gentry from southeastern England, in Massachusetts and Virginia, respectively, who largely shaped the cultural orientation of the early colony. Lower-class and non-southern speech forms from England came a little later but did become highly influential in America in the long run. Towards the latter part of the seventeenth century Quakers and other lowly folk from the midland and northern parts of England and elsewhere came to the American Midlands, via present-day Philadelphia and Pennsylvania, geographically between the two earlier settlement locations. And this regional and social foundation of American English away from

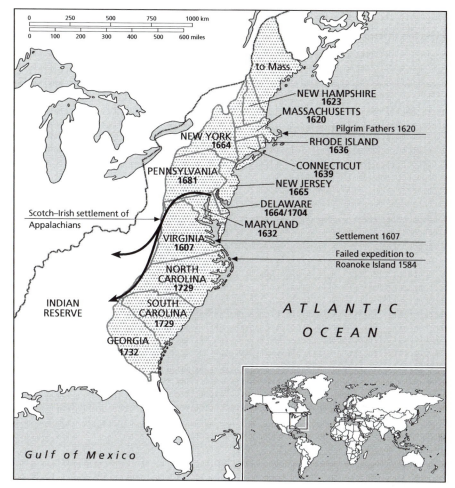

Map 9 Emerging American English: the thirteen original colonies and major settlers' streams

polite London society continued throughout the seventeenth century with the immigration of ordinary working people from northern England, Scotland, and Ireland who moved on into the interior, predominantly into the Appalachian Mountain region. Map 9 shows the location of the founding colonies and the earliest settler streams.

To some extent these early major settlement waves have shaped the most important dialectal distinctions in the United States to the present day. New England's Puritans and Virginia's Cavaliers have left their traces in the distinctive dialects of eastern New England and the conservative upper class of the Lower South, respectively. Interestingly enough, both of these regions and groups, despite being geographically separated from each other, share a number of linguistic features, and to some extent these features are also found in southern English speech. The reason for these similarities is the comparatively conservative orientation of these settler groups. They remained closely associated and upheld strong ties with the mother country's society, including the fact that many young American gentlemen from these origins were educated in England. These shared features include non-rhotic pronunciation (/ka:/ instead of /ka:r/ in *car*) and, for instance, a /j/ glide in the pronunciation of words like *tune*, *new*, or *student* (with /ju:/ rather than just /u:/ as elsewhere in the US).

Conversely, the Quaker and Midland origins of the later arrivals ulti- mately contributed most to the emerging new national variety. The reason for this is simple. It was these speakers and their descendants (and not the conservative upper class who had successfully established themselves in the east) who later felt a need to move on, further into the continent and towards the West, in search of new opportunities.

So, very roughly we might say that the standard of British English is predominantly southern and upper-class English in character (and so are, to some extent, some upper-class American dialects in New England and the South), while mainstream American English has its roots more strongly in the northern English, Scottish, and Irish speech forms of simpler folks.

As is well known, in the mid-eighteenth century political tensions between the thirteen colonies and the homeland ultimately led to the Declaration of Independence (won in the ensuing War) and the foundation of the United States of America. Interestingly enough, in the US independence triggered a wave of nationalism with linguistic ramifications. Politicians and writers called for the development of a distinct and "independent" language form which for a while was labeled "Federal English." A leading figure in this movement was Noah Webster, who published works like *Dissertations on the English Language* (1789), an *American Spelling Book*, and finally an *American Dictionary of the English Language*. But Webster was also too much of a businessman not to realize that a massive break with linguistic traditions would affect the sales figures of his book products – so the long- term practical effect of these discussions and deliberations turned out to be no more than a small number of distinctly American spelling conventions (such as *-or* for *-our*, *-er* for *-re*, etc.).

In fact, the public discourse on language matters of these days produced a number of interesting and seemingly contradictory effects on widespread attitudes to linguistic usage. The national language debate, and with it an emphasis on "good usage," became associated with nationalistic and polit- ical ideas. The idea was that access to such a new language form to "every yeoman" should become a democratic privilege. By implication, striving for such a "proper" language form was widely considered a nationalistic duty (which was one of the reasons why many American households in which no other books, except for the Bible, could be found owned a copy of Webster's so-called "blue-backed speller"). Conservative gatekeepers in society, who more or less explicitly also upheld an admiring attitude towards standard British English as the "best" language form, have continued to promote and enforce such attitudes, which is why in the United States to the present day a strongly prescriptivist tradition prevails. The ability to speak "proper English" is considered a central prerequisite for success in society, and for American school kids knowing how to spell complicated words right counts as a sign of education. Sometimes this leads to really puzzling effects. For example, in a scholarly paper on the education of African-American children I found a discussion on how to teach the spelling of the word *paleontologist* most efficiently. In real-life contexts, which black kid in the US would ever feel a need to speak, let alone write, properly about paleontologists?

In general, the notion of a "standard" in American English is a difficult and problematic one anyhow. Unlike British RP, there is no single accent or speech form which signals only the formality level of the situation and a speaker's status as highly educated but not his or her regional origin. Historically speaking, this situation goes back to the mixing process mentioned earlier, and especially to another wave of koinéization which came with the westward expansion during the nineteenth century. The Louisiana Purchase of 1803 and President Jackson's ruthless policy against the Natives had gradually opened up the Midwest and the West, first for explorers and squatters and later for wave after wave of frontiersmen and settler families. In this process, people with all kinds of origins, predominantly from the Midlands on the east coast and from the inland North, came together in new settlements, and in this continuous mixing process they developed a kind of compromise dialect which gave the impression of a high degree of linguistic homogeneity. Twentieth-century phoneticians coined the label of "General American" for an accent which appeared largely homogeneous from the inland North of the Great Lakes region to the Far West, and a modern, media-oriented era reconceptualized this at times as a supposedly neutral "network English" language form.

That is a question of how finely graded one's view is, however. Dialectologists and sociolinguists have always pointed out that even in this supposedly uniform area there are substantial regional differences in instances of word choice and on the pronunciation level. So the notion of a "General American" has been attacked as being misguided, and recently it has occasionally been replaced by the term "Standard American English," which essentially implies that in formal and supraregional contexts speakers deliberately avoid using marked regionalisms. The absence of a single standard form of American English has typically been illustrated by the fact that even recent Presidents of the United States from the South in some of their speeches displayed traces of their native southern accents.

American English is much more than the continuation of the language imported by British immigrants, however. It has been enriched by loanwords from other European languages, like Spanish *bronco*, German *pretzel*, Polish *kielbasa*, French *prairie*, Dutch *boss*, and many more. And it has been accommodated by population groups of other than British ancestry to form distinctive ethnic varieties.

The best known one of these is African American English (AAE), a dialect which has been the topic of extensive research and also much public debate. Most linguistics today agree that AAE is a variety of American English which is normally used by black speakers in informal situations, has some characteristic features, and may serve to signal ethnic identity. Its origin, i.e. how "British" or "African" it is in character, has been disputed. Nowadays, most linguists probably accept the thesis that it is closely related to Southern US English (and thus indirectly to British dialects) but that it also shows notable parallels to strongly contact-induced and possibly African-influenced varieties of the Caribbean, in addition to innovative traces.

Another family of distinct American varieties are those spoken by descendants of Spanish speakers, notably Mexican-American (or Chicano), Puerto Rican, and Cuban English. These dialects give the appearance of "a Spanish accent," even if many of their speakers do not speak Spanish at all. A similar situation obtains in Louisiana, where a seemingly French-accented dialect of English is spoken both as a second and as a first language by people who identify as Cajuns. Many Native Americans have been forced to shift to English, by the circumstances or in boarding schools, and many ancestral native languages have been lost or are endangered. Immigrant groups from various Asian countries sometimes speak English with an accent, but in many cases this appears to be a transient learners' phenomenon.

Note that many of these ethnic dialects have been shown to be growing in importance in recent decades, in line with a revitalization of ethnic pride and a community emphasis on historical roots. This fact has been epitomized also in the recent concept of a "salad bowl," with distinct ingredients retaining some of their recognizable qualities, gradually replacing the "melting pot" myth.

As was implied above, American English in reality comes in varying forms, depending upon a speaker's regional, social, and ethnic background. An interesting relationship can be observed in the United States between regional and social variation and the main language levels. Regional dialects tend to be characterized by phonological and lexical features, so lexical choices and pronunciation details depend upon where a speaker grew up, irrespective of social class. In contrast, nonstandard grammar is socially marked and stigmatized but hardly depends upon one's regional origin. Patterns like *I didn't hear nothing* or *You done this?* occur in informal situations and most likely with less educated speakers but in all regions.

Of course, there is no way of telling "how many" regional dialects there are in American English – that depends purely on one's level of granulation, on how finely graded we wish to draw our distinguishing lines. Traditional research used to suggest that along the east coast, where regional differences are most prominent, three major dialect regions can be distinguished, namely Northern, Midland, and Southern, and each of these can then be further subdivided into smaller regions with distinguishing features, sometimes down to the strictly local level. Recent research has tended to largely confirm this division, though supplemented by two important modifications. Some scholars have suggested that the West constitutes a distinct region of its own, and others have questioned the separate identity of the Midland, subdividing it into either a North vs. South Midland or into a "Lower North" vs. "Upper South." Thus, roughly speaking, regional differences in American English can be described in terms of two distinct poles, North and South, with a broad transition band between them (increasing the proportion of northern / southern features the further north / south we go). This division gets increasingly more blurred (by the results of dialect mixing in the nineteenth century) the further west one looks – with a small set of distinctly western properties coming in as well.

Canadian English is generally considered a separate branch of North American English. Historically it goes back to the speech of American Loyalists who in the late eighteenth century resisted the independence movement and then moved north to remain loyal to the British Crown. To the present day Canada has retained stronger ties with the United Kingdom, a fact which, together with the presence of French settlers, has shaped the country's linguistic setup. Canadian English stands between the two major national varieties of English in some respects. Not surprisingly, it has been strongly influenced by its large southern neighbor, thus sounding predominantly American to an outsider. On the other hand, it has retained a few distinctly British traits, for example in some spelling conventions. Very few forms and words, if any, are exclusively Canadian (a case in point being the well-known question tag *eh*) – what makes up Canadian English is its overall composition of variants. Many Canadians can be distinguished from Americans by the so-called "Canadian Raising," a tendency to pronounce the first element of the diphthongs /aʊ/ and /aɪ/ as a central vowel before voiceless stops, so that a Canadian's pronunciation of *about*, with /əʊ/, sounds more like *boat*. In recent years a change called Canadian Shift has been documented, with the vowels in words like *trap*, *dress*, and *kit* being articulated further back in the oral cavity. Canadian English has always been described as surprisingly homogeneous despite the country's horizontal extension across thousands of miles; it is only recently that early traces of regional distinctions have been described. What may be more interesting to observe is the growth of ethnic variation, caused by the country's self-projection as a multicultural nation, which attracts significant immigrant groups from the Caribbean, Asia, and elsewhere, and tends to give respect to the native population, called "First Nations" in Canada.

As an example of one distinct type of American English, let us now have a closer look at its most salient regional variety, Southern English.

4.2.2 Case study: Southern US English

Americans just simply know about Southern English, whether they speak it or not. To southerners themselves, their dialect is an important badge of their cultural identity. Outside the South, however, it is strongly stigmatized. To some extent, this reflects attitudes towards the South as a cultural region. The cartoon in Figure 8 highlights some of these aspects in a jocular fashion:

- differences between the weather in the North and South;
- the "Mason-Dixon line" (the boundary between Pennsylvania in the north and West Virginia, Maryland, and Delaware to the south, named after the surveyors who drew it in the eighteenth century), which is commonly considered the dividing line between the two cultural regions; and
- a core linguistic difference, namely the form of the second person plural pronoun which today in the North is mostly *you guys* and in the South is its hallmark form *y'all*.

Figure 8 Popular culture representation of differences between the North and the South

The economic basis of the South used to be agrarian, beginning with tobacco farming in Virginia and later expanding to include the cultivation of rice in coastal marshlands and cotton in the fertile southern plains. For a long time the region lacked the urban sophistication, appreciation of education, and also industrialization that gave the North a competitive edge. As is well known, this cultural and economic conflict culminated in what Southerners still euphemistically refer to as "The War between the States." The plantation economy of the South required large-scale and cheap manual labor, and this supply was met by the mass importation of slaves from West Africa. The infamous institution of slavery, which ran counter to fundamental principles of Christianity and human rights as spelled out, for instance, in the American Constitution, met with increasing resistance by the abolitionist movement, however. Viewing their economic basis as threatened, the "Confederate States" of the South seceded in 1861, and ultimately, in 1865, lost the Civil War which resulted from that secession. Many Southerners perceived the following decades, the "Reconstruction period," as a humiliating experience of "Yankee" dominance, and the old "Rebel flag" still flies high throughout the South and on Southern State Houses, testifying to the ongoing roots of the region's culture and identity projections in the antebellum period.

To the present day stereotypical manifestations of such a conservative, rural lifestyle and culture are evoked and conventionally associated with the South. Males are portrayed as "rednecks" or "good ol' boys" who cherish hunting and fishing, own dogs, and enjoy heavy drinking, with the liquor illegally produced themselves by "moonshining." Females are the prototypical "Southern Belles." Further components of the southern stereotype include a good-natured and friendly humor (as against the northerners, perceived as distant and cool), a slow pace of life, a deeply and conservatively religious attitude, a love for nature, country music, and southern cooking ("grits," for instance) – and, last but not least, the southern dialect.

Map 10 identifies the states which are part of the American South and suggests the core and periphery of the region. Talking of "the South" as such represents a gross simplification, in a sense – the region is vast, encompassing about sixteen states, a population of more than 100 million, and close to a million square miles, and thus a range of sub-regions with their own characteristics. In particular, it has been customary to distinguish a "Lower" or "Deep" South from an "Upper" or "Mountain" South. The former encompasses the plantation lowlands along the South Atlantic seaboard and the Gulf into the Mississippi Delta. Historically this sub-region can be traced back to a class-conscious, highly stratified society which ranged from wealthy plantation owners via overseers and skilled craftsmen to manual and slave laborers. The latter, closely associated with the Appalachian mountains and the "hillbilly" image, was characterized by a largely white, lower-class

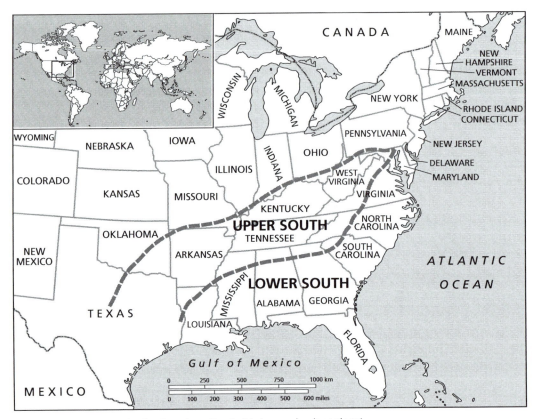

Map 10 The American South (states and sub-regions)

population with a livelihood in small-scale farming, lumbering, and mining and a decidedly local orientation. So, zooming in more closely, the South may also be viewed as a host of different lifestyles – from the Virginia tobacco farmer or the Outer Banks fisherman via the miner's family in a mountain hollow to the cotton farmer or laborer in, say, Alabama, the West Tennessee plains or the Brazos Valley in Texas. And of course, more or less subtle dialectal differences also existed between individual localities, as the *Linguistic Atlas of the Gulf States* (Pederson *et al.* 1986–91) documents masterfully and in great detail. Nevertheless, there is a shared cultural perception and there are enough linguistic phenomena shared by the region as a whole to justify conceptualizing it and talking of "the South" as a coherent and distinct entity, also on linguistic grounds.

From the present-day perspective, an additional qualification is required, however. The stereotype and culture just described is real and is being maintained, but it is also a rural and conservative one, and as such no longer typical of modern American society, even in the South. After the (for some) painful Reconstruction period of the late nineteenth century, accompanied by the restoration of ethnically segregated life patterns through the "Jim

Crow" laws (propagating "separate but equal" development of the races), all of the twentieth century has been a major period of change. The boll weevil, a pest which feeds on cotton buds, and the cotton gin caused the major source of revenue, cotton production, to decline substantially. Poverty and the industrialization of the North drove many southerners, black and white, out of the region. Participation in two World Wars widened life perspectives. Most importantly, this has turned out to be a period marked by the urbanization and modernization of the South, with the military leading and industry following. The South, formerly just the Bible belt, has become the sun belt, the site of global players like Coca Cola and of global events like the Atlanta Olympic Games of 1996. Migration patterns reverted, with northerners now moving to southern cities, and adjusting, for better or for worse.

All of this has had interesting consequences, discussed in recent scholarship, for the Southern dialect. It all boils down to the question of "When did Southern English begin?" (which is the title of an interesting article by Guy Bailey of 1997). The traditional assumption would have been that Southern English is essentially conservative in character, a mixture of British dialectal input components retained here because of the region's secluded lifestyle and lack of access to education. Bailey claimed, however, that essential components of Southern English are surprisingly young, going back to no later than the Reconstruction period. At that time Southerners needed to defend and strengthen their regional identity against the presence of northern outsiders, and they did so by selecting and reinforcing certain language forms as symbolic markers of their status as indigenous residents of the region. Following Bailey, this process continued into the twentieth century, with Southerners asserting their regional pride through their dialect as an icon of their identity. If this sounds strange to you, let me assure you it is not – over the last few decades linguists have convincingly documented a number of similar cases in which speakers of an endangered regional dialect selected and "recycled" a small number of speech forms as implicit projections of their claim to a privileged, ancestral status.

The apparent conflict between two competing notions of "Southern English" is also not as contradictory as it may seem, as Schneider (2004) showed. We are in fact talking about two different conceptualizations and forms of Southern dialect which blend into each other but which from this diachronic perspective need to be distinguished. One is "Traditional Southern," a set of dialect features associated with the old-time, rural, antebellum notion of the South. And, interestingly enough, some of these features have actually vanished by now, and others are clearly archaic or weakened, being no longer used as frequently as before by younger, urban speakers. Conversely, there is "New Southern" (coined analogously to the common catchphrase of the "New South"), speech forms associated with the modern, urban conceptualization of the South, typically spreading in frequency over the last few decades, especially among the young (as Bailey has shown). Table 3 summarizes and illustrates some linguistic features associated with these two conceptualizations, respectively.

Text 3 illustrates some characteristic features of Southern English, including both of the historical sub-dialects just mentioned, which blend in this

Table 3 *Features of Traditional and Modern Southern dialect*

Traditional Southern		
Feature	Comment / source	Example
"preverbal *a-*"	historically derived from *be on Ving*(gerund)	*He's a-comin'*
lack of rhoticity	Postvocalic /r/ not pronounced, as in StBrE (but unlike "General" AmE)	*car* [kaː], *card* [kaːd]
no "jod-dropping"	/j/ pronounced after alveolar consonants (/t, d, n/) (as in StBrE, unlike "General" AmE)	*tune* [tjuːn], *duty* [dj-], *new* [njuː]
general verb *-s*	suffix *-s* freely used with present tense verbs in all grammatical persons	*I comes, you tells me, dogs barks*
intrusive /r/	unmotivated /r/ inserted in certain words	*Washington* sounds like *Warsh-*

Modern Southern		
Feature	Comment / source	Example
y'all	distinct second person plural pronoun, derived from *you all*	*y'all know; y'all's car*
"*pin/pen* merger"	confusion or homophony of mid-high and high front vowels (/e, i/) before nasals	*tin/ten* sound alike; *think* [θɛ̃ŋk]
double modals	two (rather than one) modal verbs preceding main verb	*I might could go there*
rhoticity	postvocalic /r/ pronounced (esp. among younger speakers)	*car* [kaːr], *card* [kaːrd]
/aɪ/ monophthongization	diphthong /aɪ/ pronounced as monophthong /aː/ (in some regions only before voiced consonants)	*time* /taːm/, *I* /aː/, *high* /haː/, *ride* /raːd/
"inceptive constructions"	*get to* or *fixin'* to denote the initial stage of an activity	*Let's get to walking; I'm fixin' to leave*

TEXT 3: "Suthern like it should be spoke"

INTRODUCSHUN. . . . Heah, yawl will discovah thet the English language iz spoke like it oughta be spoke. . . . Yawl must know thet whin the settlers came ovah the big watah years ago, the smartest ones picked the mountain areas uv the Sowth to settle in . . . heah they remained isolated 'n thair speech, even aftah many, many years, remained the same az thair forefathahs ovah in Shakespeare's part uv England. Most uv thair words 'n dialect then spread all ovah the Sowth . . . the Sowth Ah sed! So you see, we got most uv the culture thet yawl desparately need! Now we have put alot uv owah Suthern knowledge down heah in this book with yawl's interest in mind . . .!

UNUSUAL WORDS: *Airish* 'cool'; *Antigoglin* 'lopsided'; *Boogeey-man* 'devil'; *Clum* 'past tense of climb'; *Evah whichaways* 'in all directshuns', *His'n 'n hern* 'hiz 'n hers'; *May can* 'may be able to'; *No 'count* 'good fur nothin''; *Shivaree* 'boisterous party fur newlyweds'; *Totin'* 'carryin''; *Whupped* 'beat up'

TROUBLESUM DEFINITSHUNS.
abode (git on 'r git left): The train's a'leavin' – all abode!
bare (a foamy drank): wuz shakily a'drankin' a bare
cot (a small baid): If'n yuh gits on thet cot wid Mamie Lou
far (sump'n whut burns): whin hiz britches cot on far
fix (about, gittin' ready): Cauz Ah ain't fixin' to go to jail. Then Ah'm fixin' to go.
hit (struck): Jimmie John dun hit me.
hit (it): 'n hit hurt mitey bad.
law (the sherrif): but thet didn't keep the law frum arrestin' me.
plum (completely): she got plum tuckahed out.
stripper (lady wid no clothes on): The stripper Ah seed warn't nuthin'
NAWTH CA-LIN-AH. Thez heah folks is often referred to az Tarheels.
CAIN-TUC-KEY. . . . Now thez folks make whiskey like crazy 'n sells it fur cash
WARNIN' NOTICE. Eny uv yawl yankees whut mite be thinkin' uv startin' the wah agin had best remembah thet we haz now got a atom bomb factory . . . not to menshun a rocket plant . . . none uv which yawl haz got! Frankly suh, yawl ain't got a dawg's chance next time . . . so don't start nuthin' agin!

Selections from *Speakin' Suthern Like It Should Be Spoke! A Dixie Dictshunary*, by Nick and Wilann Powers. Boogar Hollow, Lindale, GA: Country Originals 1975. Reproduced by permission of Mrs. Wilann Powers.

sample quite nicely. In fact, this is not a coherent text but it consists of a selection of samples (short texts or "dictionary entries") from a popular booklet which is meant to entertain a lay audience by illustrating and pointing out a few features of the Southern dialect. So, take this with a pinch of salt and as what it is, a fun piece (and I hope you find it entertaining, too) – which, nevertheless, somehow reflects or evokes aspects of reality – otherwise it wouldn't work.

Notice that cultural stereotypes play a major role in the self-definition and self-presentation of the South, and we find some of them represented even in this small sample. That includes the reference to the Civil War initiated by the North (the "Yankees") and to regional labels (like the *Tarheels*) or customs (like distilling whiskey in Kentucky). Most centrally, however, it builds upon expressions of regional pride in the southern culture and also in the region's dialect (but note that the technological advances of the "New South" are also included). An important point is the claim of historical dignity and purity of the dialect because of its direct descent from the time and language of Shakespeare, as expressed in the "Introducshun." Implications of southern politeness may also be brought up here – notice the address form *sir* (*Frankly suh, . . .*).

Southern English includes a wide range of distinctive vocabulary items and colorful expressions, some of which are illustrated in the text sample, like *boogey man, ever whichaways, shivaree,* or *tote.* Amongst the most interesting ones is perhaps *the law,* referring not to an abstract principle but to its representatives in a very literal and physical sense, 'police officer'.

Quite a number of the pronunciation characteristics of southern English are illustrated in this selection:

- The so-called "southern drawl" describes a tendency to turn simple vowels into diphthongs by adding some sort of an offglide. In the texts we find this represented in *baid* 'bed', *Cain-tuckey* 'Kentucky', or *dawg* 'dog' (the University of Georgia football team is called the *Bulldawgs* or *Dawgs,* with the respelling representing a conventional pronunciation which indeed adds an u-like glide to yield something like [dɔ:ʊg]). This may even lead to triphthongization, so in words like *town* or *cow* an e-like onset results in, for example, [tæaʊn]. Whether the spelling *Sowth* is meant to signal such a pronunciation is difficult to say.
- Conversely, the diphthong [aɪ] as in *time* is widely monophthongized, i.e. pronounced as a plain [a:] without its offglide. This is rendered as *Ah* 'I', *far* 'fire', or also (not in the above selection) *har* 'hire'.
- The "*pin-pen* merger" causes mid-high and high front vowels to sound alike before nasals, which we find represented in *whin* 'when', *agin*

'again', or *drank* 'drink'. A general tendency to substitute these vowels for each other in other contexts as well yields *thet* 'that' and *git* 'get'.

- Traditional southern used to be non-rhotic – and we find this mirrored in *heah* 'here', *abode* 'aboard', *ovah, watah* 'water', *wah* 'war', etc. But in line with current reality (though we should not assume that every single letter in the text is meant to be interpreted phonetically) we get postvocalic *r*'s represented as well, as in *part, years, thair* 'their', *hurt*, and so on.
- The preverbal *a-* onset before verbal *-ing*-forms occurs in *a'leavin'* and *a'drankin'*.
- And there is more – processes of assimilation (*sump'n* 'something', *warn't* 'wasn't'), reduction (*Cauz* 'because'), and other forms of dialectal pronunciation (e.g. *If'n* 'if', *wid* 'with').

Southern dialect has also a number of peculiarities on the level of grammar:

- Perhaps most notably, the South has a distinctive pronoun for the second person plural, *yawl* (derived from *you all*). Southern dialect thus fills a communicative gap of standard English (where the earlier distinction between singular *thou* and plural *you* got lost centuries ago), because the grammatical form *you* fails to signal whether a single individual or a group of addressees is referred to. (Incidentally, other dialects of English have felt the same need to reinstitute such a distinction – in the Jamaican sample we'll come across a form *unu* in that same function, and Americans outside the South nowadays quite regularly use *you guys* to address a group of people, even if they only consist of females.) Notice that the full integration of this form in the grammatical system of the dialect is confirmed by the derivation of a possessive form, to be observed in *yawl's interest*.
- In general, the pronominal system affords a number of special forms in this dialect (and I focus on the ones to be found in the text). In the third person singular neuter form an old *hit*, a relic of Old English days, as it were, can be observed instead of *it*. Following the model of *my* vs. *mine*, the forms *hisn* and *hern* append an *-n* (rather than an *-s* as in *hers, ours*) to generate a nominal form of possessives. Demonstratives can be strengthened by adding a deictic adverb, as in *Thez heah* 'these here' (with the same function as *these*). Finally, the form *what* can function as a relative pronoun: *sump'n whut burns*.
- The liberal use of the verbal *-s* ending, also a conservative feature already observed in the northern England sample above, is illustrated by forms like *you gits, we haz, yawl haz*, and *folks iz*. A really interesting and highly complex grammatical principle is hidden behind the example *thez folks make whiskey ... 'n sells it*, viz. the so-called "Northern Subject Rule" (or, more precisely in the present context, the "nonproximity-to-

subject constraint"), named like this because it can be traced back to dialects of northern England. The rule describes a tendency not to use an -*s* on a verb which immediately follows its subject (as in *folks make*) but then to append the suffix on a second, coordinated verb which is separated from its subject by intervening words (as in *folks ... and sells ...*). Notice that this is a really subtle condition which even speakers who apply it are not aware of consciously; so its occurrence here testifies to both the regularity and complexity of dialect grammar and to the sensitivity of the authors of this sample for such implicit regularities.

- In standard English a modal verb is obligatorily the only one in its clause, to be followed by a full verb; but southern dialect permits "double modals," as in *may can*, 'may be able to' or, even more frequently but not documented in the sample, *might could*.
- A form which has grown in importance in the more recent past is *fixin' to* to denote an incipient action, something which one is just about starting to do, as in *Ah'm fixin' to go*.
- Another characteristically southern form (at least in the US – Caribbean and creole forms of English have it as well) is a preverbal *done* to express the perfect: *John dun hit me*.
- For historical reasons, many dialects of English have nonstandard verb forms which happen to be different from the standard ones, including instances of regularization (*seed* 'saw'), the exchange of past tense and past participle forms (*spoke* 'spoken'), and an extension of the /ʌ/ vowel (as in *clum* 'climbed') to more broadly indicate the past tense.
- Similarly, many nonstandard negation patterns occur in a wide range of dialects and are thus not really regionally distinctive of any particular dialect (though they may be listed among features of southern dialect, and they are probably more frequent here than in other regions). These include the strongly stigmatized form *ain't* meaning 'am/are/is not' (as in *I ain't fixin'*) or also 'have not', and double negatives in the same clause (*warn't nuthin'*; *don't start nuthin'*).
- Finally, southern English features a set of highly characteristic intensifier adverbs, including *mighty* (*mitey bad*) and *plum* (*plum tuckahed* 'totally exhausted').

Notice that this sample, like the previous one and later ones, contains not only regionally distinctive forms but also a mixture of these together with standard forms and also nonstandard forms which can be found much more widely (including, for instance, the alveolar nasal in present participles, as in *leavin'*, *fixin'*, *thinkin'*; reduced forms of function words, such as *'n* rendering *and*; and double negatives). A further observation which is characteristic of this particular text type, dialect writing, is that there is a whole lot of so-called "eye-dialect": spellings which look strange but which on closer inspection do not signal a pronunciation deviant from general norms, as in *introducshun, iz, uv, wuz, sed, frum, mite,* and also, of course, *suthern.*

4.3 Plantation wealth and misery: the Caribbean

4.3.1 From English to Caribbean Creoles

For most people from outside the region "the Caribbean" would probably invoke just a few simple associations: pirates as portrayed in recent Hollywood movies, reggae music (and possibly calypso as well), and palm-lined dream beaches on tourist islands. Not bad for a start, perhaps, but also a far cry from a complex social reality where for most people poverty is much more of an issue than aspirations to glamour or thoughts of leisure time. But it is probably true that despite problems a friendly atmosphere is widely felt to prevail, and a rich history has produced a unique cultural and linguistic blend of European and African components. In the following few paragraphs I outline the region's history in the conventional perspective of "history from above," i.e. those in power, the Europeans. We should not forget, however, that the vast majority of the population of the Caribbean are descendants of Africans who were forced to the region as slaves, a perspective to which I will return momentarily. Timeline C puts some essential dates together.

The Caribbean – that is essentially a chain and a few blots of islands scattered in the tropical zone between North and South America, and in the

Timeline C: The Caribbean	
1624	British settlement on St. Kitts and claim to Barbados
1651	British colonization of Suriname (from Barbados)
1655	British conquest of Jamaica
1667	Dutch Guyana (Suriname) ceded by the British in exchange for New Amsterdam (New York)
1692	Earthquake destroys Port Royal (Jamaica)
1807	End of British slave trade
1834	Legal emancipation of slaves in Jamaica and other parts of the British Empire
1865	Morant Bay rebellion in Jamaica
1962	Independence of Jamaica

present context it makes sense to subsume the adjacent mainlands of Central and South America because they have largely shared the same patterns of history, language transmission, and lifestyle. A native population played only a minor role on the mainland, and a negligible one on the islands. Beginning with Columbus' explorations in 1492, for centuries the Caribbean was a battleground contested among the major European seafaring nations, whose main agents were buccaneers, settlers, traders and the military. The Spaniards led the way but were attacked soon by the French and the Dutch and, relatively late, the British. Settlement patterns were scattered, and individual places or islands changed hands, often repeatedly, by settlement, migration, battles and skirmishes, or just by contracts signed in far-away Europe in the aftermath of warfare between European powers. The colonial powers shipped settlers, laborers, and soldiers to their respective possessions, and in most cases they have left their languages. Thus, the Caribbean today is a linguistic patchwork. Spanish is still strong, dominating most of Central and northwestern South America, Cuba, and the Dominican Republic. The Dutch lost most of their possessions in the course of time (like the Dutch Virgin Islands, sold to the US) but retained their impact in present-day Suriname. The French owned Haiti, independent since 1804, and several islands and locations most of which today are politically integrated into France as "Départements d'outre Mer": Guadeloupe, Martinique, and French Guyana. Some islands, like Dominica, St. Lucia, and Trinidad, have shifted more or less strongly from French to English.

The English entered the race in the 1620s, and they were interested not in spreading Christianity (as the Spanish were) and less in trade but, recognizing the agricultural potential of the islands, primarily in settlement, reacting to a labor surplus at home. In addition to wealthy owners who secured legal titles for themselves and founded plantations, many poor people from the British Isles came as indentured laborers, who in most cases stayed after their years of service, or were shipped to the area as prisoners or debtors. The earliest British foothold, dating back to 1624, was St. Kitts, and other small points of dispersion – St. Croix, Nevis, Antigua, Montserrat – followed soon. One of the most important English-speaking communities in the region dates back to the same decade: Barbados, claimed in 1624 and settled in 1627, has been continuously anglophone since then. The largest stronghold of the British empire in the Caribbean, Jamaica, was conquered by Cromwell's troops in 1655. Map 11 shows the other countries and islands in the region which today count as English-speaking. They include larger ones like the Bahamas, Trinidad and Tobago, Belize (former British Honduras, located in Central America), Guyana (former British Guyana, at the northern edge of South America), and smaller ones like Antigua and Barbuda, Grenada, St. Vincent and the Grenadines, St. Lucia, the Virgin Islands, the Turks and Caicos Islands, and the Cayman

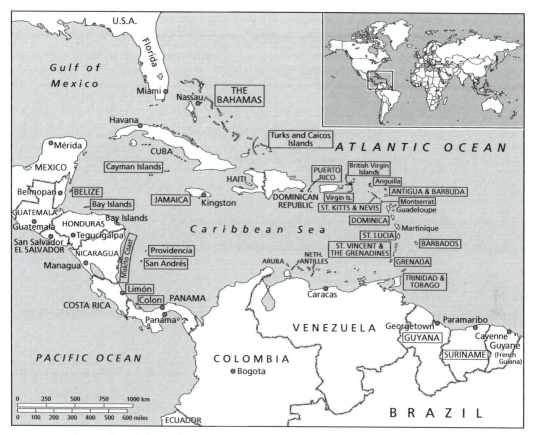

Map 11 English and English-creole speaking islands and regions of the Caribbean

Islands. In addition, English-speaking (or, in most cases, actually English Creole-speaking) communities, going back historically to groups stranded for various reasons, can be found in otherwise Spanish-speaking countries: the Bay Islands of Honduras, the Miskito Coast of Nicaragua, Panama, Costa Rica, the Islands of Providencia and San Andrés (politically parts of Colombia), and the Samaná peninsula in the Dominican Republic.

As was stated above, however, the vast majority of the region's population and substantial components of its culture are African in origin (and one question that has been discussed is to what extent its language is so, too). The major industry, promising enormous profits to owners, was the cultivation of sugar cane, introduced in the 1640s from Brazil. Growing sugar requires large units and a huge amount of extremely demanding human labor, and this demand was met by the European planters, ignoring all humanitarian or religious principles, by the infamous institution of slavery. For three centuries millions of West Africans were enslaved and forcibly transported to America to work on the plantations under most cruel and inhumane conditions. A field hand's life was hardship, and punishments for even minor

95

forms of misbehavior were cruel. Slave uprisings were a constant fear amongst the Europeans, given that the Africans constituted the demographic majority by far, and they did occur regularly, although with the exception of Haiti none was successful in the long run.

To people of African descent more attractive options than working the sugar cane were available, but only in minority instances. Blacks worked as cooks, drivers, craftsmen, and the like, and on top of their social hierarchy there were house servants with better access to the dominant white world. Some developed loyalties to the social system and their owners and oppressors, despite all, though generalizations seem problematic, and reality had many different shadings. Locally born, so-called "creole," slaves tended to despite the "bozales," fresh arrivals from Africa perceived as less civilized. And on most islands a small stratum of "brown" people, sprung typically from unions of white males and black mothers, grew into socially intermediate positions. So social realities throughout the Caribbean tended to be more complex than simple concepts of plantation societies warrant.

These complicated social relationships found their reflexes in the language situations of individual islands. The Caribbean is the main region in the world where creolization occurred, which is commonly regarded as the birth of new languages under extreme contact conditions. Certainly Caribbean creoles are derived from European languages (mostly English and French, formerly also Dutch), and show strong similarities with them especially in their vocabularies. In addition, however, they share a number of peculiar grammatical properties (like preverbal tense and aspect markers, copula omission, pronoun conflation, or serial verbs – some of which will be illustrated below) which cannot be explained by their European origins. For a long time creolists have debated the issue of where these grammatical peculiarities derive from. Some, usually called "substratists," believe that they can be explained as grammatical transfer from substrate, i.e. in this case essentially West African, languages – the metaphor suggests that these somehow shine through from underneath the current linguistic surface. Others, the "universalists," suggested that these structural options reflect innate and universal, possibly cognitively motivated or even genetically preprogrammed principles of human language organization in general, which came to effect in these special situations.

Creoles became objects of serious language study fairly late, in the 1960s, and such disputes about fundamental issues are typical of an early phase of theory formation. Both camps shared three fundamental beliefs, however:

- that creoles emerged relatively abruptly, amongst the first generation(s) of slaves who needed some sort of new code to fulfill their communicative needs because their African native languages were no longer usable in the new environments;

- that because of the demographic and social relationships between whites and blacks this process was caused by the insufficient, and mostly only lexical, input of white target language speakers to black slaves; and
- that, consequently, creoles were distinct, newly born languages, largely independent of and only indirectly related to the European languages that they resembled.

In other words, the idea was that in their daily lives the vast majority of African slaves had very little access and exposure to the target language (English, in our case – let us focus upon this from now on), and thus they were able to pick up words but no real grammar, and they filled the need to combine words into sentences by using syntactic principles from their innate or African-derived language capacity, thus creating a creole. If this were undisputedly true, then this section could be dropped from this book, because in this view English-based creoles are not varieties of English. Although such a view can still be found, especially in older sources, it no longer represents accepted wisdom, however.

Modern scholarship, in contrast, tends to view creoles as varieties of their European lexifiers, even if distant and unusual ones, strongly restructured and shaped by language contact. The reason for this reorientation lies in the increased attention paid to the existence of "intermediate" varieties (mixed between Creole, dialectal, and standard English) which can be widely heard throughout the Caribbean. Classic theory, as just characterized, predicts that there would be only two types of language in such a scenario:

- English, as spoken by whites (the so-called "acrolect," or socially "high" form), and
- Creole, consisting of English-looking words but creole (possibly African) grammar, spoken by blacks (the so-called "basilect").

But what we mostly find in reality are language forms which are somehow intermediate between the two, so-called

- mesolects: recognizably English, though with words and patterns modified a bit, but interspersed with characteristically creole forms and patterns.

And the relative proportions of the two ingredients, as it were, on any given occasion depend upon the formality of a speech situation and the social background of a speaker: the proportion of English items increases the higher a speaker's status and educational level and the more formal the situation; conversely, lower-class status and informality correlate with more creole forms. So what we frequently encounter in the Caribbean is such a continuum of forms, spread out between acrolect and basilect, correlating with these situational parameters.

Early theory formation explained this as a "post-creole continuum." The assumption was that the strongly creole systems sprung first, from the abrupt creolization process as described above, and they were then, in the course of time, increasingly infiltrated by standard English forms and choices which because of the presence and dominance of whites influenced the creole, and trickled in from above, as it were. When researchers inspected historical evidence more closely, however, both old linguistic records and demographic data, they found evidence contradicting such ideas. They observed, for instance, that even the earliest texts from many regions displayed mesolectal language, the characteristic mixture of English and creole properties, and in many cases "deep" creole characteristics appear only much later. The "abrupt" emergence scenario, closely connected with universalist views, which builds strongly upon the presence of children as language creators in the early slave communities, was also challenged by the fact that there were very few children in most of the early slave communities.

Actually, attention has increasingly been directed to the fact that things didn't even start off with the huge plantations which are essential to the abrupt creolization scenario. For the first few decades of the British Caribbean settlements, the so-called "homestead" phase, maize and tobacco were the main crops, and these tended to be grown in small family-run farms, not on huge plantations. There were slaves there even then, but in minority numbers, and probably with sufficient opportunity for cross-ethnic language contact to achieve reasonably successful second-language acquisition rather than to trigger language creation. It was only thereafter, around and after the mid-seventeenth century, when the promise of immense profits from sugar plantations caused a substantial disruption of the social patterns of earlier decades. Small-scale white farmers sold out to wealthy plantation owners, units grew constantly in size, and thus the prototypical slavery plantations, with very high slave numbers and just a few whites as owners, overseers, or agents around, became reality. But it seems likely that in a so-called "founder effect" (cf. Chapter 7) the language habits formed during this early phase amongst slaves, most likely not creoles, set a benchmark and strongly influenced the linguistic conventions of the following periods. Therefore mesolectal, basilectal, and acrolectal language forms have probably co-existed from the early days of an island community, depending on demographic and social conditions in detail.

Today we find reflexes of this situation in the fact that Caribbean English Creoles come in a "cline" from regions where there are deeply basilectal creole forms, maximally distinct from English in a number of ways, to regions where the creole (or local language variety) is relatively "light," i.e. largely looks like dialectal English, with occasional occurrences of creole forms and structures blended in (documented in Schneider 1990). Basilectal, rural Jamaican Creole, for instance, clearly is a "deep" creole, displaying practically all the characteristics of creoles in general, and the same applies to Guyanese Creole (and surely to other language varieties of the region as well). In contrast, some dialects studied on the Virgin, Cayman, or Bay Islands are so "light" and so English-looking that some scholars have called them "semi-creoles" (or, more technically speaking, "partially restructured" varieties). And many others are somewhere in between. Bajan, the creole of Barbados, for example, is fairly readily accessible to an outsider and decidedly "lighter" than Jamaican.

Historical coincidence and varying social patterns have caused all kinds of unexpected, in a sense complicated, situations. There are white speakers of creoles as well, for example – individuals and coherent groups in various locations, and a noticeable population segment, mostly descendants of poor indentured laborers of earlier centuries, in Barbados. Other creole speakers are Indian by ethnicity, notably in Trinidad and Guyana, two countries where the ongoing demand for plantation labor in the nineteenth century, after the end of slavery, attracted large numbers of Indian workers whose descendants today constitute roughly half of the populations in these two countries. In Guyana, it is the people of African descent who have established themselves as relatively more powerful, urban, and mesolectal, whereas the Indo-Guyanese are predominantly rural and basilect-speaking. Trinidad and Tobago jointly form one nation and share language patterns, but because of its smaller size and higher isolation Tobago's Creole is much deeper than that of Trinidad; Trinidad's basilect is similar to what is mesolectal in Tobago. And so on – many of these complexities, especially on smaller islands, are in fact insufficiently researched and documented.

So – there are no clear-cut boundaries between Caribbean dialects of English on the one hand and Creoles on the other. There are some structural properties typically associated with creolization, but there are no structural properties which uniquely and exclusively identify creoles as a language type (though some linguists have voiced claims to the contrary, at least for combinations of certain more abstract language properties). It has been suggested by Mufwene and is widely accepted today that creolization is strongly a social and not primarily a linguistic process, associated with contexts of European plantation settlements and slavery, and that creoles are varieties of their lexifiers, even if strongly restructured and modified ones under conditions of extreme language contact. In that respect they are similar and related to the New Englishes of Africa and Asia, which are also language contact products of colonial times and postcolonial contexts – and this observation and classification justify the inclusion of the Caribbean region and of these varieties in this book. Some Caribbean creoles and creole texts, notably those from Suriname, may indeed seem difficult to understand for English speakers from other parts of the world, but upon closer inspection, as with the text below, their close proximity with English is more than obvious and would render their classification as unrelated to English counterintuitive or even absurd.

4.3.2 Case study: Jamaica

Throughout the colonial period, from 1655 until independence in 1962, Jamaica was Britain's stronghold, her largest and wealthiest possession, in the Caribbean, and today it is the largest "anglophone" country of the region, with a population of almost 3 million. Historically speaking, it was a classic sugar colony, and today its linguistic make-up shows the continuum between a deep, mostly rural basilect, a range of urban mesolects, and an acrolectal form of standard English with a Caribbean accent.

Unlike Barbados and some of the smaller islands, Jamaica did not go through a homestead phase, as it was occupied at a time when sugar was already known to be the most profitable crop. The country did have its administrators, soldiers, and seafarers in urban settings, notably in the city of Port Royal until its destruction by an earthquake in 1692, but the dominant scenario was indeed that of the huge sugar plantation with its unequal distribution of wealth and power and all the cruelties of slavery and plantation life. Jamaica's history records a long series of slave uprisings, and cruelties in retaliation. As a consequence of the harsh living conditions for slaves, raising slave children was not the norm, so for centuries the colony's economy relied upon continuous importation of slaves from Africa. Obviously, this stream of newcomers also reinforced African cultural roots, which were stronger than elsewhere. It was reported, for example, that African languages were occasionally spoken and African rituals practiced into the nineteenth century, and certainly strong traces of these habits can be found to the present day in indigenous rites, religious practices, art forms, and the like. Furthermore, the island's mountainous interior provided a retreat for an exceptional icon of Africa's heritage, the maroons. The maroon community, going back to runaway slaves of the days of Spanish occupancy prior to the English, lived and hid in the mountains, preserved their independence, and even defended it successfully in battles against the British in the eighteenth century.

The nineteenth century brought an end to slavery. In British colonies slave trade was forbidden in 1807, and slavery ended legally in 1834, though for another four years slaves were kept in a dependent status called "apprenticeship," officially declared to prepare them for freedom, though what happened in practice was mostly quite another matter. Certainly not having to fear for one's health and life every day made a huge difference to the former slaves, and theoretically they now had new opportunities: freedom of movement, for instance. Some of them, in fact, secured small plots of lands in the countryside for themselves, and managed to earn their livelihood as small-scale peasants; this is a pattern which characterizes rural Jamaica to the present day. In general, however, the end of slavery did not really change the living conditions for most of the population, as the former slaves remained in poverty and dependence, so most of them continued to work on the same plantations as before, and the patterns of life and communication did not change drastically. In fact, an important incident in the history of Jamaica, the Morant Bay rebellion of 1865, was strongly reminiscent of earlier slave uprisings, resisting inequality, discrimination, and the lack of opportunities. Obviously, these patterns promoted the retention of basilectal (and also mesolectal) Jamaican Creole, locally called Patois (or "Patwa").

Social and political changes of the second half of the twentieth century have substantially affected Jamaica's society, cultural orientation, and language attitudes, however. Up to that time a conservative class stratification along wealth and complexion lines was largely undisputed, and the island's cultural orientation and linguistic norms were undisputedly British. After independence in 1962, the young nation started to forge a distinct cultural identity for herself, a process which strongly implied a readiness to accept African cultural roots. Reggae and the international success of Bob Marley's music, and probably also of artists like Harry Belafonte, played a substantial role in this, making Jamaica's culture known to the world and instilling pride in it locally. Increasing contacts with the outside world, through labor migration, emigration, and contacts with expatriate Jamaicans in,

Figure 9 Printed Jamaican creole in a newspaper cartoon (from the *Daily Gleaner*, Jan. 22, 1981; reproduced by permission, © The Gleaner Company Limited, 1981)

say, Britain or Canada, tourism, American business contacts, etc. widened perspectives and may have supported more liberal attitudes.

And some of these changes have affected Jamaica's language situation as well. In the old days Creole was strongly stigmatized as a bastardized distortion of English, to be avoided at all costs in public discourse. The only possible exception, illustrated in Figure 9, were jocular contexts, like for instance cartoons in a newspaper.

But for the last few decades Patwa has increasingly come to be accepted as the nation's distinct language, a part of its cultural heritage. Nowadays it can be heard in the media, in public announcements (paying credit to the fact that the majority of the population does not really command standard English), and in the mouths of politicians who wish to express their rapport with the population at large. Mesolectal forms can be found increasingly in public discourse, and at times even in writing, in culturally appropriate contexts or as explicit projections of distinctly local identities. There has even been a political initiative to recognize the Creole in the country's constitution (and thus to overcome linguistic discrimination), although the outcome of this process is not yet clear. But it is obvious that Patwa is very much a part of Jamaica's reality, and a publicly accepted one, today.

Text 4 is taken from a novel which tells the life story of a young man from the Jamaican country who seeks his fortune in the music business of the city of Kingston and ends as a rebel. In this scene he finds his long-lost mother, Miss Daisy, in miserable shape. In its stylistic mixture it nicely illustrates the manipulation of social distance and proximity between the interlocutors via their varying adoption of creole forms. (You can listen to the conversation on the website accompanying this book.) There are several ways in this text of indicating dialectal or locally typical pronunciation features, for example:

- The diphthong /eɪ/ is monophthongized in Jamaica (cf. *tek*, *mek*; this is heard most clearly in the local pronunciation of the country's name, by the way), and the back, raised /ɔː/ sound tends to be realized as a low central /aː/, symbolized by *aall*, *Gaad*/*Gawd* here.
- Dental fricatives are usually replaced by stops at the beginning of words or syllables (*de*, *den*, *dis*; *t'ing*, *t'anks*) and word-centrally (*maddah*).
- Word-initial *b-* and *g-/k-* immediately before vowels trigger gliding sounds in some words of Jamaican Creole – see *bwai* 'boy'; other common examples, *gyarden* 'garden' or *kyaan* 'can't', do not occur in this sample.
- As in many contact varieties, word-final (or syllable-final) consonant clusters are commonly reduced (*gran'mother*, *woun'*, *an'*). Even word-final single consonants are sometimes omitted in this text: *ha'* 'have', *wi'* 'will'.

As was pointed out above, however, the most characteristic features of creoles are syntactic in nature. Many features of Jamaican Creole are largely

TEXT 4: Conversation in Jamaican Creole between
Ivan and his mother

"Miss Daisy – *Mama*."

"Uh what? Is who dat?"

"Is me Mama, Ivan."

"Ivan ... *Ivan*? Arright, Ah comin'." [...]

Mother and son stared at each other.

"Mama ... You sick."

"Ivan, where is you gran'mother? Why you leave country? What you
come town for?" [...]

"Granny dead."

"Dead? How she can dead an' I nevah know?"

"We tried to get you – the telegram come back."

"Den when she going to bury?"

"She bury already."

"Bury already? *Bury already*?" Her voice cracked as understanding came
to her. "Bury already an' I nevah get to go to the funeral? Oh God, Oh
God, OOh God." [...]

"You don' ha' fe cry so."

"But is me *maddah*. Ah *mus'* cry."

He felt clumsy and helpless, embarrased that his words sounded lame and
weak. [...]

"Oh mi Gaad. Oh mi Gaad." [...]

Ivan stood fidgeting. He surveyed the room [...]

Miss Daisy was asking, "Den what happen to de place?"

"Granny sell it before she dead."

  He saw the sudden fleeting shock in her eyes as she digested the
knowledge that there was no longer that piece of earth in the "bush" to
which she could return, the traditional place, the center of their family's
existence in this world. [...]

"An' what happen to de money?"

"She say she wanted a big funeral."

"Den? She tek all the money to ha' a big funeral? An' I didn't get to go?
Oh Gawd."

"Den, de money finish?" [...]

"Little bit lef." He stalled.

"Wha' happen, you have it?"

  He nodded, still undecided, then fumbled in his pocket and thrust a
crumpled wad of notes at her. [...]

"Is only dis leave?"

"Yes." [...]

"Den how you going to get back to country tonight?" she asked
disingenuously [...]

"Ah not goin' back to country," he said softly.

"Where you goin' to dwell? You can't stay here y'know –" [...]

"Ah stayin' in town."

"You t'ink town easy? How you goin' live?"

"Ah can sing y'know, mama, I could mek a record."

She sucked her teeth in annoyed and total dismissal, looking at him as
though he were crazy, a fool-fool pickney. "You tek dis t'ing fe joke?"

"Well den, Ah can get a job." [...]

"Ivan, *Ivan*, mi pickney – what you can do? What kin' a job you t'ink you
can get? Outside a turn criminal – go pop lock an' bruk inna people house
an' shop?"

"Why you have to say a t'ing like dat to me?" he demanded hotly, his
voice rising. "Me not no criminal."

"Don't ask me any faastie question. You goin' back to country
tomorrow." [...] She described graphically and passionately the
hardships and pitfalls of life in the city. She outlined her own life, the
loneliness and fear, the hard work [...] But he insisted that he wasn't
leaving, whatever she said. He was going to make something of himself,
she'd be proud.

"Aaiie, mi bwai," she wailed, "no so *aall* a dem say, all de young bwai
dem. Likkle more you see dem gone a jail, gone a *gallows*. Dead a gun'
shot, dead a knife woun', or them tu'n drunkard."

"Mama, it *nah* happen to me, y'know. It *can't* happen. I know from I
small-small say I a' go do somet'ing ina dis worl'. Is my chance dis. Ah
can' go back. Me can' do dat." He stood before her, hurt, and defiant but
very determined.

"You hungry?" she asked softly. "Ah don' cook much any more, but you
can get somet'ing." [...]

"Arright," she said resignedly, [...]. "Since you determine, Ah wi' give
you de name of a person who will try an' help you." [...] "if you behave
yourself 'im wi' try an' get a little job fe you. See it here."

He examined the card. "A preacher?"

"Yes. 'Im can help you."

Ivan looked dubious. "O.K. Mama. T'anks." He started toward the
door.

"Ivan, wait!" [...]

"You ha' any money? Tek dis." She held out a few of the bills he had
brought.

> "Is arright, Mama, Ah sell de few goat an' pig dem Ah did have. You tek dat."
>
> "Well, an' you nevah bring as much as mango from country fe me?"
>
> "Mango season was bad dis year," he lied, and shamed he stepped quickly into the night.
>
> When the door closed behind him, [. . .] Miss Daisy Martin fixed her eyes on the Bleeding Heart of Jesus and prayed for her son, that "even doh a t'ousan' devils may tangle his feet, none should hol' him fas'."
>
> (From Michael Thelwell, *The Harder They Come.* © 1980 Michael Thelwell. Used by permission of Grove/Atlantic, Inc.)

in line with those found in creoles elsewhere. The above sample, broadly mesolectal in character, illustrates some of these; others I'll briefly mention in passing:

- The copula *to be* is generally left out, both in verb progressive structures (*Ah stayin'*) and before nominal complements (*Ah . . . no criminal*) but most commonly, and most typically of creole zero copulas in general, before stative adjectives, as in *you sick, Granny dead, town easy, you hungry*. Stative adjectives behave much like verbs in creoles, a fact which in this sample is best illustrated by the observation that the adjective follows a modal just like any other full verb: *she can dead*. Other characteristic copula patterns, such as a special form of the copula, mostly *de*, before locatives (so that *im de de* means 'he is there') are not found in this sample.

- Tense is not marked morphologically (with the time setting resulting clearly from the narrative context), so almost all verb forms with past reference (or participle function) have their base forms (*you leave, you come, what happen, granny sell, she say, she tek; leave* 'left'; but notice that the variability of usage is reflected in occasional past forms as well: *we tried, I didn't*). Basilectal creoles frequently have a form like *been* placed before a verb to suggest an earlier point in time (such as *Mary been go*). This is not found in this text, but a corresponding mesolectal equivalent, with not *been* but *did* placed before the verb to indicate past time, does occur: *Ah did have . . .*

- In general, creoles tend to express tense and aspect relations by placing short particles, so-called "preverbal markers," before the verb. A common form not found in this text, for instance, is *do/does* for the habitual, e.g. *im does go* meaning 'he always goes'. The above text has *go do* for future reference.

- A negation pattern which is distinctly creole is that of placing a simple negator, frequently *no*, immediately before the verb; here this occurs as *It nah happen*. Other negative structures are shared with other creoles and nonstandard English varieties, notably double negation (*Me not no criminal*) and the use of *nevah* for single events (and not an indefinite time period) in the past: *I nevah get to go, you nevah bring …*
- Creoles have characteristic highlighting patterns, typically with a sentence-initial copula form, as in *Is who dat, Is my chance dis.*
- Grammatical suffixes are avoided, and so the plural of nouns is usually not marked (as in *question, drunkard, de few goat*), or is expressed by a distinct morpheme *dem* placed after the respective noun, to be found here in *de … bwai dem* 'the boys', *pig dem* 'pigs'.
- A single pronoun form often fulfills a range of functions: *me* or *him* also function as subjects (*me can do, 'im wi' try, 'im can help*) or as a possessive (*me maddah*).
- Creoles often use a form *say/se* as a complementizer (corresponding to *that*) to introduce a finite object clause after verbs of thinking or talking. Here this is found in *I know … say I a' go do somet'ing.*
- Prepositions tend to be omitted (as in *town* 'to town'), or there is a single form covering a range of functions, often *for/fe*: *ha' fe cry* 'have to cry', *fe joke* 'as a joke', *fe me* 'for/to me'.
- Creoles are taken to have no separate passive construction: *She bury* and *de money finish* clearly express passive meanings but are active formally.

As to the vocabulary used in the sample, apart from the local word *faastie* 'rude' two items are of interest:

- The word *pickney* 'child' is derived from Portuguese, and similar forms can be found in creoles all around the globe.
- Reduplication is used to intensify the meaning of words: *fool-fool* means 'very foolish', *small-small* is 'very small'.

Chapter summary

In this chapter we have seen that colonization and the impact of language contact have been ubiquitous in the development of English, even in the cases of the "national standard" varieties where this might not have been expected, and certainly so for creole genesis. British English itself was shown to be a product of Germanic tribes colonizing the British Isles and of incorporating structural and lexical influences from a wide array of languages – Celtic first, Latin repeatedly in different contexts, Scandinavian in a very intense union,

French in a markedly diglossic situation after the Norman Conquest, and many other languages thereafter. American English and its main varieties – regional, social, and ethnic ones – have been shown to stem from settlement streams, migration and mixing, nationalistic tendencies, and ethnic integration and accommodation. The language situation of the English-speaking Caribbean, finally, has resulted from patchwork-like settlement patterns and political conflicts, the blend of European and African components in plantation settings, slavery and creolization, and post-Emancipation and post-Independence transformations towards regional pride and modernity.

We will now move on tracing the next major step in the expansion of English, from the northern to the southern hemisphere.

Exercises and activities

Exercise 4a   Imagine yourself being a member of a Celtic family suddenly being faced with Anglo-Saxon invaders in the late fifth century somewhere in central England, a member of a Native American tribe being faced with white settlers in the seventeenth century somewhere in New England, or a member of an Aboriginal tribe being faced with Europeans somewhere in southeastern Australia late in the eighteenth century. How would you try to cope with the situation, generally and linguistically? Do you see any possible parallels between the three scenarios? Where would you see the main differences between these situations?

Exercise 4b   Look up an interview by Ali G on YouTube, for instance the one on "feminism." How would you assess the language Ali G speaks? Identify individual features of Ali G's performance on the levels of pronunciation, lexis, and grammar, using appropriate linguistic descriptive terminology. In which other regions would you find these features as well? (Use sources available in your library for this. Compare your results to those found in Schneider [2007b], an article in which Ali G's language use is analyzed.)

Exercise 4c   Listen to the first part of "T'Barber's tale" on the website or to some of the other tales on www.yorkshire-dialect.org and identify occurrences of features which are characteristic of northern English.

Exercise 4d   Compare the dialectal division of the United States as proposed by Kurath (1949), Carver (1987), and Labov et al. (2006). Looking just at the primary-level divisions – where do you see important differences? How fundamental are they?

Exercise 4e	Look up the words *bawl*, *belly-buster*, *corn house*, *hoppergrass*, and *spouting* in dictionaries, and compare their regional distributions as described by Kurath (1949) and Carver (1987). Are they identical? If not – what might be the reasons for any differences?
Exercise 4f	If you are interested in Jamaica, get hold of Thelwell's novel *The Harder They Come* (and read it) or of the movie of the same title (also available as a DVD) – both are wonderful introductions to Jamaica's language and culture. Pick a selection from either one and identify further language features that you find difficult to understand; check if they are characteristic Jamaican or creole features.
Exercise 4g	Bob Marley's famous 'No woman, no cry' has been claimed to be the most widely misunderstood song title ever. Why? (Consider the above statements on negation in creoles.) Listen to the song and identify further features which are characteristically Jamaican.
Exercise 4h	Look at the cartoon in Figure 9 and identify characteristically Jamaican speech forms in it.
Exercise 4i	On YouTube, search for "A Fi Di Piipl," and listen to one of the programs, e.g. the one on how to get water from the water commission ("Ou fi get waata fram waata komishan"). Transcribe the text. Identify characteristic features of Jamaican language. Discuss the appropriateness of the language form chosen for the subject matters discussed in these clips and consequences this might call for in language policy.

Key terms discussed in this chapter
article reduction
acrolect
adstrate
basilect
Celts, Celtic fringe
colonial lag
koinéization
lexifier
mesolect
monophthongization
preverbal markers
reduplication
rhotic

semi-creoles

substrate

superstrate

Further reading

The settlement history of the British Isles, and the external history of English in general, have been described in numerous language histories. One of the most successful, and still highly readable, accounts can be found in Baugh and Cable (2002); other recommendable ones (for non-specialists) include Barber (2000) and Fennell (2001). The idea of a possible Celtic influence on early (and present-day) English has been voiced most explicitly in a series of books entitled *The Celtic Englishes* (Tristram 1997–2006). The dialects of England have been studied most systematically in a mid-twentieth-century project known as the *Survey of English Dialects*, with the *Basic Material* volumes providing lots of details for the specialist (Orton *et al*. 1962–71); the *Linguistic Atlas of England* shows distributions of regionally varying language forms in maps (Orton, Sanderson, and Widdowson 1978). Furthermore, various textbooks provide accessible accounts and insights (Francis 1983, Upton and Widdowson 2006; Trudgill 1990). On Northern English, the main source to consult, a masterly discussion of the subject, is Katie Wales' book (Wales 2006).

With respect to American English, there are classic sources, most notably Mencken (1963), which focus on historical aspects and lexical choices. Algeo's (2001) collection provides perhaps the most comprehensive, if a slightly conservative, survey of traditional scholarship on the variety. Tottie (2002) puts American English into its broader, cultural context, and Wolfram and Schilling-Estes (2005) is the most recommendable introduction from a sociolinguistic perspective. Wolfram and Ward (2006) is a very readable collection, geared towards a layperson audience, of short snippets which characterize a wide range of dialects of American English. Chapter 5 in Schneider (2007) provides a coherent history of the variety, and Schneider (2008) is an 800-page collection providing the most detailed descriptive accounts of the pronunciation and grammar characteristics of American and Caribbean varieties to date. Algeo (2006) looks into subtle differences between British and American English, and Rohdenburg and Schlüter (2009) document grammatical differences between the two main varieties. Classic sources on regional differences in American English, notably on the level of vocabulary, are Kurath (1949) and Carver (1987). For dialect words the *Dictionary of American Regional English* (*DARE*; Cassidy *et al*. 1986–2002) is most recommendable. Labov *et al*. (2006) is the authoritative, if a highly sophisticated, source on current details of regional American pronunciation. There is a host of books on African American English; amongst introductory texts, currently the market leader is Green (2002). For Southern American English, the collection by Nagle and Sanders (2003) gives a readable survey of current scholarship, and Pederson *et al*.'s *Linguistic Atlas of the Gulf States* (1986–91), in 7 volumes, documents just about every linguistic detail that one might be interested in. Much more accessible, however, are entertaining popular booklets like the one quoted from earlier, or Steve Mitchell's *How to Speak Southern*.

Roberts (1988) is a very accessible survey of forms and functions of English and Creole in the Caribbean, and the same applies to Christie (2003) specifically for Jamaica. D'Costa and Lalla (1989) is an interesting collection of historical texts from Jamaica, and Lalla and D'Costa (1990) surveys this development historically. Thelwell's novel, from which the above sample is quoted, makes wonderful reading and indirectly provides an understandable introduction and some exposure to Jamaican Creole; the 1972 movie, with the same title and starring Jimmy Cliff, which the novel was based on, is also highly recommendable. The language of the novel is analyzed in Schneider and Wagner (2006).

CHAPTER 5

Settlers and locals: Southern Hemisphere Englishes, transported and newly born

In this chapter . . .

In this chapter we will look at the spread of English to countries of the Southern Hemisphere, notably Australia, New Zealand, and South Africa. For the last decade or so a category of "Southern Hemisphere Englishes" has been established, because it has been found that the Englishes spoken in these countries (and also much smaller settlements like the islands of Tristan da Cunha and the Falklands in the South Atlantic) have a great deal in common both historically and linguistically. They were settled at roughly the same period, namely in the late eighteenth and early nineteenth centuries, typically in large-scale, organized settlement moves, and by similar "founder populations," predominantly lower- and middle-class people from the British Isles, with a preponderance of settlers from southern and southeastern England. They came to stay for good, so their descendants today constitute large native-speaking communities of direct British ancestry. And they faced similar situations – unfamiliar territory and climate and, most importantly (except for the small and isolated islands just mentioned), the need to deal and communicate with earlier residents of the areas they migrated to. In the long run, these peoples – Aboriginals in Australia; Maoris in New Zealand; Africans, Afrikaners, and later also Indians in South Africa – have adopted and transformed English, using it for their own purposes, and many of them have shifted to it completely. Because of their closer geographical and historical proximity the similarities are even greater between Australia and New Zealand, obviously (but don't tell a Kiwi you mistook him for an Ozzie – that's the easiest way of making yourself unpopular!), so in the following section both countries will be dealt with jointly to some extent. But all three larger regions also share some pronunciation similarities (e.g. a tendency to raise short front vowels). It has been debated why this is so. Most likely the reason lies in the continuation of articulatory trends inherited from the shared southern English input dialects of the early settlement period.

5.1 Pride in being "down under": Australia and New Zealand

5.1.1 The growth of Englishes no longer just "antipodean"

Australia and New Zealand, shown in Map 12, are sometimes referred to jointly as "the Antipodes," although this label is increasingly rejected by the people "down under" because of its Eurocentric (or Britocentric) perspective. Timeline D compiles some important dates.

In the late eighteenth century both countries were known mainly because of Captain Cook's explorations, and they promised opportunities for settlement and expansion. Australia was originally perceived as a place to which prisoners, unwanted at home, could be conveniently deported. The "First Fleet" brought the first shipload to Botany Bay in 1788. For the next few decades the transportation of convicts continued, and Australia's population grew, but it also diversified. The deportees were accompanied by soldiers, administrators, and so on. Most of the convicts stayed after having served their stint, and they joined the increasing numbers of free settlers who also came to seek their fortune in the new colony. It took several decades until free

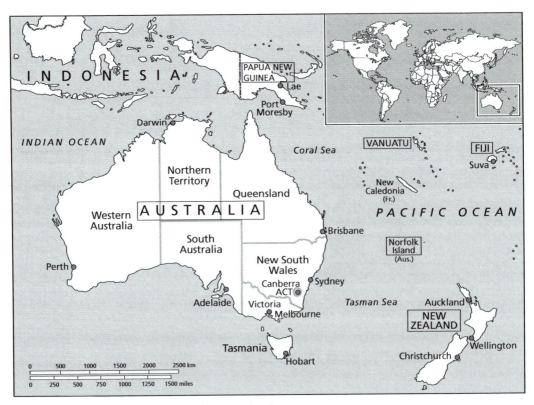

Map 12 Australia and New Zealand

Timeline D: Australia and New Zealand

1768–79   Captain Cook's voyages to the Pacific, including Australia and New Zealand

1788   Prisoner's colony established at Botany Bay in Australia (New South Wales)

1825   Colony of Van Diemen's Land (Tasmania) established

1836   Colony of South Australia established

1840   Treaty of Waitangi between Maori chiefs and the British Crown

1850   Gold rush in New South Wales

1901   Federation of the Commonwealth of Australia

1907   Dominion status in New Zealand

1947   Independence of New Zealand

1973   Great Britain joins European Union (without making special provisions for New Zealand's economy)

1976   Aboriginal Land Rights Act

1981   Publication of the *Macquarie Dictionary*

2008   Prime Minister Rudd's apology speech to Indigenous Australians

---

settlers outnumbered the convicts, but in the long run Australia ended up as a settler colony, with new waves of arrivals moving on to unclaimed lands and thus opening up more and more of the territory to European occupation.

The expansion process in New Zealand was similar, though there were no convicts. For the first four decades of the nineteenth century the islands served primarily as bases for whalers and sailors, and the number of British settlers was still fairly small. However, this changed drastically when in 1840 local Maori chiefs signed the Treaty of Waitangi in which they ceded sovereignty to the Crown in exchange for the promise of protection and privileges (though it seems likely that the consequences and the European understanding of that treaty were not quite clear to them). This document, represented in Figure 10 and publicly accessible in the National Archives in Wellington, is something like a birth certificate for the New Zealand nation. After this date, large-scale, organized settler streams from Britain migrated to the islands. So throughout the nineteenth century both Australia and New Zealand saw substantial growth through a continuous

Figure 10 Treaty of Waitangi

influx of migrants from the British Isles, primarily from southeastern England, with a noticeable Irish contingent, and a strongly Scottish enclave in the Otago district and the city of Dunedin on New Zealand's South Island.

In this process new dialects of English originated, essentially by dialect mixing (or "koinéization"), which we observed in a similar fashion in the United States. This process takes time and happens very gradually, of course, so no clear cut-off date can be given, but distinctive accents are commonly supposed to have emerged by roughly the middle of the nineteenth century in Australia and late in the same century in New Zealand. The regional origin of the majority of settlers accounts for the strongly southern English impression that both dialects give to outsiders (and a stereotypical, though mistaken, assumption for a long time was that Australian English is "like Cockney"). And their social origin (simplifying things greatly: convicts and farmers, above all) explains a markedly lower-class orientation and social stratification of both new dialects.

Dialect mixing amongst the settlers is not the whole story, of course. They met indigenous people there (even if Australia's political theory for a long time upheld the thesis that the country was "terra nullius," uninhabited land), had to deal with them, influenced them, and were influenced by them in return. Again, there are similarities but also differences between both countries. Both Australia's Aboriginal people and New Zealand's

Maoris were subdued and deprived of substantial parts of their lands in the long run, though the latter were treated with more respect (including both contracts and enmity) and have maintained more of their traditional culture. To the Australian settlers the Aboriginals remained essentially alien, it seems. Contacts were relatively restricted in the beginning, and they cost the lives of many Aboriginals because of newly introduced diseases and hostilities. In the long run, having been deprived of their livelihood and the means of continuing their traditional migrant and nature-oriented lifestyle, many of them had to get integrated more or less into the white world, work for the Europeans, and adopt their language. To the present day the tension continues between integration, with difficulties, into the mainstream, white, urbanized culture and the attempt to uphold cultural roots and traditional values and lifestyles. Sadly enough, much too frequently this ends in unemployment, cultural deprivation, and alcohol problems. The Maoris fared somewhat better in general. Relationships with the whites oscillated between explicit arrangements (which gave them contracted titles) and overt and organized military resistance (which culminated in the Maori Wars of the 1860s and then faded away gradually). On the whole, however, and in comparison, they have been able to maintain more of their culture, independent lifestyle, and language.

Both indigenous peoples have thus been assimilated, linguistically and culturally, to the European-derived mainstream culture to a considerable extent, but have also retained some of their language roots and traditional cultures. Many Aboriginal languages have died out, and the majority of Maoris do not speak their ancestral language any longer. In the shifting process both groups have developed specific varieties of English, presumably through the retention of some ancestral sound patterns, and so in the two countries Aboriginal English and Maori English, respectively, constitute distinctive ethnic dialects. The former is less homogeneous (because of a range of substrate languages involved), and the latter is more elusive (because the set of distinctive features is small and not very prominent). In Australia's North there are also regions where due to an earlier plantation history distinctive Australian creoles (commonly called Kriol) are spoken.

The English spoken by white Australians and New Zealanders has been influenced by the indigenous languages mostly in their word stock, and in two domains in particular. One is place names: it has been estimated that about one-third of Australia's and almost two-thirds of New Zealand's toponyms are of indigenous origin (take *Wagga Wagga, Woolgoolga, Muralgarra* or *Whakatane, Whangarei* or *Takapuna* as examples). The other are terms relating to plants and animals and, not surprisingly, artefacts and customs of indigenous cultures, not infrequently in a phonetically distorted form (e.g. *kurrajong* 'tree', *kangaroo, woylie, nulla-nulla* 'club', *kauri, kiwi, tuatara, whare* 'house', *mana* 'prestige', *waka* 'canoe').

These lexical borrowings are one important component which has contributed to the emergence of distinctive new dialects of English in both countries. There are other lexical innovations as well, including new meanings associated with "old words" (like *bush* meaning 'wilderness' and *station* 'outpost, grazing land, animal farm' in Australia or *dairy* 'corner shop' and *field* 'paddock' in New Zealand) or new compounds (e.g. *outback, sharemilker*). Emerging grammatical differences are few and subtle, but there are some as well. For example, Australians are reported to use the perfect construction (*have done*) more frequently and with a wider range of meanings (e.g. referring to specific points in past time), and New Zealanders use certain verbs in patterns which are unusual elsewhere – for instance, as Figure 11 shows, they *farewell somebody* (rather than *say farewell to …*).

What is probably most noticeable, however, are accent features, and I name only the most prominent ones here. Australians mostly have a more open onset of the /eɪ/ vowel, so that words like *mate* sound like /maɪt/. Hence, the country's reduced name (*'Stralian*) has produced the variant *Strine*, and in a very widespread joke a patient is shocked when told by his Ozzie doctor that he is *going home today* because he hears the last vowel differently, yielding … *to die*. New Zealanders are known to centralize their /ɪ/ vowel (in *kit*, etc.); and they raise their /e/ vowel (e.g. in *dress*) to sound almost like *i*. So when in Auckland's AUT building I took the elevator to the Institute for Communication on the eleventh floor, I always enjoyed hearing the automatic

Figure 11 Regional syntax: transitive *farewell* in New Zealand English

announcement (which you can also listen to on the website), which sounds like "*luft stopping – livel iliven*" (though the locals didn't find this strange at all).

The growth of these dialects is one thing; their recognition is another. Throughout much of the twentieth century it was perfectly clear in both countries that a "good" accent, suitable for media use and formal contexts, had to be a British one, and that the local way of speaking was "slovenly" (or something like that). By now this has changed drastically, however. Technically speaking, we have witnessed a shift from an exonormative attitude (seeing norms of correctness "outside") to an endonormative (accepting an internal norm) orientation. Such a change does not come out of the blue – it typically follows a change in political orientation, in a group's "identity" (i.e. the understanding where "we" belong and who is part of "us"). Both countries had moved towards political autonomy and independence (achieved in Australia practically in 1901, in New Zealand in 1947). But at the same time they continued to perceive themselves primarily as cultural outposts of Britain, enjoying a very special relationship with the mother country.

Both, however, had to learn that the balance was uneven, that for Great Britain they were less important than vice versa. Australians were denied the protection they had hoped for when they feared a Japanese attack during World War II, and New Zealanders were left without their main export market when in 1973 Britain joined the European Union without making sufficient provision for their former colony's interests. Consequently, both had to reorientate themselves, and they did – by redefining themselves as wholly independent nations and by emphasizing their Asia–Pacific location (allowing increasing immigration from that region, for example). And their new national accents and varieties of English have gradually come to be accepted as symbolic expressions of these new states of nationhood, as distinctive cultural assets. For Australia, Moore dates this process of "cultural nationalism" as well as the acceptance of Australian English to the 1970s (Moore 2001: 53); New Zealand follows suit some two decades later.

These steps towards linguistic independence, as it were, were strongly supported by the production and publication of reference sources which in western cultures count as tools towards good usage and indicators of linguistic dignity: dictionaries. In the latter twentieth century in both countries scholarly dictionaries appeared (some of which carried the word *national* in their titles) which formally established this independence on the language level which receives the most public attention, the vocabulary. In Australia, this important step was marked by the publication of the *Macquarie Dictionary* (Delbridge *et al.* 1981), which has therefore become something like a national icon, followed by others with similar ambitions. A *New Zealand Dictionary*, by Orsman and Orsman, appeared in 1994, also followed by others, including a major *Historical Dictionary*, along *OED* lines, three years later. Another facet that contributes to this linguistic independence is uniformity, perhaps a prerequisite to being recognizable, distinctive, and also "national." In many writings on Australian and New Zealand English from the second half of the twentieth century it was noted, often with surprise, how homogeneous the two varieties are, i.e. that practically no regional speech differences could be observed. It is only very recently that this seems to have been changing – initially in New Zealand, more systematically in Australia, where differences between regional words and also pronunciations have been increasingly documented in the last two decades or so.

Finally, in both countries the growth of nationhood has also affected the dominant culture's attitudes towards the indigenous minorities and their languages, which are receiving increasing recognition and support. Legal disputes over land claim titles in both countries have contributed to an awareness of the historical injustice that the indigenous populations had to suffer. The political reorientation towards emphasizing the status as young nations in their own territories has forced a need to reconsider and renegotiate the contributions of the indigenous peoples as part of both countries' national heritage, more so in New Zealand than Australia (where a conservative government blocked this process for a while). I do not wish to whitewash the persistent tensions between the races and the difficulties that Aboriginals and Maoris are facing due to high unemployment rates and other problems, but attitudes and perceptions, and to some extent also realities, have definitely been changing. In Australia an awareness of the injustice done to the Aboriginals and respect for their traditional culture, and interest in it, are definitely growing, and language revitalization programmes are trying to preserve as much of their linguistic heritage as is still possible. This process culminated on 13 February 2008 in Prime Minster Rudd's historic apology speech to Australia's Aboriginal peoples, delivered to the parliament. New Zealand is now officially bilingual, and efforts are made to reverse the far-reaching loss of the Maori language, which is now taught in schools and learned even by Pakehas (New Zealand's Maori-derived word, used quite naturally, for European New Zealanders).

5.1.2 Case study: Australian English between "Broad" and "General"

In contrast to the noted regional homogeneity of Australian and New Zealand English, both have been characterized by strong social speech differences. In Australia, these were categorized by Mitchell and Delbridge (1965) into three distinctive social varieties (later observed in similar ways in New Zealand and South Africa as well) which they labeled "Cultivated," "General," and "Broad." It is difficult to say when these speech level differences began to emerge. Given that from the beginnings of white settlement there were representatives of various social strata involved in the colonization effort, it seems likely that somehow they go back almost to the earliest stages. In any case, they are assumed to have stabilized as recognizably Australian social varieties by the middle of the nineteenth century.

The top, "Cultivated" end of the cline used to be close to RP, and is most likely a minority option these days. Conventional wisdom suggests that the middle, "General," variety is used most widely and the "Broad" end is restricted to lower-class and informal speech – but very little serious documentation is available to back such an assessment empirically. Australia's culture and discourse are strongly egalitarian. Differences in class and wealth are relatively small, and above all, they are not supposed to be displayed in public – Australians have a tendency to "cut down the tall poppies," i.e. to keep overachievers close to the ground. In practice, it seems clear that the postulated three social varieties are convenient simplifications, models of what in reality is a skillful manipulation of linguistic variation to signal social proximity (or distance), as well as varying levels of formality or a relaxed atmosphere.

This typically Australian appreciation for informality is particularly strong in the male subculture, marked by a desire for "mateship," which corresponds to the general male stereotype of emphasizing strength and social bonding. Thus, it is not surprising that "Broad" Australian language is more typical of male speech.

To illustrate some of the range of these socially symbolic sound distinctions and their skilful manipulation I have selected a sample (available on the website) which oscillates between standard and nonstandard features of Australian speech. For reasons just mentioned, Text 5 represents male speech (though on other occasions female public figures can clearly also be heard playing with these accent markers). And it comes from a context which epitomizes the tension between formality and mateship needs. The sample and its transcript originate in a TV sports program, a type of discourse marked by an inherent contradiction of formality level requirements. Being public media speech, the context would call for highly monitored, standard-like behavior. At the same time, however, the topic of sports as a male domain and the personae of the discussants call for the display of prototypically male qualities and "mateship," and thus for informal speech. Three male sports commentators and then, in an interview, a well-known player discuss this player's possible intentions of leaving the Brisbane team to join the one from Melbourne. The speakers discuss a distinctively national sport, namely "Footy" (Australian Rules Football) – so the topic of the conversation, by implication, requires the deliberate use of the national language variety. These parameters produce a very nice manipulation of dialect features between "Broad," "General," and "Educated." In the transcript I have inserted some phonetic symbols to

TEXT 5: Transcript of a discussion and interview from a
TV sports program, 2008

A: ... been superseded by the man J. B., who's up there at Brisbane.
      He's a Warmambool boy, he's gonna wear the Big V[veɪ] in four
      years' time, in fact he's gonna cap-, ah, four weeks' time, he's
      gonna captain that side. Is there any inkling that perhaps he might
      be looking with eh loving eyes[ɒɪz] back down[dɛːən] here?

B: A bit of mayonnaise from James earlier hasn't helped with the story
      but, eh, look, in five[ɒɪ] weeks time[ɒɪ] J. B. ... will ...

C: What does that mean[əɪ]?

B: Little bit too much topping on the story, James.

A: Ahh, that's what we do here!

B: Haha! In five weeks time, J. B. will captain the Big V, and it's now
      or never if he's to be lured out of Brisbane. Collingwood had a go
      two years ago, he's out of contract at the end of the year, he's 26,
      he's getting married at the end of the year and wants to sign a
      lifetime contract. Preference is to do it with Brisbane, but he[əɪ] will
      be[əɪ] the centre of a frenzy, even if he can't[aː] be moved, and
      particularly when he comes down in five[ɒɪ] weeks[iː] time[ɒɪ],
      given that he'll be the hottest player[æˇə] coming out of contract
      and on the market. This week[weɪk] the Footy[fʊdi] Show caught
      up with J. B. to ask him about his future plans.

JB: I[ɒɪ]'m happy up here[hɪ], but you know, you still make[aɪ] your
      decision on, you know when it's contract time[ɒɪ], you still got to
      make[aɪ] your decision and, and go through all those factors, but
      eh, certainly would ha-, would 've thought the percentage is, uhm,
      eh fairly[fɛəli] in favour[aɪ] of staying[aɪ] in Brisbane.

I: If clubs do wanna talk to you, will you have a listen like you did
      with Collingwood?

JB: Ahhm, well, uh, no doubt[dɛətʰ] you probably uh, dunno, I
      suppose first and foremost you, you deal[dɪə] with your own club,
      you deal with Brisbane, and hopefully that all works out well, see
      [eɪ], you really won't have to continue on down the line[lɔ̃n], but I
      think, you know, I always been a believer in you, you give your
      home club[kʌb] first crack at it, and eh, you know, if they satisfy
      [ɒɪ] your needs[əɪ], there's probably no need[əɪ] to really go any
      further, you don't want to turn into a Dutch auction, ehm... so... I
      think that's, that's more the process you work through.

I: I guess when you came[æɪ] up here as a sixteen [°i] or seventeen
      year old, ah, wide-eyed you probably had in the back (of) your
      mind[ɒɪ], one day, you might go back and play[aɪ] in Melbourne,

but eh, the, this will be now or never, wouldn't it and probably the opportunity would nearly pass.

JB: Yeah, that's right[ɒɪ], I, I think this is the one where you, no doubt, this is the one where you're going for the . . . the lifetime[ɒɪ].. ahm . . . the lifetime contract, really.

A: Well Hutchy what's all that mean[əɪ], I mean, he's a, he's a very smart man, J. B. He's got three[i] premierships up there at Brisbane, he's, he'll be the out[əʊ]right[aɪ] captain I reckon in a year or two . . . is there any chance whatsoever?

B: oh Gut feeling[i] is that he stays[aɪ] in Brisbane, but he[iː] will be the target of some pretty big offers . . . in Victoria.

D: They all tell you how smart he is, if you could just hang on I've got a bit of tape[æe] of J. B. ringing me, if we can locate this before the show.

A: But we're not playing anyth[ð]ing, unless[ɛ] you get permission from J. B. to play that.

D: Hey . . . he rang me, and left it on my answer machine.

C1: I know that; it was late at night though.

point out interesting pronunciation features (mostly vowel variants), which subsequently I discuss in more general terms.

Most of the interesting variation here, and in Australian English in general, is in the vowels, and in particular in the long vowels and diphthongs:

- The most typically Australian vowel, certainly from an outside perspective, is the "ei" in words like *face*, which "down under" is characteristically articulated with a very open onset to sound like "ai." Notice that the onset of this diphthong allows for quite a wide range of phonetic and articulatory variation – from the standard "e" realization, where the mouth is relatively closed and the tongue is raised fairly high in the front region, to an "a" vowel where the mouth is wide open and the tongue remains flat. This range of vocalic variation – technically speaking, from a closed [e] via relatively more open [ɛ] and [æ] to a fully open [a] – can be skillfully manipulated to signal relative proximity to the educated / standard end on the one hand and to the vernacular / regionalized end on the other. And this happens in this sample as well. Speaker D, the last discussant, is closest to the formal end, and pronounces *tape* with very little opening. On the other hand, the player JB displays the most vernacular accent, probably in line with social role expectations, and has fully open diphthongs in the words *make, favour* and *staying*. And speakers A and B, the show hosts, and the interviewer I are in between, and audibly so, I think, with intermediate opening degrees in *player* or *came* and a rather open quality in *stays*.

- Another diphthong which shows the potential for rather "broad" realizations is the one in words like *time*. In "Broad" accents the onset of this "ai" sound is articulated further back in the mouth, so that it sounds like "oi". In the sample this can be heard quite frequently with most speakers, most clearly in JB's pronunciation of words like *right* or *lifetime*. Elsewhere we hear a little less backing, and also a fairly standard-like realization in A's pronunciation of *outright*, for instance.
- The diphthong of words like *down* or *house* also shows some variation: in words like *down* or *doubts* we can hear it with a raised first element, closer to "e," and a schwa-like endpoint.
- Finally, the long /i:/ sound in words like *fleece* is also commonly employed as a style or formality marker, with the informal end being marked by increasing degrees of diphthongization. The sample displays almost the whole range of available options, from a standard, monophthongal [i:] in A's *three* and B's *feeling* and *he* via near-standard forms with little gliding, as in I's pronunciation of *sixteen*, and other intermediate realizations with schwa-like, central first elements as in C's *mean* or B's *he* or *be* to fairly strongly diphthongal, "ei"-like forms in JB's *see* or A's articulation of the letter *V*.
- Other pronunciation details, as elsewhere, connect Australian English with other dialects and may be worth noting without being really regionally distinctive. Its British origin and relationship is evident in the dialect's non-rhotic character, for instance (no trace of an r is audible in words like *here*, *favour*, *turn*, *work*, and so on). B's pronunciation of the vowel in *can't* also sounds very British, a fully open /a:/ (unlike raised American realizations).
- Notice, finally, that like some dialect speakers of English elsewhere JB vocalizes his l's: In the words *deal* or *all* the /l/ is not audible but has merged with its preceding vowel.

5.2 Nation building with language(s): South Africa

5.2.1 Differential adoption of Englishes – a historical perspective

South Africa is known to the world primarily as the country where a society managed to sweep away an inhuman and unjust system without violence: The peaceful revolution of 1994, led by Nelson Mandela (see two links on the website!), terminated the decades-old rule of "apartheid" in which the country's society was strictly compartmentalized on the basis of ethnic group membership, and introduced a process of democratization, the building of what Archbishop Tutu called the "Rainbow Nation." This has turned out to be a difficult process. While legal barriers have vanished, the country's fragmentation into ethnic groups, each with their own culture and language, largely continues, and old patterns like an unequal distribution of wealth and power or ethnic housing divisions fade away only slowly. Still, significant progress towards a more homogenous society is clearly being made. Patterns of language use – both ethnic group languages and English, and changing forms of English in particular – play an important role in this process, as they have done throughout the country's history. The main population groups have developed different varieties of English which persist to the present day.

First, for a broad historical outline, spelled out below, see Timeline E. Map 13 shows the state in its regional context, and it also illustrates the fact

Timeline E: South Africa	
1795	Short-term British occupation of the Cape
1806	British seizure of the Cape
1815	Congress of Vienna gives authority over South Africa to British Empire
1822	English formally declared the language of the Cape Colony; Cape settlers
1848–62	British settlement of Natal
1860–1911	Indian immigration to Natal
1880–81	First Boer War
1899–1902	Second Boer War
1910	Union of South Africa established
1948	National Party wins election in South Africa and leads the country into apartheid
1953	Bantu Education Act in South Africa
1961	South Africa becomes Republic (and thus formally independent)
1976	Soweto uprising
1994	Democratic election in South Africa
1996	South African Constitution, including the clause on eleven official languages
2010	Soccer World Championship in South Africa

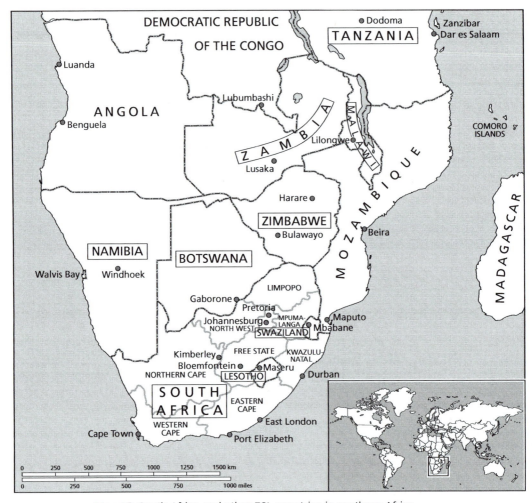

Map 13 South Africa and other ESL countries in southern Africa

that several other states in southern Africa have also adopted English as a second language of sorts.

The first European power to occupy the region of present-day South Africa were the Dutch in the middle of the seventeenth century. Dutch settlers and their descendants, later called Boers or Afrikaners, developed a language of their own called Afrikaans, a Dutch–African contact language. When they came under British dominance, reactions varied. In the nineteenth century, to some extent they gave in, adjusted, intermarried, and gradually adopted English as a second language, but they also attempted to evade foreign dominance by "Treks" to the interior, where they set up their own "free" states. In the Second Boer War, early in the twentieth century, these republics also fell under British dominance (as part of the British-dependent "Union of South Africa" founded in 1910) for almost half a century – until in 1948 an election victory of the National Party (with Africans disenfranchised) installed the infamous apartheid system and white (i.e. Afrikaner) dominance for more than four decades. However, it was also Afrikaner politicians who early in the 1990s recognized the need for a peaceful surrender and transition of power, a rare insight in human history.

Afrikaans is still their dominant language, of course, and even if it is somewhat discredited by apartheid history, the community defends it strongly. Afrikaans tends also to be the main language of the so-called "Colored" population, of mixed European-African descent, antedating as a group the arrival of the British and singled out as a distinct ethnicity during the apartheid days. Both groups tend to speak English as well, in the form of characteristic, though fairly similar, varieties known as "Afrikaaner English" and "Colored English" (or "Cape Flats English," after the coloreds' primary residential district), respectively.

Disregarding a short and transient earlier occupation, South Africa became British initially only on paper, in the 1815 Treaty of Vienna, which ended the Napoleonic Wars in Europe and redistributed some of the participants' colonial possessions. This was filled with life, however, by two distinct settler streams. Lower-class rural settlers from southern England came to the Eastern Cape in the 1820s, and middle-class settlers migrated to Natal in and after the 1840s. Through language contact and mission schools, English gradually spread to other ethnicities as well. What boosted its diffusion most effectively, however, was the discovery of diamonds and gold in the 1870s, a process which attracted many new settlers and workers and which in the Witwatersrand area established a mining industry and an urban stratified society of miners, workers, merchants, and professionals.

English was the language of political and economic power, and consequently it spread rapidly as a second language. The mixed dialects which had emerged from the two earlier regional settler streams were reallocated as social accents, because the rural Cape settlers, whose accent came to be classified as "Broad" or "Extreme," continued to occupy manual labor positions while the upwardly oriented Natalians established themselves as leaders in the new society, and their accent, called "Respectable South African English" by some linguists, became something like a speech model. It is noteworthy, however, that only about four percent of today's population of South Africa are English native speakers of British ancestry.

According to standard figures (likely to change in the future, though), there are twice as many native speakers of English living in South Africa, with the other half mostly being Indians by ethnicity. Their ancestors came to South Africa in large numbers throughout the second half of the nineteenth and into the early twentieth centuries, as contract laborers to work the sugar plantations of Natal. By now South Africa's Indian community has largely shifted to English, typically spoken with a characteristic accent, like all of the other ethnic groups. Indian South African English leans towards the Respectable, Natal-derived white accent, partly because it originates in the same province and partly because of the Indians' emphasis on education and upward social mobility.

Of course, the largest ethnic group in South Africa are the Africans themselves. Actually, this label is a cover term for ethnolinguistic groups speaking various Bantu or Khoisan languages. Amongst the Africans, English spread gradually as a second language – slowly and mostly through mission schools at first, more vigorously and by natural contact or taught by other non-native instructors later, in the mines and cities. The language had always enjoyed prestige amongst Africans, as is indicated by their resistance against perceived attempts on the side of the government to deny children access to it. This became directly evident in 1953 after the passing of the "Bantu Education Act" and in 1976 in the Soweto uprising. This prestige was increased by the fact that English became the language of liberation, the language employed by the leaders of the African National Congress even prior to the democratic turnover. And English has grown in prestige ever since, and has been spreading vigorously amongst Africans.

Whatever one may think of this – English has no doubt emerged as the language promoted most strongly by the post-1994 changes. This was definitely not intended by the authors of the fairly liberal Constitution of 1996, which explicitly lists as many as eleven languages, nine of them African (plus English and Afrikaans), as the republic's "official languages." But Afrikaans is definitely not spreading any further, for historical reasons, and the nine African languages are all used in certain regions only. Giving priority to any one of them at the expense of the others is as equally inconceivable as is the idea of promoting, spreading, and elevating all of them throughout the nation, if only for practical and financial reasons. And that leaves English as the only language which is reasonably neutral and accessible to everyone and everywhere, in addition to being prestigious as the gateway to skilled jobs, international contacts, and so on.

The post-1994 dynamism of English in South Africa, despite being spoken natively only by a rather small and ethnically disparate minority, has been amazing. It becomes transparent in many individual statements of language attitudes, in communicative realities in multiethnic settings (such as the police force or the military), and in changing acquisition patterns from one generation to another, with proficiency in English becoming increasingly important and advancing rapidly. This strong pull towards English tends to meet with some unease, because it stands in stark contrast with the national language policy, which was intended to favor an African-based multilingualism. Attempts are therefore being made to turn this policy into reality, and some political and financial support is given to the development of African languages, though it is difficult to see how far this can lead.

So where is the new South Africa heading to linguistically (which, of course, is a reflection of social changes and identity alignments)? Based on the available evidence, two trends can be discerned. One is towards multilingualism (which has always been a part of Africa's daily reality but seems to be growing strongly as well) and an explicit emphasis on cultural hybridity (reflected in the very common practice of language mixing, mostly between English and African languages and increasingly also in the media, for instance). The other is towards English, though the follow-up question, which English, is more difficult to respond to. The country's earlier ethnic fragmentation continues to be mirrored in the co-existence of various recognizable group dialects of English (Indian, Black, Colored, White – possibly subdivided into Respectable and Extreme).

However, with the gradual – if slow – emergence of a middle class for which ethnic membership is no longer of primary importance, new linguistic accommodation processes are beginning to produce new, interracial compromise accents which ultimately may form the basis of an emerging new, more homogeneous standard South African English. Naturally, these processes and their social evaluation are complicated. For instance, it is mostly young, urban, better-educated black speakers who are moving along this path of social mobility. Naturally, the basis of their accents is the Black South African English variety, but they are moving towards prestigious standard language forms, which are perceived as white. This requires complex negotiation and manipulation of accent features, between sounding ambitious and upwardly mobile on the one hand and "too white" on the other. The label "coconut" ('black on the outside, white on the inside'), after the title of a highly successful novel by Kopana Matlwa, has been spreading for such behavior. South African linguists are tracking these interesting changes. For instance, Rajend Mesthrie has shown that how far a speaker articulates the long vowel in words like *goose* with a tongue position further to the front of the oral cavity correlates with a "mainstream" orientation. Alternatively, this conflict may also explain the popularity of language mixing: sprinkling one's English with African words and expressions may be a means of asserting one's African identity.

5.2.2 Case study: South African Black English

So, perhaps the most interesting South African English accent today, and certainly with an eye into the future, is the Black one. Historically speaking, it has its origins in language contact and transfer, and in poor teaching conditions of English in particular, with generations of African learners approximating their English performance to that of target speakers who were second-language users of the language themselves. However, as was just mentioned, being the language of the revolution has given English prestige, and the new political realities also enhance its status. Black South African English is also the variety spoken by most of the country's political leaders, for example, and hence the one which dominates the media. This dialect has thus been envisioned as the basis of a possible future norm by some observers, possibly modified by the processes described in the previous section. Black South African English is mostly a second language today, acquired after one (or more) African languages (and possibly also Afrikaans), though it is also gradually appearing as a first or dominant language among Africans. Current estimates project the proportion of speakers of English amongst the African population to be somewhere between one-third and two-thirds – depending on proficiency levels accepted in such a count,

---

TEXT 6: Lions

aah . . . the animals[animals] . . . all there the old(?) . . . kudu, and eland and everything . . . they not used to lions['laɪɔns] . . . you see. So it's easy for the lions to catch[-ɛ-] . . . an[an] animal an' eat. Yah . . . but they say sometimes they can stay three days without catching . . . they don't always catch. Yah, sometimes they, they do attack what the, the animals lying . . . And then . . . most of the time those lions they full you see, they not hungry, yeah, because, ah, there's like a couple of story. Another guy was coming to Grahamstown, and then he had to go[go] hitchhike, but it is like, something like a . . . was less than[dan] a kilometer['kilomita] you have to walk but within the[ði] game[gem] reserve to the tar road, you see. An' he was walking there unexpectedly['a:nekspektedli] . . . and then . . . there's a male lion jus' as uh he was chases from, chased from the, uh, crowd from the other male, so he's a, like a nomad, walking [. . .] alone. And then this guy was like walking walking walking an' all of a sudden he look on the other side but he was k- kind of a, on the lookout all the time because he knows that he's on this zone(?) but there can be anything[ɛ-]. Few meters[mitaz] there was lions sleeping[slipɪŋ] . . .you see . . . yah, because the lion, yah, look at him[him] and then sleep[slip] again. And that guy was like [simultaneous speech, unintelligible] because of the gate getting close'. But he said the lion maybe thought about "hey there's a meat passing by" and he [simultaneous speech, unintelligible], while he was like few meters to the gate the lion came . . .

(Fieldwork sample by Lucia Siebers, reproduced by permission)

and correlating with sociodemographic factors such as urbanity, status, income, and age.

Text 6 reproduces a story told by a 33-year-old man from Grahamstown. Clearly, this is a fluent and rather educated speaker, but the sample shows a few characteristic forms, most notably on the sound level:

- Black South African English tends to avoid central vowels. In this text, for instance, the *but*-vowel in *something* and *but* is not fully central but has a low back, o-like quality.
- The unstressed central schwa also typically receives more stress and a distinctive quality which seems to depend upon either the unreduced vowel quality or on spelling: rather than the unstressed, weak vowel we might expect, in the last syllables of *animal, kilometers,* and *meters* an /a/ can be heard; in *lion* it's an /o/; in *to* it is clearly an /u/; in *the game* it is /i/; and in *unexpectedly* the weak vowel in *-ed* is /e/. This tendency contributes to a more syllable-timed impression, with weak syllables taking as much time as stressed ones, something which can be found in many New Englishes.
- A related phenomenon in many New Englishes is stress shift, to be heard here in 'unexpectedly (though meaningfully so).
- Another fairly widespread process is a tendency to reduce vowel distinctions. In particular, the "long" and "short" vowels of standard English (e.g. *bit* vs. *beat*) tend to sound alike. In this sample we can hear this in *sleep* and *sleeping,* which sound the same as *him*; and in *full,* which has a fairly high back and long quality and sounds like *fool* in other varieties.
- In a similar vein, the mid-high front vowel /æ/ of words like *trap* becomes either fully open (*animals* and *than* both have the vowel /a/) or raised (*catch* and *anything* have a closer /ɛ/ quality – though the second occurrence of *catch* also has /æ/).
- Diphthongs tend to get monophthongized: in *day, stay, game, gate, came* the vowel is /e/; in *don't, most, road* it is /o/; and in *time* /a/ can be heard.
- Variation involving consonants is less prominent. As elsewhere, dental fricatives are sometimes replaced by stops (so we have /d-/ in *an' then, the*), and consonant clusters are audibly reduced in *don', an',* and *jus'.*

Despite the brevity of this sample a few grammatical characteristics can also be documented:

- The plural marking of nouns is sometimes omitted, as in *the other male, a couple of story,* though in other cases it can be found quite normally: *lions, few meters.*
- Similarly, verb agreement is variable: we can hear both *he look, the lion look and sleep,* and also *he's, he knows.*

- A resumptive pronoun, expressing the subject a second time but by means of a pronoun, occurs in *those lions they full*.
- An overt use of the complementizer *that*, as in *He knows that he's on this* ..., is not unusual in itself, but together with the previous feature it serves to illustrate a tendency of South African Black English which Raj Mesthrie called "antideletion": forms which are unnecessary in standard English tend to be expressed explicitly in that dialect.
- Semantic intensification by means of reduplication was observed earlier, in Jamaican Creole, and occurs here as well: *this guy was walking walking walking* (meaning 'walking for a long time').
- Features in noun phrase determination (broadly, article use) which can be observed more widely in New Englishes as well include the countable use (with an indefinite article) of an uncountable noun (*a meat*) and the introduction of a new discourse referent by *another* rather than *a*, as in *Another guy was coming* ...
- Finally, the use of a singular copula form in existential clauses with plural subjects, as in *there's* ... *a couple of story* and *there was lions sleeping*, may seem noteworthy but is not typical of New Englishes (but of colloquial speech in many varieties).
- Two more examples in the text illustrate the fact that some structures which are considered typical of pidgins may occur in second-language varieties as well: the copula is left out repeatedly (see *they not used to* ..., *the lions full*, *they not hungry*); and *go hitchhike* looks like the "serial verbs" of some creoles (though, in line with other New Englishes, it may also simply be understood as an unusual type of verb complementation, with the ending *-ing* omitted).

So, the forms of English as spoken in Australia, New Zealand, and South Africa share a number of pronunciation phenomena which jointly have motivated the coinage of an overall notion of "Southern Hemisphere Englishes." For instance, they all display tendencies to raise their short front vowels (so in words like *bat* or *bet* the mouth is closer and the tongue higher up than in the British source variety from which they all stem, so that *bat*, for example, tends to sound like *bet* in these countries). With the short i sound (/ɪ/ in IPA transcription) there is hardly any space left to continue that upward movement in the oral cavity, so it either gets slightly lengthened and even more peripheral (so Australians are perceived to articulate "fish and chips" as "feesh and cheeps") or it rotates back to the center to yield schwa (so that New Zealanders are heard to say "fush and chups"). Furthermore, all these varieties display u-fronting, i.e. the vowel of words like *goose* is articulated with a tongue position further to the front, which sounds a bit like the German umlaut <ü>. Diphthongs are also undergoing similar movements. The reasons for these similarities most likely lie in the shared historical and regional origins of the settler populations, all of which came predominantly from southern England, in or around the first half of the nineteenth century. It is widely assumed that these new dialects have accelerated and intensified sound change tendencies inherited in incipient form from their input dialects at that time.

Interestingly enough, there are a few more such "Southern Hemisphere Englishes" which largely share some of these tendencies but which are most unlikely to be known to the outside world simply because they are spoken by just very few people on small, isolated islands in the South Atlantic. While many people might think these factors render them fairly insignificant, to linguists they make them all the more interesting, because shared input and history, small size, and isolation make for laboratory-like, undisturbed situations with ideal conditions for studying the effects of dialect contact and dialect mixture.

- One such place is the **Falkland Islands,** a few hundred miles off the coast of Argentina, a long-time British colony, home to a sizeable English-speaking settler community and site of a notorious war in 1982.
- Similarly, the South Atlantic island of **St. Helena,** known as Napoleon's last place of deportation, has been a British possession, a crown colony, and now a dependent territory since the seventeenth century. A few hundred to a few thousand people – British planters, settlers and soldiers, African slaves, and also a mixed bag of residents from other parts of the world – have lived there since then.
- Perhaps the most interesting of these smaller southern hemisphere locations and varieties, however, is **Tristan da Cunha,** the world's most isolated permanently inhabited island. Located roughly halfway between Cape Town and Montevideo, it is also the home of a mostly British-origin population which can be traced back to 1816, with 278 residents (and, thus, speakers of Tristan da Cunha English) at the time of writing this (and I'm tempted to say I'm proud to know one percent of the entire population personally . . .).

Both islands are exceptionally well documented in the world of linguistics because of the fieldwork efforts and other activities of the Swiss linguist Dani Schreier (2003, 2008).

Chapter summary

In this chapter we have observed the complex language contact processes between colonial settlement initiatives and indigenous populations in strongly English-speaking countries of the southern hemisphere. We have seen that these processes have typically produced new dialects of English which play a special role in their respective sociopolitical environments. The dialects spoken by the descendants of European settlers have undergone mixing processes, have been influenced by local languages, and have come to signal new status differences and social alignments. The indigenous population groups in all three countries have shifted to English, to a considerable extent and in some cases even completely. In that process they have produced new ethnic varieties which tend to be perceived as reflections not only of their membership in newly forged nations but also of their ancestral status. All territories discussed here have also experienced a growth of the respect attributed to indigenous groups and their respective contributions to the countries' cultures and language situations over the last few decades.

Exercises and activities

Exercise 5a   Search for other clips associated with "Footie" on outlets such as YouTube, and analyze the language that you hear there in terms of its socially significant features.

Exercise 5b   The late Steve Irwin, an environmentalist and TV personality who died in 2006, was a popular icon of Australian culture who skillfully employed his accent to project an Australian identity. Some of his shows are available on YouTube – watch one and analyze the language used.

Exercise 5c   Can you remember ever having seen Nelson Mandela, or other South African politicians or public figures, speaking on TV? (Samples are available on this book's website as well.) If so, what did you think of their accents?

Exercise 5d   The website includes another sample of South African Black English, entitled "In the hospital." That speaker uses an unusual pattern for indirect questions: *I think where I am*; *I asked where is others?* How would you explain this structure linguistically? Consult the *Handbook of Varieties of English* to find out how widespread it is.

Exercise 5e   Listen to this second sample of South African Black English and identify other characteristics in the speaker's pronunciation.

Key terms discussed in this chapter
Aboriginal English
antideletion

"Broad" accent
Cape Flats English
"Cultivated" accent
dialect mixing
endonormative
exonormative
"General" accent
Maori English
South African Black English
Southern Hemisphere Englishes

Further reading

Australian and New Zealand English jointly were the topic of a book written in the early phase of interest in varieties of English, with strong emphasis on their distinctive vocabularies (Turner 1966). During the 1990s and early 2000s, both varieties, separately now, were analyzed and discussed in a few collective volumes of a slightly more technical nature, e.g. Blair and Collins (2001) and Bell and Kuiper (2000). In recent years, finally, accessible survey monographs were devoted to both varieties. For Australian English, Moore (2008) constitutes a highly readable outline of the history of the variety from the beginnings, and Leitner (2004) covers the same ground on an even broader basis, documenting a wide range of aspects of the topic. For New Zealand, Gordon and Deverson (1998) and Hay, Maclagan, and Gordon (2008) wish to introduce a general audience to properties and the emergence of the variety, and Gordon *et al.* (2004) is an authoritative linguistic study of its historical evolution, based on audio recordings with speakers born in the late nineteenth century and later.

The linguistic situation in South Africa, and the evolution of its varieties of English, has been described in books and publications which mostly are a bit more technical, meant for a readership of linguists rather than lay observers. De Klerk (1996) is a recommendable and comprehensive collection of work specifically on varieties of English. Mesthrie (2002) surveys the language situation in the country authoritatively, and many of his other writings, including books on South African Indian English and on sociolinguistics, are also recommendable.

For readers interested in the remote South Atlantic islands: Schreier and Lavarello-Schreier (2003) is a wonderful and highly accessible survey of not only the speech but also the culture of the Tristanians; and Schreier (2008) presents an in-depth analysis of St. Helena's English, a model of a community study which, of course, also tells a lot about the history and the characteristics of the island and its population.

CHAPTER 6

Missionaries, merchants, and more: English is useful, English is ours

In this chapter ...

In this chapter we will have a closer look at the historical background and the current usage conditions of English mainly in countries which Kachru termed the "Outer Circle," i.e. typically postcolonial countries where English holds a strong position as a widely used second language (and it is sometimes becoming a first language, as we will see). To these world regions English was brought as the language of traders and missionaries, and later, when the British held a tighter colonial grip, administrators and soldiers. Basically, however, their stay in colonies was planned as being target-directed and transient – except for small expatriate communities we typically do not find large resident settler groups of British ancestry in the localities discussed here. The diffusion of English to these countries has been a long-standing process which, interestingly enough, has gained special momentum only fairly recently, after the end of the colonial period. In regions like West Africa and India the advent of English dates back to the seventeenth century, but it was only in the nineteenth and twentieth centuries, with English becoming the language of political dominance, education, and social advancement in general, that it gained special prominence. Since then, however, and particularly after independence and for the last few decades, in many places it has mushroomed, and frequently it has been transformed substantially in this process. So today in many countries it serves both as the primary means of upwards mobility, in a standard form, and, with indigenized pronunciations, patterns, and words, as a symbol of community solidarity. Similar motives and effects, albeit in a weaker form, are visible also in the "Expanding Circle" countries, about which we will hear a bit towards the end of the chapter.

6.1 English for administration, English for the marketplace: Sub-Saharan Africa

6.1.1 West and East African Englishes: a historical survey

During the colonial period European powers like Britain, France, Germany, and Belgium competed for possessions in Africa. They contributed to infrastructure development and created political structures (including states which in most cases have been ethnically heterogeneous and thus unstable), but their primary interest was economic – to gain wealth by trade and also exploitation. In all of Sub-Saharan Africa English was employed and spread as an administrative language for a social elite, with restricted access to it, until after World War II, when a change of policy towards mass education and national development diffused it more widely. Circumstances were quite different in West, East, and southern Africa, so let us look at these in turn. Map 14 shows the region as a whole and identifies the countries in which English has a special status.

Timeline F gives some important historical dates from this region.

English came to West Africa early, but for centuries it played a very insignificant role. In the seventeenth century coastal fortifications were established to secure trade routes and to serve the slave trade, but Europeans hardly ever ventured into the hinterlands. Communication needs were restricted, and a West African Pidgin English emerged and was in use for centuries to facilitate rather superficial contacts with indigenous peoples. It was only in the nineteenth century that the British political involvement and interest began to grow, with trading posts expanding, some plantations being established, and the British outreach gradually growing into the interior in various forms. Missionaries were the first to venture further, spreading their faith and also, to some extent, their language. Late in

Map 14 English-speaking countries in Sub-Saharan Africa

the nineteenth and early in the twentieth century British colonial control, after earlier protectorates and involvement of the Royal Niger Company, became firmly established in The Gambia, Sierra Leone, Ghana, Nigeria, and the British Cameroons. The English Pidgin continued to be in use throughout the region, and was strongly promoted further by the increasing ethnic and social mixtures brought about by urbanization. In general, familiarity with English spread, associated with an elitist position in society and frequently transmitted in missionary schools. In the twentieth century many African leaders adopted and used English as a symbol of prestige and power.

There are two smaller nations in West Africa where the language situation is different from their other neighbors because of an American and Caribbean connection and thus the impact of American Creoles. Freetown in Sierra Leone was founded by the British in 1887 as a home for liberated former slaves from North America. The city, soon a colony, later assimilated further waves of "repatriated" New World Africans: blacks from Nova Scotia, Jamaicans, Africans from intercepted slave ships, and others were transported there and, in the absence of shared ancestral roots in Africa, formed a new community. All this linguistic input forged a creole language known as Krio, spoken there to the present day. Supported by the same spirit of abolitionism in the United States, the country of Liberia was founded in 1822 as a place where African American slaves were "returned" to, Africa's first democracy. Not only Liberia's culture and political system but also the language, with "Settler English" or "Merico" presumably a creole, are strongly shaped by their American background. Sadly enough, in both countries the newcomers from

Timeline F: Sub-Saharan Africa

17th c.	British trading forts established along West African coast
1672	Royal Africa Company chartered
1787	British settlement of Sierra Leone
1822	American settlement of Liberia
1824–26	British protectorate of Mombassa
1861	Lagos becomes British
1874	British Gold Coast Colony established
1884–1919	Cameroon established as a German protectorate
1885	Berlin conference assigns formal authority over parts of East Africa to Britain and over Tanganyika to Germany
1885	British protectorate of Bechuanaland
1886	Royal Niger Company chartered
1890	Zanzibar became a British protectorate
1900	Northern and southern Nigeria become Protectorates
1902	Construction of railway between the East African coast and Lake Victoria
1914	Nigeria was unified and became a colony
1919	Tanganyika became British League of Nations mandate
1919	British Cameroons became British League of Nations mandate
1920	Kenya became a British colony
1952–59	Mau Mau rebellion in Kenya
1957	Independence of Ghana
1960	Independence of Nigeria
1961	Referendum in British Cameroons, leading to the northern part joining Nigeria and the southern part being united with French Cameroon
1963	Independence of Kenya
1963	Independence of Zanzibar
1964	Formation of Tanzania as a union of Tanganyika and Zanzibar
1967	Arusha Declaration in Tanzania (socialist policy, promotion of Kiswahili)

the New World felt themselves superior to the indigenous Africans and established themselves as a leading elite in power, thus creating tensions which have
persisted into the twenty-first century and were a major cause of civil wars and
cruelties in the recent past.

East Africa's linguistic ecology differs from the West African one in one
major respect: there is no Pidgin English. This has to do with the absence of
slavery (and thus of "slave factory" fortifications) and with the fact that
Kiswahili had grown as a regional lingua franca, influenced by Arabs and
their trading routes. English came in the nineteenth century, via the usual
steps of coastal establishments supporting naval routes, missionary and
trade expansion into the interior. It was essentially during the first half of
the twentieth century that protectorates and colonies (or, after World War I,
mandated territories) were formally established. Throughout this period the
teaching of English was not really promoted widely, for a simple reason.
Access to English also implied access to power – so the demand for it kept
growing, but it decidedly retained an elitist status.

Kenya was special in this region because it was the site of a systematic
British settlement activity. In the 1910s, after the railway opened up the
interior and fertile lands offered profitable farming, large numbers of British
settlers were attracted. They did little to spread a knowledge of English
amongst the Africans, however, and adopted some Swahili for their own
purposes instead. Descendants of these white settlers still live in today's
Kenya. On the way to independence, the country went through a period of
turmoil and violence during the Mau Mau rebellion of the 1950s, which
ended with independence in 1963.

In southern Africa, Britain held the protectorates or colonies (in some
cases these were subsequent stages) of Bechuanaland (which became today's
Botswana), Northern Rhodesia (now Zambia), Southern Rhodesia (also a
site of fairly large-scale white settlement, traces of which, however, have
almost completely disappeared from today's Zimbabwe), and Nyasaland
(renamed Malawi after independence). In all these cases Britain's colonial
grip remained fairly loose. Today English in these countries tends to be an
elitist second language which is found useful and attractive but is clearly
secondary to indigenous languages. The geographical proximity to South
Africa strengthens the role of English and influences the forms of the
language used in this region.

The British reluctance to spread their language and culture in the colonies
changed drastically, as in all of Britain's African possessions, after World
War II. Growing nationalism and self-confidence in the colonies after the
war experience and the example of India's independence made it clear that
the other colonies would follow into independence sooner or later. Linguistic
and cultural anglicization was therefore deliberately supported in that

Table 4 *Domains of English use in some eastern and southern African states*

	Uganda	Kenya	Tanzania	Zambia	Zimbabwe	Malawi
High court	+	+	+	+	+	+
Local court	*	*	–	*	*	*
Parliament	+	+	–	+	+	+
Civil service	+	+	–	+	+	+
Primary school	+	+	–	+	+	+
Secondary school	+	+	+	+	+	+
Radio	+	+	+	+	+	+
Newspaper	+	+	+	+	+	+
Local novels	+	+	+	+	+	+
Local records	+	+	–	+	+	+
Local plays	+	+	–	+	+	+
Films (not dubbed)	+	+	+	+	+	+
Traffic and vehicle signs	+	+	–	+	+	+
Advertising	+	+	*	+	+	+
Business correspondence	+	+	+	+	+	+
Private correspondence	+	+	–	+	+	+

Key:
+ English used
* English only sometimes used
– English not used
(adapted from Schmied 1991: 41. Reprinted by permission of Pearson Education)

period, to build lasting ties with Britain for the days ahead (a relationship which was to become formalized in the Commonwealth of Nations). So around the middle of the twentieth century English became well established in the public life and educational institutions of these countries, and in many of them this effect continued into the period of independent statehood.

Since then, different policies and developments have produced a range of varying degrees of penetration of today's societies by English. In most of Britain's former possessions in Sub-Saharan Africa, English is a strong second language today, and in some it is an official or co-official language. It is typically the language of specific domains of life, including politics, jurisdiction, the media, the education system, and so on. Table 4 illustrates this principle as applied to a few select states from eastern and southern Africa.

Nigeria, to be discussed in greater detail below, is the region's most strongly anglicized country, a fact which can partly be explained by the strength of Pidgin, locally perceived as an informal variant of English. In Ghana, English is an official language, widespread in formal domains, and

Pidgin is also spoken, though more strongly stigmatized. Cameroon, German until 1919, was then divided between France, which established French in the majority of the country, and Britain. Two of today's provinces, adjacent to Nigeria, have had a continuously "anglophone" history and population and are struggling to maintain their ethnolinguistic identity against a francophone majority. But Pidgin English is fairly widespread and growing everywhere, and there are signs of English becoming an attractive target for French speakers as well.

In Uganda, a former British protectorate, English is also the official language, though in practice it is not as widely spread as elsewhere in East Africa. Kenya's political and economic orientation to the west, together with the colonial heritage, has resulted in English playing a very strong role, ranging from formal uses in politics down to a grassroots spread among the urban poor (though Swahili has also been established as a national language). In contrast, Tanzania pursued a nationalist language policy after independence, promoting and developing Kiswahili successfully and reducing the role of English to a small range of business domains and international functions (although the country's "elite" and many others still speak and uphold it).

Thus, English in Africa today, rooted predominantly in former British territories and colonies, comes in a wide range of forms and functions, but in general it is a vibrant language which is rapidly growing, spreading further and getting indigenized. Two trends are most noteworthy: a process of grassroots diffusion and nativization, and young people's love of mixing it with local languages.

To start with the latter: code-switching and code-mixing are widespread in many countries, especially among young and typically educated speakers. This is a trend which reflects linguistic creativity and playfulness but clearly also expresses hybrid orientations, identities which deliberately incorporate both the speakers' African heritage and western, modernizing influences. Some of these new varieties (if that's what they are) have stabilized and been given names: Camfranglais (a mixture of English, French, and African components) in Cameroon, Engsh (more English than African), and Sheng (more African than English) in Kenya. Text 7 briefly illustrates these two language forms. The Sheng sentence, clearly African in character, is essentially from Kiswahili, though it incorporates elements from Kikuyu (*wathii* 'passengers') and English (*mushii* 'lady' including *she*) or words mixed between English and Swahili (*alidondoka, konkodi*). The Engsh sentence, on the other hand, is recognizably nonstandard English with some African words interspersed.

The process which is most likely to shape African English in the long run, however, is its indigenization. English is no longer just the formal, elitist

---

TEXT 7: Sample sentences of Sheng and Engsh

Sheng: *Maze, huyo mushii alidondoka kutoka kwa wangora akadunda ile noma. Usikii konkodi na wathii walibaki wamepasua!* 'Hey, that lady alighted from an old matatu and fell down badly. Imagine the conductor and the passengers broke into laughter!'

Engsh: *We chomokad with the beks that that chile had been pewad by her kid bro.* 'We took off with the cash that that lady had been given by her younger brother.'

(kindly provided by Alfred Buregeya and Cedricc Anjiji Voywa, Nairobi)

---

expression of educated speakers, close to "standard English" except, perhaps, for a few lexical items or some distinctive pronunciation features. It is used by market women, taxi drivers, manual workers, all kinds of people today, in all kinds of situations and for down-to-earth purposes, and thus, obviously, also in locally characteristic forms. In West Africa in particular it blends with Pidgin – speakers think of pidgin as an informal version of educated English, Pidgin usage spreads into formal contexts (such as radio news), and conversely the Pidgin has lost some of its most distinctive, conservative forms, approximating to formal English at times. And finally, English is not only spreading widely as a second language – increasingly it is becoming a mother tongue, children's first or even only language. Obviously, this is predominantly an urban phenomenon, associated with higher education and interethnic marriages, but not only so. There is also documentation of small tribal communities who are giving up their ancestral languages and shifting to English.

6.1.2 Case study: Nigeria

The above processes can be most vigorously observed and documented in Nigeria, the country which, as was mentioned before, has been penetrated by English most fundamentally. The number of English speakers in Nigeria counts by the tens of millions, though it is impossible to provide reasonably accurate figures, not only because it is difficult to define how much knowledge of English is required in such a count, and whether Pidgin English should be included. The current population is estimated to be close to 150 million, of whom roughly a fifth have been estimated to speak English reasonably well and more than half are assumed to speak Pidgin English.

The special role of English in Nigeria has most likely been promoted by its ethnically neutral status in a highly multilingual nation. More than

500 languages are spoken in the country, and three big, regional ones (Yoruba, Igbo, and Hausa) are also mentioned in the constitution as national languages, but in the interest of national unity English is the "official" language. The ongoing rapid diffusion of English (and Pidgin) is a consequence of this special status, going hand in hand with its practical importance and usefulness. Certainly English and Pidgin are mostly second (or third, etc.) languages, acquired in addition to tribal and regional languages. Both have been found to increasingly become mother tongues of African children as well, however. English is becoming a first language primarily in educated families and in urban contexts, and Pidgin in certain regions and amongst the less affluent. Strictly speaking, Pidgin is thus a creolizing language. It is noteworthy that the number of its native speakers has been estimated to be as high as three to five million.

Historically speaking, restricted, coastal uses of early forms of Pidgin may date back to the seventeenth century, thus predating serious applications of English by some two centuries. Lagos became a British colony in 1861. The Royal Niger Company was founded in the 1880s, and the country became a protectorate in 1900, which attracted more soldiers, government officials, and other personnel. Nigeria's formal status as a British colony lasted from 1914 to independence in 1960. For most of this period English was the property of a rather small elite, taught in formal contexts and a means of signaling social superiority, of explicitly "showing off" one's status. So, for example, there are reports of high-ranking Nigerians deliberately using English rather than the African languages which they also commanded and which their audiences would have understood. Ken Saro-Wiwa in his novel *Sozaboy* repeatedly presents government representatives as using what he calls "big big words" and "grammar" (see Exercise 6a). It was only later, after World War II and even more so after independence and in the recent past, that English began to spread vigorously. And it seems that this former elitist attitude towards it continues today to some extent in the ongoing esteem attributed to "standard English" as against "broken" forms of it or the Pidgin.

Actually, the relationship between English and Pidgin is more complicated than one might think, with social and linguistic aspects to it and considering the presence of a growing range of intermediate forms. For many educated Nigerians, including government officials and education gatekeepers, it seems clear that "English" means "standard English," the "ideal" form of which, and the target of local education, is still British English. Typically, some local lexis is tolerated, the fact that most Africans have an accent which is far from RP is ignored, and grammatical "deviance" is scorned. Linguists have documented grammatical patterns which are incipiently typical of Nigerian formal usage, but so far such insights have not informed official language policy.

In practice there is a range of stylistic varieties, from that formal "standard" end to what has been termed "Nonstandard" or "Popular." The formal types of English dominate higher domains of public life and formal discourse: political debates, the media, business transactions, the education and legal systems, formal interethnic conversations, etc. In contrast, Pidgin English is the language of the less educated and of informal encounters: market places, public transportation, sports, the armed forces, and informal conversation amongst the young, even the educated ones. As we will see in a moment, it is set off from English by specific grammatical properties, like preverbal markers for tense and aspect relations, a reduced set of pronoun distinctions, distinctive copula forms, reduplications, and the like.

But the distinction is getting increasingly blurred, because forms intermediate between English and Pidgin, with one borrowing from the other, have been emerging. Pidgin is now used in some public and formal contexts, for instance, such as in advertisements, TV entertainment, politicians' speeches, and radio news, and in these contexts it tends to borrow more words, paraphrases, and also structural properties from formal English. Conversely, informal English usage or even learners' forms of it may be interspersed with items characteristic of Pidgin, more or less deliberately.

Whether there is, and even more so whether there should be, a distinctive Nigerian form of English, acceptable in local contexts, is very much a matter of ongoing public debate (and some linguists have argued that the most effective way of extinguishing Nigerian English would be to publicly discover it). Although many articles and books describing properties of English in Nigeria have been published, there is no authoritative grammar or dictionary available. An educated form of Nigerian English seems very much to be in existence in reality, and proposals to accept an endonormative orientation are increasingly voiced. But conservative observers and users deny its existence and have opposed such moves so far. Thus, the West African Examination Board still prescribes British English, even if in reality it tends to tolerate or ignore many local forms.

On the other hand, the majority of Nigerians of whatever persuasion probably just don't care. They find English attractive and useful and do their best to acquire as much of it as they can; they use whatever suits their purposes without bothering about issues of normativity or correctness; and they thus simply contribute to the daily diffusion and nativization of the language, Pidgin or otherwise. Most uneducated Nigerians who speak Pidgins do not draw a distinction anyhow – they just assume that what they use is English. Pidgin has actually been suggested as a language of national unity and development, being spoken so widely and being ethnically and socially neutral (and also being African in origin). So far its stigma seems so strong that elevating it to some form of an official status seems unlikely in the not-too-distant future, but its use in some formal domains – by politicians, in radio news, in advertisements and public announcements, etc. – may foreshadow a change of attitude in the long run.

One form of language usage in which both English and Pidgin have spread widely, also beyond the country's borders, has been literary adoptions, e.g. in Nigerian novels, in various styles and contexts. Probably the best-known representative of this is Chinua Achebe, who deliberately wrote in English and defended this language choice. In his first and best-known novel, *Things Fall Apart* of 1958, and also in later works, his characters speak a distinctively Nigerian, partly Pidgin form of English. The same applies to the poetry and other works of Nobel Prize Laureate Wole Soyinka, or to the late Ken Saro-Wiwa's impressive (and partly depressing) book *Sozaboy*, which is explicitly subtitled *A Novel in Rotten English*. On a more popular level, novels and stories collectively known, after their main place of distribution in the 1950s and 1960s, as "Onitsha market literature" (cf. Obiechina 1972) also represent spoken Nigerian forms of English very nicely and accessibly.

Text 8, which can also be heard on the website, presents a sample of news from Radio Nigeria 3, thus illustrating the fact that Nigerian Pidgin has progressed into public domains and usage contexts which in earlier times would have been reserved for standard English. This sample, together with many others which are also made directly accessible on a CD, is originally provided in Deuber's (2005) impressive study of Nigerian Pidgin.

TEXT 8: Nigerian Pidgin news

Check your time dere you go see na five minutes e take dodge two o'clock, e don reach di time for our Pidgin news for today wey be number seventeen day for di month of May wey be number five month for di year two thousand. But before I go chook leg for di news proper, I go tell una di ones wey carry kanda for inside. [. . .]

One hand no dey carry heavy load put for head o. Na im make di Lagos Mainland Local Government don set task force wey go follow put eye to monitor how private sector people o wey dey do dirty carry-carry work to do am well well and proper proper. Na di oga for dat council, Alhaji Bashir Bolarinwa, tell our newtory people say di work of di task force na to make sure say people wey dey stay dat Local Government Area cooperate with di law wey di council put on top dirty matter for dat area. Alhaji Bolarinwa come take salute o rub di body of Lagos State House of Assembly on top di new step wey dem wan take on top dose wey dey do street trading for Lagos State now. [. . .]

Na tree wey want noise o, na im dey grow flowers o. Na im make di number one ogbonge group on top Igbo people matter, Ohaneze Nd'Igbo, don dey tell every Nigeria people say di celebration of dem Igbo Day wey wan show face for on di twenty-nine of May no go cause am make people no celebrate di first year of dis government for office, because pikin no dey senior im papa. One former oga on top ofofo and talk-talk matter o, Chief Uche Chukwumerije, say dem no go dance dat day o and dem no go do any oder kind of celebration (da#) but make everybody wey be Igbo man (ta#) tabi Igbo woman wherever dem dey o to keep quiet tabi silent for three minutes by twelve o'clock dat day to show say dem dey mourn abi dey squeeze face on top dem broders and sisters dem wey kpai during di Civil War.

Translation

Check your time, you'll see it's five minutes past two, time for our Pidgin news for today, the seventeenth of May two thousand. But before I enter into the news proper, I'll give you the headlines. [. . .]

You can't lift up a heavy load with only one hand. That's why the Lagos Mainland Local Government has set up a task force to supervise the work of private waste disposal companies. The Local Government Chairman, Alhaji Bashir Bolarinwa, has told our reporters that the task force is meant to enforce the council's regulations on waste management in the area. Alhaji Bolarinwa also applauded the new measures introduced by the Lagos State House of Assembly to curb street trading in Lagos State. [. . .]

A tree produces flowers to attract bees. The prominent Igbo cultural group Ohaneze Nd'Igbo has made it known to all Nigerians that the celebration of Igbo Day on the twenty-ninth of May won't interfere with festivities to mark the first anniversary of the present government, because a child can't be senior to his father. The former Minister of Information Chief Uche Chukwumerije said there will be no dancing nor any other kind of celebration, but that every Igbo man and Igbo woman will be called upon to observe three minutes of silence at twelve noon on that day in commemoration of the Igbos who died in the Civil War.

(From Dagmar Deuber, *Nigerian Pidgin in Lagos: Language Contact, Variation and Change in an African Urban Setting*. London: Battlebridge, 2005, Appendix, N04-1. Reproduced by permission given by Dagmar Deuber and Battlebridge)

There is no reason to be frustrated if you find this difficult to understand, particularly the aural version. Pidgin is quite different from "regular" English in some ways, so this text requires a translation. But on the other hand with a fresh mind and the strategy of searching for word-by-word equivalents in English, and of trying to just make sense of their combinations somehow, much of it is actually transparent at a second glance. Take a sequence like *no go cause am make people no celebrate di first year of dis government for office*, which, despite what to an English speaker might at first look like odd ways of expressing things, is not really difficult to follow, for example.

As Deuber also points out very convincingly, this text type shows a tension between pidgin proper and the intrusion of anglicisms to denote complex and abstract concepts (which a news program obviously needs to be able to express but which may not be topics typically discussed in Pidgin). So, for example, *task force* is left like that, with an English expression, but 'waste disposal regulations' is rendered in a pidgin paraphrase as *di law wey di council put on top dirty matter*. Similar paraphrases include *follow put eye*, *people wey dey do dirty carry-carry work* 'waste disposal companies', *new-tory people* 'reporters', *come take salute* 'applaud, praise', *talk-talk matter* 'information', etc.

The words of this sample illustrate the composition of the vocabulary of West African Pidgin from multiple sources.

- Obviously, the majority of lexical items can be recognized as deriving from English, though some show modifications of the word form, as in *newtory* 'news story'.
- Some words are borrowings from West African languages. The most frequent and most widespread one of these is *oga*, an honorific title of a leader or chief. Others include *ogbonge* 'authentic', *ofofo* 'gossip' (Yoruba), or *kpai* 'die'.
- Notice the item *una* – an African second person plural pronoun which has moved into a wide range of pidgins and creoles.
- The same applies to the Portuguese-derived word *pikin* 'child'. Remember that we already encountered both of these words in the Jamaican text.
- Two words in this text seem particularly characteristic of Nigerian Pidgin, if only because they occur so frequently. The form *o*, mostly placed at the end of a clause, ranges between a discourse marker and an interjection; typically it adds emphasis and stresses the truth of the statement it comes with (but it may also imply empathy). The form *na* counts as a copula, corresponding to English *be*, but it has adopted a much wider range of functions, primarily that of highlighting (or empha-sizing) the following constituent.

Note that the sample also illustrates the impact of traditional West African culture, for instance a discourse convention of putting the moral of a story up front: Each news item begins with a short proverb which in a nutshell and by using indigenous metaphors spells out the core message, the gist of the matter, and connects it to folk culture and traditional wisdom.

A number of systematic differences to standard English can be observed on the level of phonology:

- The number of vowel sounds is reduced, and some vowels which are kept distinct in other varieties have fallen together. For example, the short raised front vowel /æ/ is replaced by a low /a/, as can be heard in the words *hand*, *carry*, or *dat*. Similarly, the central raised /ʌ/ falls together with a low back /ɔ/, e.g. in *month*, *done*, *body*, and *broders*.
- The English diphthongs with mid-high onsets are generally monoph-thongized: in words like *day* or *Lagos* we hear not a diphthong /eɪ/ but a monophthong /e/; correspondingly, *load*, *Local*, etc. have not /əʊ/ or /oʊ/ but a plain /o/.
- Nigerian Pidgin lacks the dental fricatives, so /ð/ is replaced by /d/ (in *dere*, *di*, or *dose*), and its voiceless equivalent /θ/ is realized as /t/, audible in this sample in *month* and *thousand*.

But the more noteworthy phenomena, as is usually the case with a pidgin or creole, can be observed on the level of grammar.

- In the verb phrase, temporal and aspectual relations are expressed by preverbal markers. In this sample we find *go* for the future (*you go see, before I go chook leg, dem no go dance*, etc.), *don* for the completive (*e don reach di time, Government don set . . ., done . . . tell*), and *dey* for ongoing actions (labeled an "incompletive" or "imperfective" marker), e.g. *One hand no dey carry . . ., we dey do . . ., im dey grow flowers, dem dey mourn*).
- Negation is achieved by simply placing the invariant negator *no* in front of the verb phrase: *no dey carry, no go cause, no celebrate*.
- The form *am*, derived from *him*, is commonly analyzed as a third person singular "bound" object form, sometimes even as a clitic, something like a grammatical dummy element. It indicates that its preceding verb is transitive, i.e. that a direct object will be following or is to be understood. Hence in *do am* it is implied that "something," formally suggested by *am*, is to be done; and *cause am* indicates that the entire following statement (*make people no celebrate . . .*) is to be understood as what is caused.
- The form of the copula, also in finite clauses, can be *be* in a purely equative function before a noun phrase (e.g. *wey be number . . ., wey be Igbo man*); *dey*, derived from *there* (e.g. *pikin no dey senior*), especially

147

when it combines a subject with a locative, as in *wherever dem dey*; or *na*, typically understood as a highlighter, as in *di work of di task force na to make sure* 'the work ... is to make sure ...'.

- In line with a similar pattern in many pidgins and creoles, the copula-like form *na* is also frequently found clause-initially as a sort of focusing or connecting device. So *na five minutes* roughly means 'it is five minutes ...'; and *Na im make* is best translated as 'So he makes ...' or even 'It is him who makes ...'.
- Verbs of saying or thinking, but also predicates denoting other activities like *make sure* or *show*, typically connect their object clauses by means of a complementizer form *say*, corresponding to English *that*, so *to show say dem dey mourn* literally corresponds to 'to show that they are mourning'. So, in a sentence like ... *tell every Nigeria people say di celebration ... no go cause* the speech activity is expressed by the verb *tell*, whereas *say* has the purely grammatical function of introducing the following clause.
- The masculine singular pronoun form *im* can be both a subject (*im make*, *im dey grow*) and a possessive (*im papa*). The form *e* in *e take dodge* and *e don reach* represents 'it'.
- The relative pronoun *wey* ('who, which, that') is invariant, i.e. always the same irrespective of whether the referent is human or not (cf. *news ... wey be ...*, *di ones wey carry*, *task force wey go follow*, *tree wey want ...*, etc.).
- Pidgins have little or no inflectional morphology – notice, for instance, that all verbs stand in their base forms, without third singular suffixes or past tense endings. However, in this text the plural -*s* comes up repeatedly (e.g. in *minutes*, *flowers*, *broders*). Reportedly, this English-style type of plural marking has increased in frequency in the recent past at the expense of the "deeper" pidgin or creole plural marker, a post-nominal *dem*, which is also to be found once here (in fact, this is an instance of double marking, with both -*s* and *dem*): *dem broders and sisters dem*. (Notice that the *dem* preceding these nouns is a demonstrative marker corresponding to *those*, a form widely found in dialects of English in this function.)
- A word modification principle which is widespread in pidgins and creoles, however, and also found frequently in this text, is reduplication to express intensification: *carry-carry* 'carry heavily', *proper proper* 'very properly', *talk-talk* 'discuss intensely'.
- Finally, the preposition *for* may express a variety of meanings, broadly of one entity having to do with another: *news for today*, *day for de month*, *load put for head*, *di oga for dat council*, etc.

Notice that quite a number of the phenomena just listed (vowel reduction, dental fricative replacement, a second person plural pronoun *unu/una*, the word *pikin*, preverbal markers, plural *dem*, multifunctional pronouns, a complementizer *say*, an invariant relativizer *wey*, reduplication) were also found, at least in a very similar form, in the Jamaican Creole sample discussed in Chapter 4. These shared traits, an ocean apart, have continued to puzzle creolists, and testify to some form of relatedness of creoles, at least those on both sides of the Atlantic (though we will find that even Tok Pisin and Bislama, in the south-west Pacific, have a few similar properties).

6.2 More than just colonial traces: South and South-East Asia

6.2.1 From the Empire's jewel to global cities: English becomes an Asian language

Together with Africa, Asia has been the continent to which English has been spreading most vigorously, and perhaps surprisingly, over the last few centuries and, even more so, decades. In a strong form, with English nativizing as a Second Language, this concerns in particular the postcolonial "Outer Circle," consisting of South Asia (India, Pakistan, Sri Lanka, and Bangladesh) and South-East Asia (Malaysia, Singapore, Brunei, Hong Kong, and, as a product of American colonization, the Philippines). In this region English has been spreading largely "from above," via formal education, though the language has moved far beyond the confines of such elitist social settings and also of the area defined by a former colonial status. Take East Asia, discussed at the end of this chapter, as a case in point. Or consider the decision of ASEAN, the Association of South-East Asian Nations, stipulated in Article 34 of their 2007 Charter, to establish English as their sole "working language." Some member states of ASEAN, such as Vietnam, Cambodia, Thailand, or Indonesia, have had no historical exposure to English through a colonial background. Their decision to accept such a clause clearly testifies to the importance which is attributed to English in Asia also internally.

See Timeline G for a first, brief summary of the history of this region.

To India, once the "jewel" of the British Empire, English came gradually, with the activities of the East India Company, which was founded in 1600. Throughout the seventeenth century this remained largely restricted to the establishment of trading "factories" along the coast and missionary activities. In the following century the Company increasingly gained political and military control over more and more parts of India, until the Crown also assumed responsibility – jointly with the Company in 1784, and then solely in 1858. Throughout that period, and into the early twentieth century, the English language and a western education became much more widely

Timeline G: South and South-East Asia

1600	British East India Company founded
1661	Bombay ceded to Britain by Portugal
1757	Battle of Plassey gives Britain authority over Bengal
1786	Penang colonized by the East India Company
1795	East India Company conquers Dutch Ceylon (today's Sri Lanka)
1819	Foundation of Singapore by Stamford Raffles
1824	Melaka taken over by the British from the Dutch
1842	Treaty of Nanking ends First Opium War: Hong Kong island ceded to Britain
1849	Punjab in India annexed by Britain
1857–58	Indian Rebellion results in end of East India Company rule and crown colony status
1874	Treaty of Pangkor extends British authority in Malaysia
1889	Straits Settlement (later Malaysia) became a crown colony
1896	Federation of Malay States founded as a protectorate
1898	American authority over the Philippines
1942	Japanese seizure of Singapore
1946	Independence of the Philippines
1947	Independence of India and Pakistan
1957	Independence of Malaysia
1963	Separation of Singapore from Malaysia
1965	Independence of Singapore
1976	National Language Act in Malaysia, removing English as a co-official language
1997	"Handover" of Hong Kong to China
2003	English re-introduced as the language of teaching sciences in Malaysia; decision reverted in 2010

accessible in India. Based on contemporary documents there must have been a huge demand amongst the Indian leadership for such an "Anglicist" education. The English, following Macaulay's famous "Minute" of 1835, essentially a statement on India's educational policy, were willing to grant it – but only to a leading minority of local rulers who were expected to collaborate with the British and serve their interests. In the twentieth century, independence dawned (and was won in 1947), and the role of English remained strong, partly because it was the language of the Indian National Congress and the new political leadership (Gandhi, for instance, had been exiled in South Africa before returning to India).

Post-independence India originally intended to do away with the former colonial language, but this simply did not work out. The idea, formalized in the "Three-Language Formula" of the Language Act of 1967, was to develop Hindi into a new national language and to strengthen regional languages as well, until English would become dispensable. However, essentially the Hindi north and the Dravidian south were unwilling to yield ground and to acquire the other language, respectively, so English has remained an official and highly important language in public life and all formal domains. Clearly, a distinctive Indian English, partly with some regional pronunciation differences, has evolved and has become one of the world's main varieties, based on speaker numbers (even if in a local perspective only a minority really speaks it). Uses of Indian English are clearly associated with and partly symbolic of a high social status and a superior education on an individual basis and with formal domains of life (education, politics, the judiciary, and so on). However, this sociolinguistic restriction, while being reasonably typical and true, has never been the whole story, and increasingly less so in recent decades with all their mobility and social changes. Even in earlier times amongst the soldiers and staff stationed in India there were many lower-class and middle-class dialect speakers who were in touch with ordinary Indians who also picked up and used some English. Reportedly, even some long-resident British people, so-called "white babus," adopted Indian ways of using English. In the recent past the association of English with access to better-paid jobs and thus greater income and prosperity caused it to spread also into the lower strata of society, through some form of schooling or even informally and through natural acquisition. Language mixing between English and indigenous languages (a form called "Hinglish," for example) has also come to be enormously popular and is spreading vigorously.

The British Empire in South Asia also encompassed today's independent countries of Pakistan, Bangladesh, and Sri Lanka, and in all of them English is also still widely used as a second (and in Pakistan also an "official") language, typically restricted mostly to formal domains. Map 15 shows the South Asian countries mentioned here.

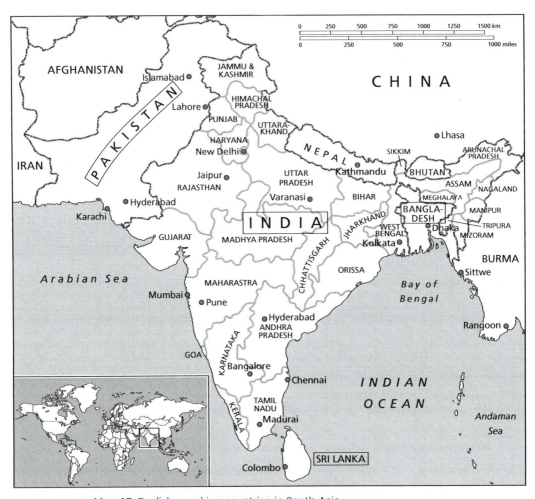

Map 15 English-speaking countries in South Asia

On the Malay peninsula, the Dutch were the earliest colonizers, and Britain's activities, beginning in the late eighteenth and early nineteenth centuries and steered from India for a while, originally were directed against these European competitors (from whom they took Melaka in 1824, for instance). The Straits Settlement, consisting of Penang, Melaka, and Singapore (which was somewhat different and will be discussed separately below), became a colony in 1889 and constituted the basis for a gradual regional expansion of the British influence on and grasp of the region (through various kinds of arrangements with local Sultans and rulers). Similar to the African and Indian patterns, local elites were anglicized to some extent and admitted to the role of sharing and administering power structures, supported by missionaries and later also state-run schools. Chinese and Indian immigrants, today significant minorities in Malaysia's population makeup, adopted the English language much more readily than the local Malays, who to the present day have less incentive to acquire it for their traditional, rural life patterns.

Malaysia has successfully reduced the role of English and promoted and developed Bahasa Malaysia as a new national language after independence. In the twenty-first century the importance of a sufficiently high level of national competence in English has been recognized again and has resulted in a reintroduction of English as the language of teaching sciences in secondary education. The most recent decision is to revert to the earlier stage again in 2012 – a back-and-forth movement which is quite indicative of the ambivalent attitudes toward English in the country: it shouldn't get too strong, but it is equally unthinkable to let it go.

A Malaysian form of English is widely recognized and widespread in the country, associated with a speaker's level of education and social status, and more strongly with urban life and an Indian or Chinese ethnicity. However, it is also frequently reported that a mesolectal, informal form of Malaysian English is also an indicator of social proximity and a relaxed situation, so it seems to some extent the language is becoming symbolically loaded with internally indexical social functions.

A language habit that is spreading very vigorously in the country, as practically anywhere in the region, is the practice of mixing indigenous languages with English, an explicit symbolic indicator of the multilingual and multicultural makeup of Malaysia, and her young and educated population in particular. Text 9, a selection from an informal letter between two female friends, illustrates this usage.

In Hong Kong, English has also always marked an elitist status, although in a number of informal contexts, such as the night market represented in Figure 12, English is going strong. Today it is considered a "value-added" language and a symbol of middle-class status and an outward business orientation.

The 1840s Opium Wars established Hong Kong Island as a British colony, and some twenty years later the Kowloon peninsula was leased. In 1898 the British-controlled territory grew again, with a treaty that brought a 99-year lease of the New Territories. In the "handover" of 1997 the region was returned to China and became a Special Administrative Region of the Republic of China. Throughout the colonial period English was essentially the language of the colonial power and a small educated indigenous elite. But after the 1960s, when Hong Kong redefined herself as a global city and became an international trading and banking center, the demand for a knowledge of English, for utilitarian motives, also grew tremendously, and speaker percentages increased substantially, to reach a proportion of more than 40 percent of the population speaking English "quite well" or "well" today, according to recent surveys. In practice, as elsewhere in Asia, English

TEXT 9: "Manglish": Selection from an informal letter between two female Malaysian friends

Oohhh...guess what?! I accompanied Angie to this air-stewardess walk-in interview two days ago, and guess who I saw? Suraya! You still remember-*kah* which one? *Haiyaa*, the short-short one *bah*! The long hair one, *yang gila* check-in the crew *punya-bah*. The one *yang* looks okay, *tapi bila* start to *cakap*, *suara macam katak* that one-*bah*! You should know by now-*lah*! So, I saw her-*lah*, plus her 1-*inci tebal punya* make-up! While waiting, one of the captains (I *lupa* the name) passed by. So, *ini perempuan nampak, kasi jack-lah* the captain! I guess she saw me too, *tapi tak tegur pun*. Well, not that I care anyway!

Glosses and explanations: *kah* 'particle used in questions'; *haiyaa* 'exclamation (predominantly used by Chinese population)'; *short-short*: reduplication in Malay expresses emphasis (and more commonly the plural); *bah* 'particle, used like *lah*, mainly in Sabah'; *yang* 'relative pronoun'; *gila* 'crazy'; *punya* 'possessive marker'; *tapi* (short for *tetapi*) 'but'; *bila* 'when'; *cakap* 'to talk, speak'; *suara* 'voice'; *macam* 'like (for comparisons)'; *katak* 'frog'; *inci* 'inch'; *tebal* 'thick'; *lupa* 'to forget'; *ini* 'this'; *perempuan* 'woman'; *nampak* 'to see, look; here: saw (Malay does not have a form for the simple past)'; *kasi* 'give'; *jack* 'butter up, kiss ass (slang)'; *tak* '(short for: *tidak*) negation'; *tegur* 'acknowledge'; *pun* 'too, also'.

(Reproduced by permission; thanks to Sebastian Hoffman and the author of the letter, a friend of his wife, from Sabah)

is the language of education, business, and formal domains. Given the largely monolingual Cantonese background of the city (although Putonghua is becoming increasingly important because of the new political situation, language policy, and immigration patterns) there has never been a need for an interethnic link language. But the strife for English has continued to be enormously strong, as has been witnessed by the post-1997 debate on school policy. Many parents have resisted the political goal of turning many "English-medium" schools into "Chinese-medium." Actually, in practice, based on local reports, this may not mean that much, given that even in so-called "English-medium" schools Cantonese is very widely employed simply to secure comprehension, but even so – attending an English-medium school counts as prestigious, an asset. This resistance has been partly successful. So English continues to be considered important in Hong Kong, especially in formal domains (though it is also spreading in the manual workforce) and in writing, and it is also liberally mixed with Cantonese by the young. Linguists have documented some locally characteristic features of pronunciation,

Figure 12 Hong Kong – trilingual, biscriptural, and multicultural metropolis

grammar, and, of course, word choice (consider *dim sum* or *lucky money*, for instance).

The Philippines, formerly a Spanish colony, were turned over to the United States in 1898, as a consequence of the Spanish–American War. The Americans decided to anglicize and to culturally "develop" the country, and to that end they sent large numbers of English teachers, locally remembered as the "Thomasites," after the name of the ship that carried the first load. Their work was exceptionally successful – English spread enormously rapidly and widely, also after independence in 1946. Consequently, in addition to a number of indigenous features on all language levels, Philippine English has an American rather than a British touch (and teaching target, for that matter). English was promoted by those teaching efforts and a bilingual language policy and simply by the fact that it was perceived as the language of social aspirations and opportunities, promising access to well-paid jobs. Speaker numbers are remarkable: according to recent figures, about three quarters of the population are able to read or understand English, and more than half are reported to speak it. My own (naturally limited) impression is also that nowhere in Asia except for Singapore is English found and used so regularly.

On the other hand, the government soon decided to pursue a national language policy, with the goal of developing a form of Tagalog, later renamed as Filipino, into a new national language, and to a considerable extent this policy has also been implemented successfully. The outcome of all of this is somewhat ambiguous. Filipino / Tagalog has clearly been established as a national language (with limitations, given that in the country Tagalog is also a regional language only), and together with other indigenous languages it fills the role of social intimacy, so for English there is little symbolic space left in the personal domain. English, on the other hand, is still associated with job opportunities – most recently with the massively growing call center industry in particular. But again, this is a double-edged process: call center jobs are desirable and comparatively well paid, but they deeply affect life patterns because work needs to be done mostly during the night hours, when North American customers are at work – a new, subtle type of dependence and quasi-colonialism. Furthermore, English has been associated with local political and business elites, which in the eyes of strong segments of the population is not really a positive image. Thus, attitudes towards English seem ambiguous at this point – useful and desirable but also a bit alienating and sniffed at at times. Interestingly enough, "mix-mix," or "Taglish," a heavily mixed code combining elements from Filipino, English, and also commonly regional languages, seems to be spreading vigorously, even in the media, advertising, and the public domain. Apparently it is perceived as a language choice which symbolically combines the local associations and the international aspirations of its input languages.

Despite all their differences the varieties of English in South and South-East Asia share a number of interesting traits. Typically their roots lie in "exploitation" colonization, the desire of the colonial power, usually the British Empire, to gain material profits from trade, cultivation, and political dominance. Consequently, the diffusion of English usually has had an elitist touch – it used to be a language reserved for the ruling classes, and proficiency in it is still tied up with access to quality education, by no means a generally available good in this region, and thus with a higher social status. On the other hand, the last few decades have seen an expansion of the language beyond those confines almost everywhere, a grassroots growth of English, motivated by its utilitarian value, to less educated or uneducated speakers by whatever means available, and thus in whatever form accessible. Nowhere is this process more visible (and audible) than in the city state of Singapore. Map 16 shows Singapore's location in relation to its South-East Asian neighbors.

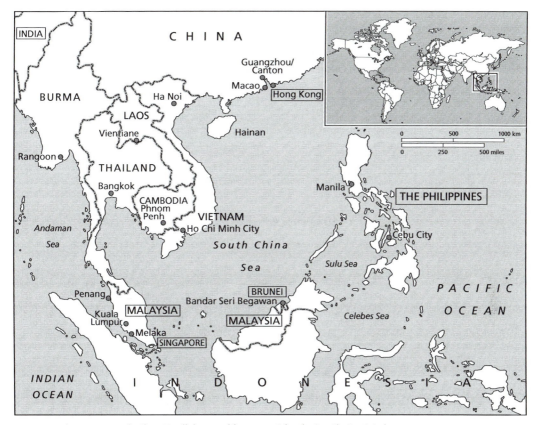

Map 16 Singapore and other English-speaking countries in South-East Asia

6.2.2 Case study: Singapore

Singapore, an island city state on the southern tip of the Malay peninsula, was founded by Sir Stamford Raffles, who recognized its strategically ideal location, in 1819, so its very existence goes back to British colonial activity. It expanded rapidly as a maritime trading center, and attracted new residents from various Asian origins who still make up the state's multiethnic population setup today: a Chinese majority, and substantial Indian (mostly Tamil-speaking) and indigenous Malay minorities. Throughout the nineteenth and early twentieth centuries we also find the typical colonial pattern of a small British resident community and of English spreading mainly through somewhat elitist channels to a growing group of indigenous professionals.

The real boost for English came only after independence, however (beginning in the 1960s and fully achieved, after earlier periods of self-governance and unification with Malaysia, in 1965). The country, led autocratically by the People's Action Party, adopted a western business and lifestyle orientation and combined it with an emphasis on Asian roots and values. This

Figure 13 Singapore, the Merlion city

culturally hybrid orientation supported the state's self-definition as a leading global city, resulting in the most prototypical of Asia's "tiger states." Singapore became the Merlion city represented in Figure 13, a major international center of business, trade, and technology.

As it turns out, the English language, in a local form, has become not only the tool and vehicle but also the symbol of this enormously successful development. Since the 1960s English has spread massively and developed local roots to an unprecedented extent. From an ethnically neutral link language it has grown to become practically the language in which the country is run, and increasingly the country's first and most important language. The roots of this exceptional development lie in the young nation's educational policy, which projected an "English-knowing" bilingualism. Since the 1960s, every Singaporean child has had to learn an Asian "mother tongue" (a politically loaded term in the country) in school and English as a second language. The Asian languages, however, vary from one ethnic group to another, and have also been weakened by discrepancies between standard forms taught at school and dialectal varieties spoken in families. So English soon became the one vehicle shared by everybody.

The result is a model case of how deeply English can penetrate an Asian society. English is the predominant language in the public domain, and more than in any other country in which "New Englishes" are spoken it has been turning into a native language of many young speakers. According to the most recent census statistics, roughly one-third of Singapore's children grow up speaking English as their first language, and even higher percentages are quoted for the use of English in communication among children and siblings, especially in educated strata and interethnic conversations. This is truly an enormous number, considering that we are talking about an Asian country and about speakers without British ancestry. Certainly we should not overestimate this process: Mandarin, promoted by the government, has also spread (but only amongst the Chinese), and which language or language variety is chosen in a given encounter may be a complex sociolinguistic decision with potential symbolic implications. Singapore is and will remain multilingual and multicultural. But we do see stages of a language shift towards English at least in parts of the community.

Actually, in the local context the use of English as such is not an issue at all – what's under discussion is the kind of English that should be used. The status of the informal indigenous variety, commonly called "Singlish," is a hotly debated and highly controversial topic in the country. Some observers, especially in public statements concerning the notion of "Singaporean English," mistake one for the other. There is a recognizable standard form of Singaporean English, spoken by educated society leaders in formal situations and marked by a few features primarily on the levels of lexis (with loans like *kiasu* or *kelong*) and phonology (including reduced vowel contrasts, consonant omission, and syllable timing). In addition, there is Singlish, a strongly dialectal contact variety (with some grammar patterns transferred mostly from Chinese and Malay) for use in informal situations amongst locals. Both the labels applied to these two forms of English and the varieties themselves are often confused.

Singlish has emerged only since the 1970s, a product of both the rapid gain in importance of English and the country's multilingual and multicultural roots. Many Singaporeans have embraced it enthusiastically as both an informal symbol of a national identity and an indicator of social proximity and a relaxed atmosphere in situations when it is appropriate to use it. The government, supported by conservative language observers, critics, and teachers, has opposed it vehemently, however, for fear that this "corrupted" language form might interfere with Singaporeans' international communicative abilities. This results in a highly paradoxical situation. On the one hand, TV sitcoms, movies, or websites employing Singlish are immensely popular and successful (and some have been banned, on the government's initiative, for that very reason), and the variety is stubbornly defended and cherished by the people. (Search for the movie and website *TalkingCock* on the internet or look for Singlish in YouTube, for instance!) On the other hand, given the government's strong hand, a "Speak Good English Movement" (SGEM) has been promoted for many years, the use of Singlish is strongly discouraged and frowned upon in public discourse, and Singaporean scholars would be ill-advised to carry out research that would attribute any positive qualities to the dialect. The struggle is ongoing, and it will be interesting to see what it leads to in a few decades from now. Perhaps there is a hidden agenda behind it – the question of how much liberalism or nonconformism is considered permissible (or desirable, for that matter) in Singapore's society.

Text 10 illustrates an informal conversation in Singlish. This sample, kindly provided by Lisa Lim, stems from the Grammar of Spoken

---

TEXT 10: A Singlish conversation

B: So just go down ... ya just go down go straight down.

C: Go straight down and turn into Zion Road *ah*.

A: Careful! The *ah pek* ('old man', H)!

B, C: (laughter)

C: You remember that guy that was running across the other day?
        {Just run across like that. (laughter)

B: {****

A: Hey, you know that Razid in Pizza Hut, right?

B: Which one?

C: Razid *ah*, Razid...the other { *mat* ('Malay male', M slang).

A: { Razali ... Razali's friend ... you know what he was doing or not?

B: The one who always like to *kow peh* ('complain', H){ is it?

A, C: { Ya ya ...

C: The one who always making { noise ...

B: { I don't like him, you know ... he *ah* ... like *macam* ('like', M)...

C: The *botak* ('bald', M) *botak* { fella

B: { *Ah*... the like ****

A: The fella centre *botak* three side hair {*one* ...

C: {Eh, that guy got problem *ah*, that fella ...

A: Lee was calling me his buddy yesterday.

B: He quite poor thing also *lor*, come to think of it.

C: Why?

B: At first, I dunno *lah*, I didn't really like him because he's just too ... his P.R. is quite bad *ah*.

C: Oh, P.R.

B: That's why. That's the point *ah*. Come to think of it, okay *lah* ... he also *kena* ('get', M) play out *lor*.

C: By who?

B: He *kena* sabotage *what*, the airport ... last minute, they send him to Brunei, you know, instead of Taiwan.

C: But is that a true story, or is he making a fast one?

B: I dunno *lah*.

C: It's a bit difficult to believe that they do that to him at the last minute ... right? But I mean ... I mean, by virtue of the fact that he accepted the overseas posting so willingly *ah*, it does say something about the family situation. Most people won't be too willing to run away like that.

B: Money is good *ah*.

C: True *ah*.

B: Good, you know, and the fella still dare to { complain about ****

C: { **** signal, you can still turn on this lane. *Ah chek ah, ka kin tam po ah, ah chek!* ('Youngest uncle, go a little faster, youngest uncle!', H) Horn the fella, horn him! Horn him!

C: In the States, this fella with the Volkswagen Beetle put a Porsche engine under the hood. All the { coppers couldn't catch him

A: { all the *mata* ('police', M) couldn"t catch him.

Coding conventions: ****: 'inaudible or unintelligible'; { (over two or more rows): overlapping speech; ...: 'pause'; M: 'from Malay'; H: 'from Hokkien'

(Source: GSSEC [see Lim 2004]; reproduced by permission given by Lisa Lim)

Singaporean English Corpus (GSSEC), a set of data described and analyzed in Lim (2004). The corpus consists of recordings of natural, everyday interactions between young Singaporeans, the generation which grew up with English as their main language. The speakers in this sample are three young male undergraduates who have had English-medium education. Ethnically, A and C are Indian, B is Chinese. The sample is clearly mesolectal and remarkably natural. Notice that the speakers are clearly able to produce complex English expressions (like *by virtue of the fact that he accepted the overseas posting so willingly*). Their use of informal language is a matter of deliberate style choice and identity projection, not inability.

You may have to listen closely to the sample (available on the website), but then you'll hear a number of pronunciation features which are characteristic of colloquial Singaporean English:

- There are no length contrasts in vowels, and so vowels of corresponding height levels tend to fall together: the i-sounds in *bit difficult* and *believe* are the same, as are the u-sounds in *true, virtue,* and *good.* The vowels of *fast* and *last* are very short.
- The syllable-timing tendency, together with vowel neutralization, produces vowels which in unstressed syllables receive a full quality identical to the main syllable ones. For example, the words *minute* /minit/ and *other* /ada/ have two identical vowels in both syllables (whereas in many other varieties the second one would be reduced). The same effect is also audible in *remember* (/-ba/), *difficult,* or *family situation.*
- As in many other varieties, the diphthongs with a mid-high onset in *go, road* and *straight, day, say* (and many related words) are monophthongized and sound like /oː/ and /eː/, respectively. The other mid-high vowels have a fairly open quality, as in *across, story* with /ɔ/, and *remember, friend, send* with /ɛ/.
- Final stop consonants tend to be omitted, not only in clusters (so *fact* becomes *fac'*; and the same happens in *fast, last*) but also on their own: in *straight, that, but,* and other words no -t in the end is audible.
- The interdental fricatives are generally realized as stops, so *that* has initial /d-/, the consonant in *other* is /-d-/, and *three* and *think* start with a /t-/.

The words used in this sample illustrate the mixed origins of Singlish:

- All three speakers use loans from Malay, even if none of them is ethnically a Malay.
- A few of the other borrowings can be traced back to Hokkien, a southern Chinese language. Notice that these expressions are used by the Indian speakers – so they are not switching to their own native language but paying tribute to the mixed nature of Singlish itself.

One of the most characteristic elements of Singlish, at the crossroads between lexis and pragmatics, are its distinctive discourse particles. They typically occur clause-finally and express a specific attitude towards the proposition expressed. The text illustrates quite a few of them:

- The particle which is most stereotypically associated with Singlish is *lah.* Its meaning is fairly general, indicating any mood or attitude on the side of the speaker, like strengthening a suggestion, persuasion, or objection (e.g. *I dunno lah, okay lah*), or also softening a negative reaction, thus marking solidarity.
- *Ah* is a variant of it, with the same functions (cf. *got problem ah, his P.R. is quite bad ah, That's the point ah*).

- *Lor* marks the statement under discussion as obvious, and implies a sense of resignation, describing a situation which cannot be improved – as is obviously the case in the occurrences in the text: *He quite poor thing also lor, he also kena play out lor.*

- The particle *wat* (spelled *what* in this transcript) also presents information as obvious, implying some sort of contradiction to a previous assertion. So one possible interpretation of *He kena sabotage what* might be that the unfair treatment that this person suffered conflicts with the previous assessment of not liking him because of "bad P.R.," with the change of attitude also indicated in *Come to think of it.*

Furthermore, the text illustrates a few more typical grammatical properties of the variety:

- Reduplication for intensification, observed elsewhere as well, occurs here with a Malay loan word. In one instance *botak* 'bald', is repeated, yielding *botak botak*, to describe a fellow who apparently is 'very bald'.

- Colloquial Singapore English has a distinctive passivization structure, the so-called *kena*-passive. The passive meaning is expressed by the Malay-derived particle *kena*, meaning 'get', with the syntax itself and frequently (as here) also the verb morphology not otherwise indicating the passive meaning: *he also kena play out* 'he was also tricked'; *He kena sabotage* 'he was sabotaged'. Note that the *kena*-passive has an adversative reading (as also in these examples), so it is not possible with predicates which express a positive quality or a desirable event (like *praise* or *like*).

- Like most pidgins and creoles, Singlish has zero copulas in equative structures: *He quite poor thing, who always making.*

- As elsewhere especially in Asian Englishes, articles are frequently omitted: *got problem, he ... poor thing.*

- The character of Singlish as a contact variety is also indicated by a tendency to reduce morphological marking. Here there are verbs which fail to mark the third person singular (*the one who ... like to ...*) or the past tense, with the time reference indicated lexically (*just run across [the other day]*), and in one instance a redundant plural suffix is not expressed: *three side.*

- The question tag is frequently an invariant *is it*, irrespective of verb and polarity of the main clause: *The one who always like to kow peh, is it?* Another common and also invariant tag, also illustrated in this sample, is *or not?*: *you know what he was doing or not?*

- The verb *got*, without an additional auxiliary, has a range of functions. Here the most standard-like, the possessive, is found (*that guy got problem*); other meanings are perfective (*got buy* 'has bought') or existential (e.g. *Here got ...* 'There are ...').

- Colloquial Singaporean English has a highly distinctive relative clause structure, in which the invariant relative pronoun *one* is preceded by the modifying constituents. Consider *The fella centre botak three side hair one* (which is made even more complicated by the fact that verbal constituents meaning 'is' or 'has' are implied but not expressed): The noun phrase *the fella* is postmodified by the following words up to and including *one*, meaning something like 'who is bald at the centre and has hair at three sides'. (Some scholars have suggested alternative analyses of this strange-looking pattern, suggesting that *one* is a "reifier" or a "singulative" which marks a particularly salient property or exemplar of a category.) Notice that of course "regular" relative clause constructions also occur, as in *that guy that was running* . . . .
- Singlish is frequently described as a "pro-drop" language, in which an understood (pronominal) subject can be omitted. So, for instance, *Can* can be a complete utterance, as can, with the above-mentioned tag, *Can or not?*. In this text we find examples of this which might be conceivable in other varieties as well: *go down* 'you go down'; *True*. 'This is true'. This is a feature which Singlish clearly has inherited from its areal substrate languages.
- Questions are indicated by intonation rather than inversion of an auxiliary: *You remember* . . . ? 'Do you remember . . . ?'.

6.3 Thousand Islands: The Pacific

6.3.1 Explorers, plantations, migrants: the spread and transformation of English in the Pacific region

Since Captain James Cook explored the vast waters of the Pacific Ocean in the eighteenth century, English has always been a strong second language in this region in one form or another. Explorers, whalers, traders, and missionaries, and later the growth of plantation economies, diffused English in the Pacific region, and have left it in various functions in some island nations. For some dates, see Timeline H.

Many of the islands and nation states of the Pacific region have adopted or inherited English somehow. Map 17 points out the ones which have.

In the Polynesian Kingdom of Tonga, for instance, English is a co-official language together with the native Tongan, although Tonga was never formally colonized (from 1900 to 1970 it was connected to the Empire through a Treaty of Friendship and a protectorate status). Similarly, in the Cook Islands and Niue (both island nations in free association with New Zealand), in Tokelau (a New Zealand territory), in Tuvalu (a former

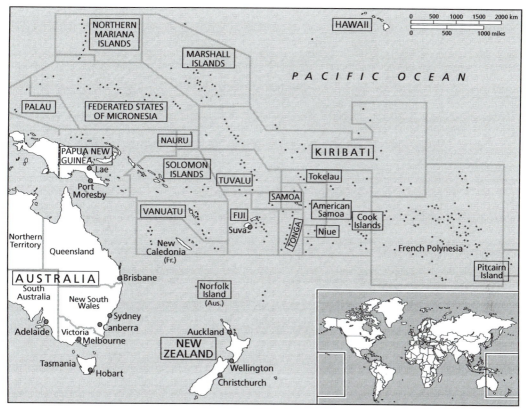

Map 17 English-speaking islands and nations in the Pacific region

---

Timeline H: The Pacific

1768–79	Captain Cook's voyages to the Pacific
1789	Mutiny on the Bounty, followed by settlement of Pitcairn by mutineers
1874	Fiji became a British colony
1893	Solomon Islands protectorate
1914	German New Guinea became Australian
1962	Independence of Samoa
1970	Independence of Fiji
1975	Independence of Papua New Guinea
1978	Independence of Tuvalu and Nauru
1979	Independence of Kiribati

Figure 14 Cook Islanders' traditional dancing at Auckland's Pasifika Festival 2008

British colony under the name of Ellis Islands, independent since 1978), in Kiribati (formerly the Gilbert Islands, independent after a protectorate and colonial period since 1979), and in Nauru (independent since 1978, and formerly an Australian League of Nation mandate) English is the official language in addition to an indigenous tongue. The Samoan archipelago shares the same bilingualism between Samoan and English, although it is politically divided into eastern American Samoa (a US territory since 1900) and the western Independent State of Samoa (formerly a German colony and then a New Zealand League of Nations trustee mandate). While limited documentation is available on the linguistic makeup of these nations, it is clear that English is associated with high status and education there.

Interestingly enough, Pacific Islanders from all of these nations have migrated in significant numbers to New Zealand, especially to the Manukau district in the south of Auckland, were they are perceived as constituting a newly emerging "Pasifika" ethnic grouping. Of course, as Figure 14 implies, they cherish their cultural heritage. They speak a variety of English which is increasingly labeled "Pasifika English": closely related to New Zealand English and especially its Maori ethnic form, with signs of mutual accommodation and homogenization, although the ethnic island origins still remain recognizably distinct.

An interesting case amongst the larger English-speaking nations in the Pacific is the island state of Fiji (also with a branch in New Zealand's Pasifika community). The English heritage goes back to Fiji's period as a British colony between 1874 and 1970. This period affected the social composition of the islands permanently, however, because the British established a plantation economy and brought in tens of thousands of Indian contract laborers. Their descendants have remained and today constitute about half of the population. Ethnic tensions and power struggles between these two groups have characterized the nation's political situation to the present day, including a few recent military coups. Both groups command their own ethnic languages (Fijian and a Hindi koiné, respectively), so the role of English is largely restricted to that of an interethnic lingua franca and the medium of formal domains, although Fiji English has developed some distinct properties of its own.

An extremely remarkable and unique case of linguistic development can be found with the varieties which are nowadays commonly labeled Pitkern or Norfuk, derived from the names of the islands where they are spoken. It goes back to the mutiny on the Royal Navy ship HMS Bounty of 1789. Most people would probably associate this with successful movies (the best-known films being the ones from 1962, with Marlon Brando, and from 1984, with Mel Gibson and Anthony Hopkins) but might not know that the story reflects a true historical incident. The mutineers, who needed to evade the long reach of British retaliation, took some Tahitians, mostly women, with them and hid on the remote island of Pitcairn. With hardly any outside contacts influencing the development of the community and the origins of the sailors and settlers known exactly, linguistically speaking this settlement constitutes a unique, laboratory-like contact situation. A new English contact variety, with strong maritime and biblical components and a Tahitian substrate, emerged on its own. When the population grew too much to be sustained on the small island, in 1856 they were relocated to Norfolk Island, east of Australia. A few years later some of them were so homesick that they returned to Pitcairn, however, while others stayed; so today there are two mutually intelligible branches of this exceptional dialect of English (considered a creole by some linguists). Both branches are endangered – Norfuk, with a few hundred speakers left, because of increasing tourism and assimilation, and Pitkern because of the small size of the community (just a few dozen residents) and their continuing extreme isolation.

Thus, language contact has been extremely important in the Pacific, a highly multilingual region. In Melanesia a few English-based pidgins have emerged which have highly distinctive properties and are unique insofar as they are the world's only pidgins which have achieved national language

---

TEXT 11: National anthem of the Republic of Vanuatu
(in Bislama)

Chorus:	**English translation:**
Yumi, Yumi, yumi i glat long talem se	We, we, we are happy to proclaim
Yumi, yumi, yumi i man blong Vanuatu	We, we, we are the people of Vanuatu

Verses:

God i givim ples ia long yumi,	God has given us this land
Yumi glat tumas long hem,	We have great cause for rejoicing
Yumi strong mo yumi fri long hem,	We are strong and we are free in this land
Yumi brata evriwan!	We are all brothers!
Plante fasin blong bifo i stap,	There were many ways before
Plante fasin blong tedei,	There are many ways today
Be yumi i olsem wan nomo,	But we are all one
Hemia fasin blong yumi!	Despite our many ways
Yumi save plante wok i stap,	We work hard
Long ol aelan blong yumi,	on our many islands
God i helpem yumi evriwan,	God helps us in our work
Hem i papa blong yumi!	He is Our Father!

---

status. There are three main branches of this Melanesian Pidgin, which are closely related, presumably because they go back to shared origins in a South Seas jargon and late nineteenth-century sandalwood plantations in Australia, Fiji, and Samoa:

- Tok Pisin will be looked at more closely as a case study below.
- Pijin, another very similar language, is the main lingua franca of the Solomon Islands.
- Bislama is one of the official languages of the island state of Vanuatu.

The name Bislama derives from "Beach-la-mar," directly transferred from French *bêche de mer*, the name of sea cucumbers which were commercially harvested on the plantations.

Text 11 provides not only an illustration of Bislama. This is Vanuatu's national anthem, so it also illustrates the elevation of a pidgin to a highly formal role. (In case you wish to listen to the anthem, on the website there is a link to a choir singing it.) Notice that the translation renders some of the appropriate style, but the text itself is more accessible when you try to think of the nearest English word from which the Bislama expression most likely has derived. As an example, let us just have a closer look at the first line. With a little creativity, *yumi* can be identified as coming from "you [and] me" and thus, quite naturally, as meaning 'the two of us' or 'we'. *i*, *glat* and *long* are not too far from *he*, *glad* (translated as 'happy'), and *belong*, respectively. And *talem se*, translated as 'proclaim', turns out to have been a sequence of "tell (th)em say" – perhaps a bit harder to trace but, again, not impossible to connect semantically.

Another very specific, multi-faceted but tightly circumscribed contact situation has emerged on the Hawai'ian islands. Beginning in the 1820s, American missionaries began to christianize the native population (eradiating much of their native culture in that process, it should be added), and opened the islands to western colonization, after earlier whaling contacts. In the nineteenth century, sugar plantations were established, and caused a huge demand for manual labor. Successive waves of plantation workers were contracted from regions where the demand for labor was highly pressing, and so Portuguese, Chinese, and Japanese people came in large numbers. Around the turn of the twentieth century the contact between them, English speakers, and Hawai'ians produced a creole, commonly labeled "Hawaiian Pidgin," which today serves as a local in-group code. Figure 15 is an excerpt from *Pidgin to da Max*, a highly successful entertaining booklet with cartoons and mock "dictionary entries." It illustrates distinctive features of this dialect, here the use of the generic preposition or complementizer *fo'*, introducing a purpose clause much like English *to* or *in order to*, and of course the distinctly local (and somewhat distancing) ethnic term *haole* for 'whites'.

6.3.2 Case study: Tok Pisin in Papua New Guinea

Tok Pisin (the name is derived from "Talk Pidgin"), spoken in Papua New Guinea (commonly called PNG), represents one of the rare cases where a pidgin has been accepted as a national language. This is one of the reasons why this language is so interesting for linguists; another one is its wide range of uses found simultaneously. Tok Pisin is an auxiliary code and a lingua franca for many speakers but also, especially in urban contexts, increasingly a mother tongue for others, so it serves to illustrate the wide range of functional options of and the fuzzy boundary between pidgins and creoles. Furthermore, it is also highly instructive to point out the linguistic transformation which English has undergone in this case. Just like Bislama in the above example, Tok Pisin looks very different and completely alien at

Figure 15 Hawai'ian Pidgin as represented in *Pidgin to da Max*
(from Simonson 1981; reproduced by permission)

first sight, but many of its words and features can be accounted for by very simple and straightforward adjustment processes – as you will find out shortly.

Together with the other Melanesian Pidgins, Tok Pisin emerged as a lingua franca on late nineteenth-century plantations set up primarily in Queensland and, for workers from this region, especially Samoa. The origins and composition of the laborers reflected the highly multilingual makeup of this region. So, broadly speaking, Melanesian Pidgin developed as a mixture of English words, which were frequently phonetically reduced and adjusted to indigenous customs of building words, local vocabulary, and some grammatical modification – either simplification or transfer of structural habits and even specific forms from indigenous languages. Laborers returning to their home villages after their work terms ended brought the pidgin with them, and there it was still found useful as a lingua franca and thus spread further and got rooted in the region. Historically speaking, parts of PNG had been under German and British dominance, respectively, but for most of the twentieth century, until independence in 1975, the country was mandated to and politically steered by Australia – a fact which, quite naturally, gave English a special status and also strengthened the impact of the English vocabulary component in certain styles.

PNG is a country with a rugged, mountainous topography (which makes many regions difficult to access and isolated), and thus an unusual degree of multilingualism and cultural fragmentation has developed and prevailed. Many areas and tribes still count as underdeveloped. Conversely, its cities, like elsewhere in the world, are also marked by modernization and increasing immigration. One consequence of these developments is a rising number of interethnic marriages, and in these not infrequently Tok Pisin is chosen as the couple's and family's language. Hence, there is now a rapidly increasing number of children who grow up speaking the language as their mother tongue. Technically speaking, thus, Tok Pisin is creolizing, and it is estimated that up to a million people, about a quarter of the nation's population, use it as their first language.

Tok Pisin is also used in the media and in writing (there is a weekly journal, *Wantok*, and a bible translation, for instance), and it is recognized as one of the country's national languages in its constitution. Figure 16 shows its use in politics, where it is found useful to reach a wide segment of the population. This is an election poster from the year 1977 which lists the political goals and demands of the Pangu Pati, both at that time and later the party in government.

This complex situation also means that Tok Pisin comes in a wide range of different forms which reflect the language's varying functions, from a rather simplistic, jargon-like pidgin used for limited interethnic communication in remote regions to a highly developed language which fulfills all functional needs in urban contexts. The following sample, Text 12, represents a fairly rural and conservative form of the language. To ease understanding and the identification of words, I am providing a word-by-word gloss and then a free translation. Notice that the elements glossed by CAPITALS are grammatical particles – with obvious English sources but radically different functions in the Tok Pisin system.

Text 12 is the transcript of an interview carried out and recorded by Peter Mühlhäusler in Urip village, West Sepik Province, in October 1972. The

171

Figure 16 Election poster by the Pangu Pati, Papua New Guinea 1977

speaker, Jakobus, has a German name, given to him by one of the many Catholic missionaries operating out of Wewak along the coast and on adjacent islands. German influence was still strong in this area, with Pidgin German surviving on some mission stations. The variety spoken by Jakobus is traditional Rural Tok Pisin, which is particularly evident is its discourse structure, with very little subordination. The text illustrates some highly frequent and characteristic features of Tok Pisin.

TEXT 12: A narrative about the early German days

Nem bilong me Jakobus. Na me wok bilong Magwe. Me laik   toktok long sampela stori
Name of   me Jakobus. And I work in   Magwe I   want talk   about some story

bilong Siamani taim ol   i   kamap nupela yet   long hia. Nambawan taim ol   i
about Germany when they PR arrive newly EMPH at   here. First   time they PR

kisim Tumleo Ol   i   stap long Tumleo, pinis, den i   go daun long Aitape, i   stap
reach Tumleo They PR stay at   Tumleo, finish, then PR go down to   Aitape. PR stay

long Aitape, bihain ol   i   kamap long ailan Wallis, orait, ol   i   go long Borom, orait,
in   Aitape, then   they PR arrive at   Island Wallis, well, they PR go to   Borom, well,

long hap   bilong mipela, ol   i   go long Borom na i   kirapim plantesin long Borom,
to   place of   we,   they PR go to   Borom and PR set up   plantation at   Borom,

bihain ol   i   stap long Borom ol   i   kam bek long kirapim tesin   long Nom, em
then   they PR stay at   Borom they PR come back to   set up   plantation at   Nom, it

dispela hap   bilong mipela long hia long Sepik long hap   bilong Wewak na Aitape, bipo
this   place of   we   at   here at   Sepik at   place of   Wewak and Aitape, before

Siamani kisim dispela ples pas. Orait, long hap bilong New Britain ol   i   bin kisim
Germany owned this   place first. Well, at   area of   New Britain they PR PAST own

Kokopo na Ikupa na liklik ples Kokorol na ol   i   stap long dispela ples, orait, tu
Kokopo and Ikupa and little place Kokorol and they PR stay at   this   place, well, two

ples i   bin yet   me bin   lukim, i   stap long Rabaul, Siare, Siar, wantaim Mikron na
place PR PAST EMPH I   PAST see,   PR stay at   Rabaul, Siare, Siar, once   Mikron and

i   stap long Rabaul na wanpela i   stap long Rapopo. Olsem me stori   long Siaman me
PR stay at   Rabaul and one   PR stay at   Rapopo. Thus I   tell_story of   German I

bifo   me harim ol   papa ol   i   bin stori   na me harim na me stori   gen
earlier I   hear PLURAL father they PR PAST tell_story and I   hear and I   tell_story again

long pasin   bilong Siaman ol   i   kamap nupela yet   long yumi. Em toktok bilong
about fashion of   German they PR arrive new   EMPH to   us.   It talk   about

Siaman em tasol. Olsem em   me stori   liklik, me no save tumas   long stori
German it   all.   Thus EMPH I   tell_story little, I   NEG know too_much about story

bilong Siaman. Em tasol.
about German. It   all.

Liberal translation

My name is Jakobus. And I work in Magwe. I'd like to tell you something about the Germans, when they arrived here for the first time. First they came to Tumleo and stayed there. When they finished their business there they moved on to Aitape and stayed there, and afterwards they arrived at Wallis Island. Well, they moved on to Boron, to our place, they went to Borom and set up a plantation there and then stayed there. They came back to set up a plantation at Nom, that was our place here at Sepik, at Wewak and Aitape, the Germans had owned this place earlier. Well, in the area of New Britain they owned Kokopo and Ikupa and the little place Kokorol, and stayed there; well, there were really two places that I saw. They stayed at Rabaul, Siare, Siar, and once at Mikron, and they stayed at Rabaul, once they stayed at Rapopo. That's what I tell you about the Germans, I had heard all this from my ancestors who had told it, and I heard it and I tell you again about the way it was when the Germans first came to us. That's all the story about the Germans. I really have little to tell, I don't know too much about the Germans. That's all of it.

Grammatical markers in the glosses: PR = pronoun ('he/it'); EMPH = emphasis marker; PAST = past marker; PLURAL = plural marker; NEG = negation marker ('not')

(Kindly provided by Peter Mühlhäusler; reproduced by permission)

As was mentioned above for Bislama, texts in this language are not as difficult and different from English as they may seem at first sight, and analyzing and playing with them may actually be a lot of fun. To find the connection to English, however, and cross the bridge of the foreign impression of these texts on the surface, a helpful strategy is to try to identify the English words from which Tok Pisin words (may) have derived. This may require a little imagination and an awareness of the fact that word meanings in such situations are not stable but tend to change, and of course word forms are also adjusted, often simplified. For illustrations, have a look at the following words in the text (and I indicate the source word and, if necessary, a broader translation): *kirap* < "carry up" 'go ahead, develop'; *wantaim* "one time"; *kamap* < "come up" 'arrive'; *nambawan* "number one" 'first'; *orait* < "all right"; *tasol* < "that's all."

The text contains relatively few phonetic adjustments, but three tendencies can be illustrated:

- Consonant clusters tend to be reduced, so at the end of words the final consonant is dropped, as in *ailan* 'island', *bihain* 'behind'.
- The number of vowel contrasts is reduced. Vowels which are distinct in English fall together under the same sound; so *talk, all, go,* or *bilong* all produce a simple *o* (*tok, ol, go, long*).
- Affricates and palatal fricatives are replaced by stops or alveolar fricatives: *German > Siaman; catch > kis; plantation > plantesin; fashion > pasin; much > mas.*

Furthermore, it is necessary to recognize a few grammatical characteristics. I start with two highly frequent and highly characteristic affixes and move on to other grammatical markers.

- The suffix *-pela*, derived from *fellow*, marks adjectives or prenominal determiners, e.g. *sampela* 'some', *nupela* 'new', *dispela* 'this'.
- The suffix *-im* appended to verbs, a transfer phenomenon from Melanesian languages, marks the verb as transitive, targeted to some object, so that *luk* (< *look*) is 'see' but *lukim* is 'watch, look at'. Further examples in the text include *kisim* (< "catch him" 'get to, reach'); *kirapim* 'set up, establish', *harim* 'hear, listen to'.
- The form *i*, derived from *he*, seems comparable to English dialect forms with "double subjects" as in *John, he works for . . .*, but in Tok Pisin it is fully grammaticalized and has become a predicate marker; so in the gloss of the text this has been rendered as PR.
- The form *bilong/blong/long*, from *belong*, occurs very frequently and serves as practically an all-purpose preposition, corresponding to a wide range of grammatical words in English. In the above text I have rendered it as *of*, *in*, *at*, *about*, or *to*, depending on context.
- As is usual for pidgins, there are normally no grammatical endings: no past marking in *kamap*, *kisim*, *go*, etc.; no plural in *Siaman*, *papa* (except for the marker *ol*), etc.
- There is no copula: *Nem bilong me Jakobus* 'My name is Jakobus'.
- Time and aspect relationships are expressed by preverbal markers, as is generally the case in pidgins and creoles. The text has *bin* for past, as in *i bin kisim*, *mi bin lukim*.
- The generic preverbal negator *no* is used: *me no save*. (Note that *save* is a Portuguese-derived word which is also very widespread in pidgins and creoles.)
- Word classes are assigned fairly liberally (as in English conversion), so *bihain* "behind" becomes a time adverb ('afterwards, then'), and *stori* functions as a verb 'tell a story'.
- Reduplication is fairly common. In the text we have *toktok* (from *talk*) and *liklik* (presumably *little bit* crossed with Tolai *ikilik* 'small').
- Pronouns are invariant (*me* 'I'), and the third person plural form is *ol*. A transfer feature inherited from Melanesian languages is the distinction between inclusive and exclusive reference. The text form *yumi* ("you me" 'we') is inclusive, i.e. it includes the listener (in this text it is used erroneously); in contrast, *mipela* is exclusive, i.e. 'me and others but not you'.
- Characteristic discourse markers include *orait*, which typically introduces a new section, and the formulaic *tasol*, which typically ends a story and confirms a statement.

6.4 Future aspirations: East Asia

6.4.1 Expanding: attractions of a global language

In this last section of my regional survey of global varieties of English I am also stretching the topic to its boundaries, as it were. In Asia in general, and especially in East Asia, shown in Map 18, the role and the diffusion of English essentially as a Foreign Language (cf. the notion of EFL, or Kachru's "Expanding Circle," discussed earlier) has been changing drastically over the last few decades. Of course, this does not really compare with what we find in, say, Singapore, which is on the verge of moving to an ENL/Inner Circle status, or also to countries like India or Hong Kong, classic cases of ESL/Outer Circle constellations. But still, the direction is the same, and the vibrancy of ongoing developments is remarkable. It has been claimed (in the title of a conference series and some books resulting from it, for instance) that "English Is An Asian Language" (e.g. Bautista 1997), and this is clearly also implied in B. Kachru (2005) and Y. Kachru and Nelson (2006). A journal called *Asian Englishes* and a book series entitled *Asian Englishes Today* have been launched, and a range of other scholarly activities is regularly devoted to this topic. The adoption of English as the sole working language of ASEAN, mentioned above, marks an important point in that development.

Map 18 East Asia

On the other hand, the question is whether we are still talking about "varieties of English" here. Distinct varieties as such need to be stable and distinguishable (on the basis of a few characteristic features, for example), need to be identified as such and have characteristic contexts of use – conditions which clearly apply in the cases of, say, Indian or Singaporean English. But this is less clear in other cases, and linguists vary in their readiness to assign the status of a distinct variety to some of these dialects. Whether there exists a "Hong Kong English" or it just makes sense to talk about uses of "English in Hong Kong" in general has been disputed for a while, for instance (though I suppose the majority of scholars would accept and back the distinct identity of this variety by now). The South-East Asian countries without a colonial history are a similar case in point, but removed one step further from such a classification. In Thailand, for instance, English is used widely for business and tourism, and linguists have used the label "Thai English" and investigated properties of this variety (vowel sounds, for instance, using acoustic–phonetic methods) – but the question is whether this is really more than just a learners' interlanguage in a second language acquisition process. And the same question applies to East Asia, with China (discussed below as a case study), Japan, and Korea. It is true that there is enormous interest in learning English in these countries, and there is also a fair amount of scholarly writing available there on English. In practice, however, much of this is about its utility for international functions and about language pedagogy.

The topic of English in Japan is an interesting case in point. A major East Asian power with strong self-confidence and a highly developed culture of its own, during the Edo period from the seventeenth through the nineteenth century Japan had deliberately cut itself off from the world until in 1853 Commodore Perry forced the Empire to establish diplomatic and trade relations with the outside world. Since then the country has been involved in international affairs and participated in military alliances and warfare, especially in the Asian–Pacific region. The most efficient real change and outside influence on Japan's culture, however, came with the country's huge economic success as a global technology producer and trading nation in the last third of the twentieth century. In Japan, globalization and westernization are almost exclusively viewed through the window of the English language, so it does not come as a surprise that today in Japan's public discourse there is a lot of emphasis on the teaching and learning of English.

English is mainly perceived as a vehicle for western culture in Japan, and as such it has transmitted a number of western concepts. It has been estimated that about 12 percent of the Japanese vocabulary consists of European borrowings, and of these about four-fifths are from English. So English loan words in Japanese are not infrequent – they include *biiru* 'beer', *nyuusu* 'news', *supootsu* 'sports', *terehon* 'telephone', and *basu* 'bus'. Such words are broadly documented in Stanlaw (2004). It is stated that millions of Japanese enthusiastically study English, and the language is taught widely. English is an obligatory subject in Japanese Middle Schools and High Schools (Grades 7 though 12), and it is increasingly also taught in Elementary Schools (though this is highly controversial). On the other hand, in my view claims about the existence of a "Japanese English" lack substance at this point. Outside of some tourist spots, such as Kyoto, English does not appear in Japan's public life; even in major cities most subway lines have no English announcements, for example. Compare Figures 17 and 18: The entry gate of a temple in Kyoto provides a little help to tourists with some English; Tokyo's subway ticket machine does not. And, as Stanlaw also concedes, most Japanese people are unable to communicate fluently in English even after several years of schooling, perhaps because the emphasis of teaching is on learning grammar rules and vocabulary rather than on speaking. My own experience tends to confirm this. Asking passers-by on the road, including young people, for help or directions in Japan usually produces friendly gestures but hardly ever a verbal response in English.

Figure 17 Temple entrance in Kyoto

Figure 18 Ticket machine in Tokyo's subway

In South Korea, the demand for learning English is also reported to be extremely high, and the country regularly attempts to recruit native-speaking ESL teachers; the government's goal is to have one native speaker of English in each primary and secondary school! Private language schools and immersion institutions are mushrooming, even for children as young as 5 years of age. In the school system English is obligatory from Grade 3, at the age of 9, and University entrance is based upon exams which test the applicants' fluency in English. The importance of knowing English well to succeed in education and business life is widely debated and emphasized. In fact, one of the recent topics of public awareness is what has come to be known as "English fever": many Korean parents send their children abroad for an extended period of time at a very early age, or attempt to move with their families to English-speaking countries such as Singapore, Australia, the US, or the UK. Their intention is mainly to give their children an opportunity to acquire fluent English in a natural setting, and thus to provide them with a competitive edge – despite all the strain that such a strategy obviously puts on family life and, as has been deplored, on the acquisition of the children's native Korean culture and language. But "English only" exposure is considered to be immensely valuable.

6.4.2 Case study: Learning English in China

A similar situation obtains in China, and it is obvious that because of the sheer population size and the economic opportunity and future potential of the country this is a topic of global importance. It is frequently stated that the number of learners of English in China is larger than that of native speakers anywhere else – a claim which may or may not be true, depending upon how we define a learner's status and proficiency benchmarks. The demand for English is buoyant, and knowledge of the language is spreading through various channels, from formal education via commercial forms to grassroots acquisition processes. Speaker numbers are notoriously difficult to provide and to define, of course, but whichever way we look at them, they are high, quite simply. David Crystal reports a figure of 220 million "speakers" in the late 1990s, then expected to rise significantly with the motivation of the Beijing Olympics of 2008, and quotes observers' assertions, unchallenged, that today about half of the population (of more than 1.3 billion people, that is) have at least some basic conversational command of English.

The history of English in China goes back a very long time, in fact. Trading exchanges along the South China coast produced a Chinese Pidgin English, also called "China Coast Pidgin," in the eighteenth century, which later was assumed to have had some influence upon the emerging South Seas Jargon which in turn produced the Melanesian Pidgins. It is supposed to have died out, though some continuity with broken forms of English as used by some speakers especially in Hong Kong cannot be ruled out.

In the second half of the twentieth century the importance placed upon the learning of English in China changed drastically, largely in line with the country's current attitudes towards the West. As in Japan, English has been perceived as the main vehicle of transmitting western ideas, technology, and business opportunities, though this has needed to be balanced against the threat this has posed to the retention of traditional Chinese values and culture. After the "Cultural Revolution" of the 1960s, English, even if it was still taught to some extent, was the language of the enemy. In the 1970s and later, however, the "Open Door" and "Four Modernizations" policies initiated by Communist Party leaders, and then of course the opening of the country's economy to become a global trade and manufacture leader, resulted in a tremendously growing importance placed upon learning

English also in the public school system. Today, a reasonable command of English is mandatory both for University entrance and for certain attractive civil service professions, and thus English is an important subject in the school curriculum. International communication in business and technological production, for example with foreign company representatives or engineers who may be resident in China for a while, is usually conducted wholly in English.

Of course, this also gives some value to the teaching of English as a commodity, so private tuition is growing. Perhaps the best illustration of the commercial value of teaching English and also of the general demand for English is provided by the success of the "Crazy English" enterprise. Since the late 1990s Li Yang, a charismatic teacher, has carried out a mass education campaign that essentially builds upon the simple method of having large crowds repeating and chanting phrases and slogans loudly, an oral pattern drill performed with audiences as large as sports stadiums, integrating patriotic messages and a strong self-development component. In this fashion Li Yang has taught some English to millions of Chinese people, and apparently made a fortune for himself in passing, now heading a major national language teaching enterprise. In a 2008 article the *New Yorker* called Li Yang "China's Elvis of English, perhaps the world's only language teacher known to bring students to tears of excitement."

The "Crazy English" campaign vividly illustrates the fact that learning English in China has moved far beyond the confines of educational institutions and formal teaching: China is experiencing an unprecedented grassroots growth of English learning. Certainly this should not be overestimated: formal teaching in schools remains the most important means of spreading the language, and a vast number of Chinese people, including most Beijing taxi drivers, for instance, have no command of English. But, surprisingly, many people work hard at picking up some of the language and acquiring it in natural contexts, frequently in contact with international visitors. Figure 19 provides an example, and also indicates some rapid change in this respect. Before I visited the Great Wall at Simatai in 2008, I read a guide book which announced there would be farmers' women there, selling goods and souvenirs but not speaking any English, for lack of education. But the lady vendors I met there, charming and with a determined business sense, communicated very successfully in English, not only on their sales activities and facts about the Wall but also about the usual social niceties in such an encounter, like one's age and family situation. And they had acquired their English locally and naturally, just talking to outside visitors, with practically no formal input.

Clearly, English has enjoyed particularly strong official support and a most welcoming general attitude since in 2001 Beijing won the bid for the

Figure 19 English-speaking vendors on the Great Wall

2008 Olympic Games. Language teaching campaigns were launched and intensified, especially in the Beijing area, and new curriculum guidelines now call for the introduction of English as a compulsory school subject in the third grade, several years earlier than before. It remains to be seen whether these trends will continue in the post-Olympic era, and possibly also whether the growing popularity of Mandarin Chinese as a foreign language studied in western countries will interfere with the role of English.

"Chinese English" is used as a term by some linguists, and there is a growing body of descriptions of characteristic features of English as spoken by Chinese people. This is not a stable variety, but there are a few characteristics which have been found to recur. Some of them can be explained as transfer phenomena which reflect properties of the Chinese languages spoken as a first language.

Text 13, twelve sample selections from recordings which I made with students from mainland China, illustrates some of these. The sample can be heard on the website; in the transcript here I have indicated a few noteworthy pronunciation details by inserting phonetic transcriptions (partly rendered by conventional orthography here in the text for the convenience of readers without phonetic training), and word omissions have been symbolized by "∅."

Languages have different rules as to how words are built from sounds (a principle known as "phonotactics"), and some of these rule differences

TEXT 13: Selections from recordings with Chinese students

(1) when[wẽ] I was a chi(l)d[tʃaɪdˀ] my parents move(d) Sh-... move(d) to Shenzhen from[frɒ~] Hunan province. Ø Is a province ...uh... which is a province in[ɪŋ] ...uh... South of China and then[ðẽ] we move(d) to Shenzhen in my childhood [tʃaɪldəχʊdə].

(2) he almost['ɒlmosə] forget[tʰ] all about it, I think. Yeah. Because they[deɪ] are old[oʊd] times[tʰ-]. Uh they... they are study–ing Ø old[oʊd] times[tʰãis] of China. So in[ɪŋ] that[dæ] time [tʰaɪm] ...mh... most peop(l)e do not[nɒt] speak English, do no[nɒ] know English[ɪŋgəliʃ].

(3) You mean[mɪŋ]...Young people[pʰɪpʰəw]. But [bʌtʰə] the midage people[pʰɪpʰəw] or the[dɛ] older[oʊdə] people almost[-tə] don't[dən] know about[tʰ] English.

(4) We are the M.A. studentØ, only one[vã] year, and the o(th)ers are M.Phil. studentØ, two years[-s].

(5) we are also the northern dialect, we are belongs to the no(rth) dialec(t)s..., because the whole Chinese can Ø divided into four dialect [tʰə] districtØ and we are... belongs to the north[s] dialect and[ændˀ] the [də] Shanghai people belong to the Wu dialec(t)s and also[ɔːlθəʊ] the[də] people[pʰɪpʰəw] here in [ɪŋ] Guangdong province and Fujian they ... they maybe ... belongs to Cantonese, uhm ... it's also..uhm.. Ø different dialect,

(6) I don't like sports, except[-tə] swim[-ŋ].

(7) I would like to, uhm, study overseas[-s], bu(t) the problem is abou(t) the money.

(8) maybe first[fɜsə] let[s] my fath[z]er or moth[ð]er let them[hɛm] pay for me, and then[ðẽ] I will pay back to them[ðẽ] after[afə] I earn[ɜnə] my money

(9) of course I don('t) know much abou(t) ... uhm ... how English was being taught in the pas(t) in China

(10) for example, let's[lɛs] take ... uhm ... the p(r)onunciation pattern of Chinese['tʃaɪnis] speakers[-s], right[raɪ], I think many people[pibl] have a certain [sɜdən] ... certain kinds[kãɪz] of uhm ... p(r)onunciation patterns[-s], right,... in Chinese [tʃaɪniːs] ... in China

(11) actually I Ø also from mainland[-lən] China. Uhm. I stayØ here jus(t) for one month.

(12) it is not[nɒʃ] allowed[-t] to have[hæf] tests[tʰæsts]. All the[də] students will go to the[də] junior school naturally from primary school in China, because this[dis] is[is] compulsory, but[bʌtə] our school is Ø only school that has the right[raɪtʰ] to have a test[tʰæstʰ] before admitting students into my school.

surface when the pronunciation of English words is modified by the application of Chinese phonotactic rules. Here are a few examples.

- In Mandarin Chinese, syllables typically end in a vowel; and in English words this effect is achieved by either omitting final consonants, as in *tha(t)* (sample 2), *bu(t)*, *abou(t)* (7, 9), *ri(ght)* (10), *no(t)* (12), or by appending an additional vowel, mostly schwa, at the end of a word or a syllable, as in *childahooda* (1), *Engalish* (2), *excepta* (6), *earna* (8), *buta* (12).
- The latter process sometimes combines with a reduction of consonant clusters, as in *almos(t)a* (2), *firs(t)a* (8).
- Consonant cluster reduction is also common in itself; cf. *mos(t)* (2); *af(t)er* (8); *pas(t)* (9); *jus(t)* (11).
- Chinese has no voiced stops or fricatives, and no dental fricatives, so these sounds are commonly replaced by others in English: voiced consonants become voiceless, as in *years* (4), *Chinese* (5, 10), *overseas* (7), *speakers* (10), *allowed, have, is* (12); and for the "th" sounds we find [s] in *north* (5), [z] in *father* (8), or [d] in *the, this* (12), or it is simply omitted, as in *o(th)ers* (4), *no(rth)* (5).
- Voiceless stops are strongly aspirated, as in *forget^h*, *t^{h}imes* (2), *about^h* (3), *right^h*, *t^{h}est^h* (12) – this may be caused by the fact that such aspirated stops are distinct sounds (phonemes) in Chinese.
- Vowels before nasals are frequently nasalized, which corresponds to the presence of nasalized vowels in Chinese, e.g. *whẽ, frã, thẽ* in (1), *tĩ(m)es* (2), *õ(ne)* (4).
- Word-final nasals are frequently velar, i.e. *in* sounds like *ing* (1, 2, 5), *mean* like *ming* (3; notice that the "long" and short" vowels also sound alike) and even *swim* like *swing* (6).
- An /l/ after a vowel is frequently vocalized, a process for which we find models both in Chinese and in English dialects – cf. *chi(l)d* (1), *o(l)d* (2, 3), *peop(l)e* (2, 3, 5).

On the level of grammar, some likely transfer phenomena can also be observed:

- Chinese is a highly analytical language, i.e. it has practically no grammatical endings, and so it is not surprising that Chinese speakers sometimes omit inflectional suffixes in English, e.g. *move(d)* (1), *the ... student* (plural) (4), *four ... district* (5), *stay* (past) (11). Conversely, hypercorrection, the unmotivated insertion of a form, indicating insecurity on its usage conditions, is also found: *we/they belongs* (5).
- In Mandarin, grammatical subjects can be left out if their reference is clear, and this process is also found in sentences like *Is a province* (1).

- Sometimes other sentence constituents, mainly the verb *be*, can also be left out, e.g. *can divided* (5), *I also from* ... (11).
- The determiner system is structured differently, which may account for a tendency to omit articles, e.g. *old times* (2), *our school is only school* (12).

Notice, by the way, that many of these phenomena occur variably – sometimes we find them, but at other times speakers regularly do produce things like their plural *-s*'s, *th*'s, and so on. The command of English of my informants in general is very good – for instance, we also find complex constructions such as *was being taught* (9).

Furthermore, Chinese uses of English may display interesting pragmatic characteristics, not illustrated in the above samples and rooted in different cultural conventions. For example, as in most Asian cultures social status is more important, and probably more formally displayed, by Chinese people than by many westerners, who practice a more egalitarian communicative style. Thus, for example, addressing a new acquaintance or a newly intro-duced business partner by their first name immediately might be considered impolite by a Chinese speaker of English, while conversely an American might mistakenly interpret a Chinese person's reluctance to use the first name as deliberately distancing himself. But the truth of the matter is that the conventions of politeness and of negotiating proximity and distance are just different. For such reasons cross-cultural encounters may be more difficult than expected, and require mutual respect and sensitivity.

Chapter summary

In this chapter we turned our attention to regions of the world which would not have counted as parts of the "English-speaking world" just a few decades ago – so when the talk comes to the globalization of English, these are the regions where things are really happening, as it were. We have found English to be thriving in large parts of Africa, Asia, and the Pacific region; we have seen the language used as a strong second language and gradually becoming even more than that, moving into the home domain, for many individuals and in some groups and countries; we have seen it promoted by educational institutions and by commercial profit-makers, and also sought after by many people who lack formal, educational access to it, an unprecedented grassroots spread in addi-tion to all the policy-making. We have observed English to be moving in directions which not infrequently are independent of and even against the official goals promoted by state authorities (as in Nigeria with respect to Pidgin or in Singapore with respect to "Singlish"). We see the language being adopted, appropriated, and taken over by all kinds of people. And we have seen that this diffusion process has ramifications of various kinds, and two in particular: the linguistic processes and properties that have characterized these newly emerging dialects of English, and their social embedding in their respective communities, not infrequently a controversial topic. It is these two types of processes and observations that we will be turning to in the next two chapters.

Exercises and activities

Exercise 6a   Here are a few very brief selections from African literary writings in English:

> Talk your mind, me I go talk my head and we go sabi who be massa for dis house wey I builded twenty years before your mama born you.
> <div align="right">(from "Veronica makes up her own mind", by Ogali A. Ogali;
in Obiechina 1972, <i>Onithsa Market Literature</i>, p. 45)</div>

> these Dukana people, they are not talking anything good oh. I can see they are all fearing, [...] The man with fine shirt stood up. And begin to talk in English. Fine fine English. Big big words. Grammar. [...]
> Oh my father wey don die, help me today. Put power inside my body. Make I no tire. I can hear the sozas saying "You are now a soza. [...]" Na lie. Na lie. (from Ken Saro-Wiwa, 1985. <i>Sozaboy: A Novel in Rotten English</i>. Port Harcourt: Saros, pp. 46, 47)

Which forms do you find unusual? Describe them, using appropriate linguistic terminology. Discuss the stylistic effect of these forms.

Exercise 6b   Provide a word-by-word translation of Vanuatu's national anthem in Text 11. How does your translation compare semantically and stylistically to the "official" one?

Exercise 6c   On the website you will find another text (with sound) representing Nigerian Pidgin English, taken from Deuber (2005), entitled "NigP: minimum wages for Lagos workers." This is a part of an interview with a female University of Lagos student in her twenties.
    Listen to this text sample and identify (a) preverbal markers, (b) complementizer occurrences, (c) forms of the copula, and (d) pronoun forms.

Exercise 6d   In case you are interested in Singlish, the internet provides you with lots of materials and further samples. Search for "Phua Chu Kang" on YouTube, for instance – you'll find a number of shows from that popular TV series, and if you like comedy you'll definitely enjoy them! Select one of them and translate difficult passages into standard English. Identify constructions which you find unusual, and see whether they constitute syntactic conventions which are characteristic of Singlish!

Exercise 6e	Which language forms in the Hawai'ian cartoon do you find noteworthy? Employing the terminology and familiarity with other Englishes you have acquired so far, describe and try to explain these forms.

Exercise 6f	Have a closer look at the text of the Tok Pisin election poster in Figure 16, and see how far you get in understanding it! To do so, employ the two-step procedure introduced earlier. First, read the text out aloud word by word and let your imagination play to identify the English words from which the Tok Pisin words have been derived (so-called cognates), with modifications of their form (e.g. *bilip* < *believe*). Second, allowing for some liberty again, try to make sense of these word sequences, to understand the meaning intended. For instance, for the top right-hand line before the ad proper this might look like this:

> *Dispela spes Pangu Pati i baim* < this[fellow] space Pangu Party he buy-him => "this space was bought by the Pangu Party" => 'paid advertisement'

Exercise 6g	Have you ever been to an East Asian country, or do you know anybody who has? Collect personal experiences and assessments on the usefulness of English there.

Key terms discussed in this chapter

Bislama
Camfranglais
complementizer
copula
discourse particles
Engsh
indigenization
invariant
Melanesian Pidgin
negator
phonotactics
Pidgin grammar
Pijin
preverbal markers
pro-drop
reduplication
relativizer
Sheng
Singlish

Tok Pisin

transitive

Further reading

Schmied (1991) provides a fine introduction to the uses and forms of English in various parts of Africa (though, given the dynamics of the language there, this description may be getting a little dated by now). Jowitt (1991) competently surveys English in Nigeria, and Deuber (2005) documents current forms and uses of Nigerian Pidgin English, including audio samples of media uses on an accompanying CD-ROM. For readers who wish to get an accessible and nontechnical exposure to African forms of English, the literary works mentioned above are recommendable, including novels by Chinua Achebe, Ken Saro-Wiwa, and many others in the "African Writers Series," or Obiechina's (1972) collection of Onitsha market stories.

Surveys of Asian English are available in B. Kachru (2005) and Y. Kachru and Nelson (2006). Sailaja (2009) is a recent introduction to Indian English, a variety which has been analyzed grammatically in Sedlatschek (2009) and illustrated by a wide documentation of sample texts in Mehrotra (1998). On Singaporean English, see Lim (2004), Low and Brown (2005), and Deterding (2007). The most important sources on English in Hong Kong and China are Bolton's books (2002, 2003). The status of English in the Philippines, with a strong emphasis on language mixing, is vividly discussed in Thompson (2003).

For a comprehensive survey of Pacific contact languages and their history, see Tryon and Charpentier (2004). Sakoda and Siegel (2003) is a nicely readable introduction to Hawai'i's Pidgin. A very interesting documentation of how Tok Pisin is currently used by young speakers, including rich grammatical explanation, is provided by Smith (2002). If you are interested in analyzing further texts of Tok Pisin, the book to consult is Mühlhäusler *et al.* (2003), a collection of samples from the earliest records to transcripts of recent conversations.

Stanlaw (2004) is a very rich documentation of uses of English, and English loanwords in particular, in Japan (though I disagree with his conclusion that a "Japanese English" should be recognized – I think he shows an Anglicized Japanese instead). The history of English in China is documented in Bolton (2003) and in Adamson (2004), with a strong emphasis on its changing roles in education after World War II.

CHAPTER 7

Language development: a general perspective

In this chapter . . .

This chapter provides a brief, non-technical introduction to the strictly linguistic aspects of the evolution of World Englishes. What are the reasons for the fact that New Englishes have developed distinctive forms of their own, and which are the processes that have brought these new properties about? We will find that from all the speech forms and habits used by anybody involved in a contact situation (conceptualized as the available features in a "feature pool"), an interplay of language-internal and extralinguistic factors determines which will be successful in the long run. Secondly, do World Englishes share not only such evolutionary trajectories but also specific forms and features? It will be shown that on the levels of vocabulary, pronunciation, and grammar it is possible to identify a few features and feature types which are relatively widespread, though none of them serves to identify New Englishes as a class.

7.1 The mechanisms of producing new varieties of English

Why all of this, one might ask from an outside perspective. Why do we have all these new varieties emerging, why do people from these regions speak "funny" (in biased Inner-Circle eyes, of course), why doesn't everybody keep speaking "the good old" way, the way they have been taught? Well, for one thing, we found earlier on that hardly anybody speaks "proper English" only, that language variability is intrinsic to speech, a way of skillfully manipulating relationships of proximity and distance. But the question deserves to be taken seriously, and if we do we find that there are a number of factors and issues which play a role here.

First, we need to understand how language works. Some linguists cherish the idea of an "**internalized language**" in one's head, a cognitive, "systematic" representation which helps to stabilize it all. Maybe so, but there is no direct way of accessing such inner knowledge, and there is no way of knowing whether or to what extent any two people share it. It is more appropriate to conceptualize **language** not as an entity, a product, but rather **as a process**. It exists whenever anybody is speaking, and with any new utterance in a conversation it is activated, revitalized, reconstructed. In speech the forms and features of language are continuously "replicated," and we may view language in essence as an ongoing sequence of zillions of such replications (Kretzschmar 2009). Each and every utterance realizes and also disseminates it further, and bits and pieces of it are likely to be picked up and replicated. Thus, language is continuously re-enacted, as it were, and in this ongoing process there is always the possibility of modification, of changing the set of and the balance between the forms and features it consists of. Everything that is said and heard has a chance of being replicated (or not!), may or may not be picked up and repeated by others. In this way some features are spread, while others fall into disuse. Frequency plays a major role in this – forms and patterns which are frequently repeated become natural, subconscious habits; linguists call this "cognitively entrenched." So, let us view language as a huge set of "features" (sounds, words, set phrases, syntactic rules and patterns, etc.) which are continuously activated and replicated, with some potential of being modified in form or frequency in this process.

So, where do all the constitutive and distinctive forms and features of New Englishes come from? The simple answer is: from pretty much any-where in the communicative environment. In a typical situation which in the long run will produce a new variety of English we see people interact-ing with each other – Englishmen from all walks of life, speaking standard English or any regional dialect, and locals who speak their native lan-guage(s) and some English influenced by it. Whatever any of them utters may be more or less communicatively successful, understandable to all the others in the given situation or perceived as useful somehow by them, and will thus be likely to be more or less frequently replicated. Mufwene (2001), in a useful and highly influential metaphor, conceptualized this as a "feature pool" to which people bring all of their own linguistic features just by reproducing them, by speaking. Especially in new contact situa-tions a new mix of features is then produced. Some disappear, while others are successful and get "selected" to become features of newly emerging varieties.

Figure 20 brings together and relates a number of factors and influences which play a role in this process, although, as the open-ended nature of

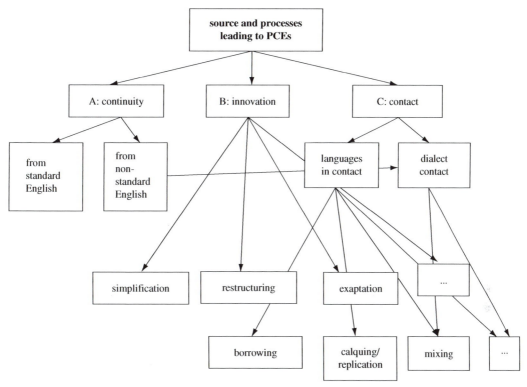

Figure 20 Sources and processes leading to the emergence of Postcolonial Englishes
(from Schneider 2007a: 100; reproduced by permission)

some branches suggests, this is merely suggestive and certainly not exhaustive. Some features are simply transmitted without much modification from one generation of speakers to another. Some seem different from anything that has been around in any of the varieties involved, hence "new," possibly originating from cognitively motivated innovative process such as simplification, possibly from restructuring or the alignment of new functions to old forms. Some are products of contact effects, from other languages or from related dialects which mutually influence each other.

Analogously to the growth of creoles, also in contact situations, it has become customary to talk of "superstrate" and "substrate" influences, respectively. The terms reflect the social status of the languages involved. English is the **superstrate**, coming "from above" and from those in power. Not exclusively so, however, for the notion also includes nonstandard English forms used and brought to the contact situation by lower-status British people. The **substrate** denotes the contributions made by indigenous languages, and like many things coming from underneath ('sub-'), it may not be immediately visible.

- Loan words are readily identified as such, of course.
- Pronunciation features may represent the transfer of indigenous articulatory habits, without this becoming obvious. For example, the English dialect of the north-eastern provinces of India has a rather unusual articulation of the /r/-sound which is identical with how this sound is pronounced in one of the regional Tibeto-Burman languages. So this represents an articulatory gesture which happened to be successful in the feature selection process, and which is now used also in the English of speakers of other regional languages (Wiltshire 2005).
- On the grammatical level, substrate influence may be most difficult to identify because there are so-called "camouflaged" forms – words which seem to be plainly English (and in terms of origins they are, of course) but which are used in patterns which replicate indigenous syntactic habits. For example, the Singaporean linguist Zhiming Bao (2005) identified the word *already* in Singaporean English as functionally expressing a perfective aspect category, directly rendering a Chinese particle *le*.

Which factors are responsible for letting features succeed in this selection process is immensely difficult to single out, given the multitude of options and the complexity of the entire process. The growth of a new variety is like the product of an equation with a very large number of input terms, as it were. The English sociolinguist Peter Trudgill (2004) even suggested that the process is "deterministic," i.e. if we knew everything about the relevant input we could mechanically predict the outcome (though this is assumed to apply to "tabula rasa" situations only, which rarely ever occur in reality; and most likely the claim is much too strong). In any individual case, we can identify many factors but we can usually only roughly assess their respective contributions.

It is customary and useful to distinguish language-internal factors, those rooted in the nature of language itself and its physical or cognitive manifestations, from language-external, mostly social factors.

The most fundamental of the language-**internal** restrictions are those resulting from the physical shape of our **articulatory** organs, which determine which (and also how many) sounds we can produce. For example, given the small size of the oral cavity, there is only a limited set of vowels which can be kept distinct, and given the limited flexibility of lips, teeth, and the mouth in general, and also the tongue, there is only a small number of places where frictions or closures, i.e. consonants, can be effectively produced.

More importantly, **cognition** imposes conditions on how language develops. The acoustic signal and the units and constituents of an utterance are processed in the mind, and so the ease of such processing certainly has an effect on which features are more likely to be successful. There is probably a connection somewhere between cognition, Second Language Acquisition (SLA), and the emergence of New Englishes (which typically started out as second languages acquired by locals in contact with English speakers). Learning a second language is strongly constrained by how the mind analyses and processes the input received by perception. The assumption is that when speakers do not (yet) "know" the conventions of the target language there is more room for cognitive principles to become directly effective and to guide the process. Again, however, it is not always clear which cognitive factors play a role and what their effect is.

Take the issue of **simplicity**, for example. It has been claimed repeatedly that New Englishes are in some respects "simpler" than other varieties, perhaps because complex properties were omitted in the acquisition process. It is not clear at all, however, what it means for one variety to be simpler than another. Actually, what we frequently find is a trade-off such that what looks like simplicity in one respect causes increased difficulty in another. For example, take pro-drop, the possibility of leaving out the subject of a sentence, observed in some examples in the previous chapter. Doing away with one major syntactic constituent leaves us with fewer words and units to deal with in a sentence, which gets shorter – clearly this should result in a simpler structure, right? So – the Singlish sentence *Can la!* looks maximally simple, when compared to a possible translation like 'But of course I/you can!' (with only two words as against five, for a start). But then – is it really when we consider the listener's perspective, the issue of understanding? The Singlish sentence doesn't even tell us who the speaker is talking about (context makes that clear) and it carries a number of implications which the hearer may fail to grasp, so in terms of its communicative efficiency this is clearly far from a simple, effective example. So what?

Actually, some cognitive principles appear to be in conflict with each other, and the above example seems a case in point: easy to produce but difficult to understand. More generally, maximizing ease of production seems to be a fundamental principle. We tend to omit sounds or constituents in casual conversation, for example. Put it negatively: as humans we are lazy buggers; positively viewed, we save our energy for more important activities. Conversely, ease of perception seems equally strong and important. After all, we need to understand what was said, so from that perspective it makes sense to maximize transparency, i.e. to spell out each piece of information separately (a principle known as "isomorphism," a one-to-one relation between meaning and form). Thus, for example, in Indian or Cameroonian English *that*-clauses are reported to be preferred over non-finite complement clauses (in sentences like *I want that he comes* for *I want him to come*) because they explicitly express the dependence relationship.

So, both tendencies are supported by reasonable, if competing, principles, and both are strong in New Englishes. There are patterns which strengthen the economy of production, like the omission of a plural -*s* after numerals, as in *all our subject* (Black South African English). On the other hand, there are also tendencies towards hyperclarity, i.e. towards expressing the same piece of information repeatedly and redundantly. A case in point is shown in Figure 21, from the Philippines, where in the phrase *visit with us* the preposition *with* is in a sense unnecessary because its meaning is already implied in the verb *visit*, but it is spelled out nevertheless. Another widely attested example is the doubling of conjunctions in a sentence, as in *Although you are away, but you do not forget* (from West Africa).

Actually, it seems that individual languages may prefer one or the other of those tendencies, economy vs. hyperclarity. Mesthrie and Bhatt (2008: 90) hypothesize that there are in fact "deleter" and "preserver" varieties, the former more generally in Asia and with a Chinese substrate, the latter preferably in Africa. In fact, Mesthrie (2006) provides a very convincing analysis of one variety along such lines. In South African Black English, he points out a consistent tendency towards what he calls "antideletion." Whenever other languages can omit constituents, or tend to do so, this one doesn't (e.g. an infinitive marker: *let him to speak*; dummy subject: *As it is the case elsewhere*;

Figure 21 Redundant preposition in *visit with* (Philippines)

gapped pronouns: *I can read them and write them*), and elsewhere it inserts redundant forms (double conjunctions like *Although ... but*, redundant prepositions like *discuss about*, and resumptive pronouns as in *the kind of education that these people are trying to give it to us*). Note that this may be viewed as a tendency which maximizes explicitness and simplifies understanding, in line with SLA principles! So, we have come full circle.

Another property of many New Englishes which seems strongly in line with cognitive and SLA principles is the one summarized by Williams (1987), in an article which very fundamentally works out the possible impact of SLA, as "avoid exceptions." One manifestation of this principle may be the avoidance of irregularities, i.e. *knowed* for *knew*, *mouses* for *mice*. Another is the force of analogy, i.e. a desire to structure one sub-system on the model of another. Examples for this include the processes of generalizing one question tag to all contexts, e.g. *you are coming, isn't it?* (India), and of transferring the inverted question word order to dependent interrogative clauses, e.g. *I asked him where is he?* (Pakistan).

There are other cognitively motivated principles of language change which seem to steer language development (and selection) processes in World Englishes just like they do in other languages. This is a potentially vast field, and one that in some respects is somewhat fuzzy and insufficiently understood, so it should suffice here to provide and illustrate two such tendencies as examples.

One is **grammaticalization**, a tendency found in many languages in which lexical items get formally weakened and semantically "bleached" and ultimately become grammatical function words. Wee (2003) claims that in Singlish *know*, reduced from the English discourse marker *you know*, is on this path (in utterances like *The coffee very hot, know*), adopting properties of the characteristic Singaporean discourse markers mentioned earlier and thus joining that class and giving up the properties of the lexical verb.

Another is **exaptation**, also called "functional reallocation," in which a form available in the feature pool is "recycled" to adopt a new function. For example, in many Caribbean varieties *does* has become a marker of habituality (*im does go* then means 'he goes regularly'); and *fit* in Cameroon is said to express a polite request (*We fit go sinema?* 'Shall we go ...?').

External causes, on the other hand, have something to do with the social evaluation and embedding of linguistic forms. In emerging new varieties, options from the feature pool may be successful just because they are the majority choice or happen to be associated with some desirable social group. Let us briefly look at some of these factors.

Demography is clearly a key player here. The larger the number of speakers of any given variety, the more frequently will their speech forms be produced and replicated; size simply increases the chances of selection and survival. Higher numbers of English speakers also mean more access to English as a target language. Obviously, settler communities, with a strong majority of English-descendant migrants dominating a territory, establish and perpetuate the dominance of English and are least susceptible to indigenous language influences. Conversely, in trade colonies and, less so, exploitation colonies the proportion of English speakers is much smaller, and learners of English are more influential in the community's language ecology.

In a historical perspective, a **founder effect,** argued for by Mufwene (2001), increases the linguistic influence of the earliest settler groups in a new territory. In a *tabula rasa* situation, the earliest generations of migrants find no pre-existing linguistic norm to adjust to. So in the course of time, typically a few generations, they create one of their own – through koinéization or the other components of the formative process which Trudgill (2004) considers "inevitable." Later waves of immigrants, however, find some social and linguistic habits already established and prevailing in a community, which for them constitutes a target to gradually adjust to – even if of course they themselves contribute to the feature pool. Thus, the "founder principle" states that earlier immigrant strata in a newly forming community have disproportionally more influence on an emerging language form than later ones.

But it's not all about numbers and chronology. Language is also an instrument to exert power or to signal **solidarity**. And in language matters, as with other social norms, those in power usually establish their own behavior and expectations as the guideline for the entire community. Today's instrumental motivations to learn English in so many countries, with knowledge of the language viewed as a gateway to economic opportunities and a better life, may be regarded as a reflection of the (economic) power of the language, or rather, its speakers as the owners or representatives of big international companies. Conversely, however, the argument may also backfire. Those in power are not always loved and do not always constitute a model for all others. Solidarity considerations, a fundamentally human desire for bonding and community, may strengthen peer group forms of (linguistic) behavior, however nonstandard or refuted by gatekeepers they may be.

The notion of **prestige**, with its two main qualities suggested by Labov (1972), is closely related to this, the linguistic reflection of social evaluation. Overt prestige is officially attributed typically to formal language usage, standard English, by the authorities. However, covert prestige is frequently assigned in a community to those speakers (and their language use) who are really admired and respected by the people, often at the opposite end of the social scale. It has been found that females are more susceptible to overt prestige and public norms, while men, perhaps in line with a stereotype demanding male strength, toughness, and independence, more often reject prescribed formal norms and are carriers or copiers of covert, informal prestige forms.

Another facet of this topic, closely related but not quite the same, is added by viewing linguistic differences as a means of signaling group membership. Linguistic variants typically carry a socially symbolic function and serve as **identity** markers. Such symbolic linguistic usage may reflect actual reality (with all members of a certain group speaking alike in some respects), but it may also be a means of projecting desired identities that a speaker is striving for: we may not be quite there as yet, but nevertheless we may be signaling where we wish to belong by speaking in a certain way. So, language variability is a powerful tool to actively manipulate one's social relations and ambitions.

So – put speakers of different origins together in one locality; add all the above ingredients to varying proportions; shake it all over by letting time pass by for a few generations and seeing social relationships and realignments evolving – and out comes a new variety of English.

7.2 **Widespread outcomes**

Of course, all the "World Englishes" share a common core of characteristically English features and properties; otherwise we wouldn't be able to identify them as varieties of English, or members of the "English Language Complex," to use Mesthrie and Bhatt's (2008) term. For example, they all have the words *house*, *dog*, and *sister*; they all have voiceless fricatives like /s/ and /f/ or high front vowels, for instance in words like *hit* or *heat*; and they all have SVO word order or some means of embedding a clause into a noun phrase as a relative clause. But the attention of observers is not attracted by the commonalities but by the differences – and there are many, on all levels.

As was stated earlier, it is the peculiar mix of properties which makes up any individual variety. Typically, there are **stereotypes** – features that speakers tend to know about and that are associated with a certain region and its language. So, for example,

- Americans, unlike Brits, pronounce their /r/'s (e.g. in *car*) and go on *vacation* rather than on *holiday*;
- Indians confuse /v/ and /w/ and have *wallahs* for all kinds of odd jobs;
- Ozzies have *mates*, which they pronounce with /aɪ/,

and so on. But of course that's just the tip of the iceberg, a gross simplification. In reality there's a myriad of differences, and especially, though below the level of anybody's awareness, there are all those tendencies to prefer or disprefer one or the other form or pattern in any given variety.

Still, while obviously there is a whole lot of variability and unpredictability, certain common tendencies in newly emerging World Englishes have been observed. It is difficult to say why this is so. Some shared features may be explained as products of cognitively influenced language acquisition processes. Others, perhaps, reflect shared tendencies of change in English, or the transmission of the same nonstandard British forms through time and space. Others, again, just leave us puzzled. In the following few paragraphs I will provide a few examples and will work out some possible shared tendencies. Note, however, that naturally this discussion represents a rather rigid selection which by necessity is illustrative of some processes and phenomena but far from exhaustive.

On the level of **lexis**, the most conspicuous forms are obviously **loan words** from indigenous languages, typically used freely and frequently and without any indication of a special status in texts from Outer Circle Englishes. Loan words tend to infiltrate English in a characteristic chronological sequence.

- The earliest borrowings are topographical terms – names of places, rivers, and mountains taken over in large numbers from indigenous populations (think of Indian place names in North America, Aboriginal ones in Australia, and Maori ones in New Zealand).
- Names of indigenous plants and animals follow soon, and constitute a quantitatively significant proportion of words borrowed from local languages – for example, *dingo, koala, kookaburra* (Australia); *kiwi, kauri* (New Zealand); *yaqona* 'kava' (Fiji); *simba* (East Africa), *tsetse* (southern Africa); *marula* (South Africa); *orang utan, rambutan* (Malaysia).
- Objects and customs alien to British settlers, i.e. typically those associated with indigenous culture, are also taken over together with increasing familiarity with the concepts themselves.

Various domains can be subsumed under this heading:

- physical objects, e.g. *tanoa* 'bowl' (Fiji), *nulla-nulla* 'club', *kylie* 'boomerang' (Australia), *hangi* 'earth oven', *waka* 'canoe' (New Zealand), *matatu* 'collective taxi', *jembe* 'hoe' (East Africa);
- food, e.g. *fufu* (West Africa), *ugali* (East Africa);
- clothing, e.g. *akwete* (Nigeria), *makgabe* (Botswana), *sulu* (Fiji), *dhoti* (India), *kaross* (South Africa);
- social standing and customs, e.g. *oga* or *igwe* (Nigeria); *fon* (Cameroon); *nawab* (India); *bumiputra* 'native, lit. son of the earth', *datok* 'ruler' (Malaysia); *mana* 'prestige', *hui* 'meeting' (New Zealand);

- terms for religion and superstition, e.g. *taboo* (Polynesia), *tagathi* 'witch-craft' (South Africa), *thahu* 'curse' (Kenya); etc.

The creative embedding of these words in the English recipient language varieties is also signaled by their readiness to enter firm **word formation** relations with English lexical material in so-called hybrid compounds, e.g. *talanoa session* 'chat' (Fiji), *hoisin sauce* (Hong Kong), *whare boy* (New Zealand), *nobat drums* (Malaysia), *botak head* 'bald head' (Singapore), *dhobi-washed* (India). Indigenous languages also exert indirect influence by motivating calques, i.e. word-by-word translations of indigenous phrases into English (*lucky money*, Hong Kong) or the rendering of cultural meta-phors (*second burial*; *shell palm kernel for the fowls*, 'waste time in an unproductive activity', from Igbo, Nigeria).

Etymologically English words may also gain a special status in New Englishes. In some cases we find the retention of **archaisms**. For whatever reason, some words which in the ancestral variety were dialectal or mori-bund and were carried to a colony by migrant dialect speakers were success-fully selected and revitalized from the pool of forms available and have survived in new varieties. Conversely, of course, there are also **innovations**, systematic ways of creating new lexical items using familiar lexical material. These processes may happen on two sides, the semantic and the formal one. Some word forms acquire new or retain old regionally restricted meanings. Figure 22 suggests that in South Africa *scholars* refers to a different kind of people than in Britain or the US.

Other examples include *shoot* 'falls, rapids' (Canada), *dairy* 'corner shop' (New Zealand), *knock* 'remove a dent from a car' (Singapore), *astronaut* 'long-distance commuter' (Hong Kong), *cut* 'overtake' (South-East Asia), *plastic* 'supermarket bag' (Fiji), *heavy* 'pregnant', *globe* 'electric bulb', or *drop* 'longest distance in a taxi for the minimum fare' (Nigeria).

On the formal side, the conventional word formation patterns described for standard English can all be found to be effective in coining new words in World Englishes as well (Biermeier 2008). It seems, however, that in these varieties combining morphemes to build new complex words is much more common than the reductive types of clipping and abbreviating words. We commonly find

- new compounds, e.g. *dragonhead* 'top leader of a triad' (Hong Kong), *big father* 'father's elder brother' (Fiji), *sharemilker* (New Zealand), *airflown* 'freshly imported (food)' (Singapore), *cow-eater* (India), *blue-ground* 'diamond-bearing ground' (South Africa), *wife inheritance* 'widow inherited by brothers of the deceased husband' (East Africa), *motor park* 'bus and taxi station' (Nigeria); including the
- hybrid compounding just mentioned and illustrated.

Figure 22 Semantic change: *scholars* in South Africa

New words are also frequently coined by

- derivation, i.e. by appending formative prefixes or suffixes (like *-y*, *-dom*, *-ism*, *de-*, etc.), as in *mountie* (Canada), *cooliedom*, *goondaism* (India), *overlisten*, *impressment* 'burden' (Kenya), *destool*, *pregnate* (Nigeria), *condomise* (Botswana), etc.

Another example of the same type is provided by Figure 23, which shows the most prototypically Philippine of all words and things, a *jeepney*. We might say that somehow the word has been derived from the familiar word *jeep* in much the same way as the objects originally were derived from leftover army jeeps – by fixing something to it and thus manufacturing something new.

Note that not only idiosyncratic new words are coined in various places. We also find regional preferences for specific word formation types and formatives, i.e. evidence for the divergence of new varieties of English through the emergence of systematically varying habits and hence, in the long run, patterns. For example, as the second part of compounds we find some elements particularly productive in certain countries: *holder* in the Philippines (*flower holder*, *record holder*, *degree holder*), *monger* and *master* in Kenya (*catastrophe monger*, *rumour monger*; *careers master*, *drugmaster*, *paymaster*), etc.

Figure 23 A Philippine *jeepney*

Pronunciation tendencies across varieties of English are more difficult to generalize, perhaps because here the impact of substrate languages tends to show most directly, and the wide range of typologically unrelated substrate languages spoken in regions where New Englishes have developed is thus responsible for influences fostering differences. But of course there are both pronunciations stereotypically associated with certain regions (some of which were mentioned earlier in this chapter), and there are regional and a few general tendencies. Schneider (2007a) provides fairly long tables of forms which are preferred in and correlate with certain regions, and also, for instance, with ESL varieties. For example, /a/ in *trap* and /ɔ/ in *strut* primarily characterize the Caribbean (though both are also found in Africa and elsewhere), /æ/ in *bath* suggests North America, peripheral [i] in words like *kit* and [u] in *foot* (etc.) are mostly typical of Africa and Asia; etc.

Interestingly enough, pronunciation trends shared more widely across New Englishes tend to be **reductive**, i.e. to reduce complexities and distinctions found in, say, British English and its dialects, so these are probably tendencies which lend some support to the recurrent claims that New Englishes are "simpler." For example, a widespread trend can be observed to conflate corresponding tense and lax (or "long" and "short") vowels, so that in many Asian and African Englishes the vowels of *beat* and *bit*

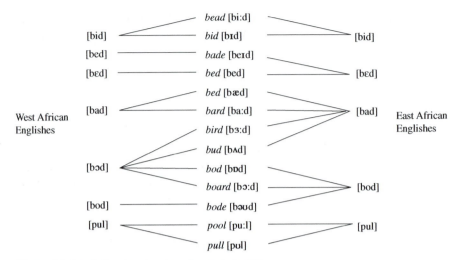

Figure 24 Conflation tendencies of vowels in Africa

(adapted after R. Angogo and I. Hancock, 1980. "English in Africa: Emerging standards or diverging regionalisms?" *English World-Wide* 1, p. 75)

sound alike. In African varieties the short vowel system of English tends to be reduced, sometimes to just five basic types (roughly corresponding to *i, e, a, o* and *u*). Figure 24 suggests how thirteen different vowels of British English are thus conflated to essentially yield seven different types in West Africa and only five phonemes in East Africa.

What this diagram also illustrates is the fact that central vowels tend to be avoided. The short central /ʌ/ of RP *cut* either moves down in the vowel space to yield /a/, or back to sound like *lot*. The long central /ɜ:/ in words like *nurse* moves to the periphery (to come out, depending on regions and specific words, as close to *e, a,* or *o*). And the unstressed schwa (/ə/, e.g. in *about, father*) tends to receive fuller stress and a non-central sound quality, frequently close to /a/ in Africa.

This latter change has to do with another tendency which is extremely widespread in New Englishes, namely a **syllable-timed** rhythm in which all syllables (including the ones which in RP are unstressed and even deleted) tend to take a roughly equal amount of time and a full vowel quality (so a word like *comfortably*, unlike its reduced British pronunciation, will have four distinct syllables and vowels).

Another widespread process modifying vowels is the monophthongization of diphthongs, especially those with a mid-high onset: the vowels in words like *face* and *goat*, /eɪ/ and /oʊ/ respectively, loose their gliding movement in very many regions (throughout the Caribbean, in Africa and Asia; but note that this also characterizes Scottish English, for instance), and are pronounced as long monophthongs, /e:/ and /o:/.

Consonants count as more stable and display less variability, but two types of "simplification" are also noteworthy. One is segmental and concerns the dental fricatives of English (spelled *th*, i.e. voiceless /θ/ in *thing* and voiced /ð/ in *this*). Typologically, i.e. when comparing languages on a global scale, these are rare sounds which many languages do not have, so, not surprisingly, in many varieties of English they are replaced systematically by either /t, d/ or, less commonly, by /s, z/. The other is suprasegmental and concerns the process labeled "Consonant Cluster Reduction." Several consonants in a row are difficult to articulate, so there is a widespread tendency to leave out the last of two word-final consonants (so we get *tes'* for *test* or *wes'* for *west*). This is very common in ENL dialects as well, but Schreier (2005) showed that the frequency of this process correlates directly with the amount of contact a language has been shaped by, so this occurs most commonly in creoles (see the Jamaican and Tok Pisin text samples on pp. 103–5 and 173).

Most of these forms would probably be classified as "**innovations**" – even if it is disputed whether there is ever "anything new under the sun," especially on the level of pronunciation, given that the range of our articulatory motions is naturally restricted. It is not possible to "invent" new sounds, so it seems likely that certain pronunciation options are continuously "recycled," rising or falling in frequency in certain varieties – but still, in a new variety in comparison with the donor language many of them are "new." But of course the **retention** of English dialectal forms also plays an important role in the emergence of World Englishes; after all, they were available in the pool in the first place. This is fairly straightforward and obvious in settler dialects: there has been a long tradition of attempting to trace American English features back to specific British dialect forms. It can be shown that much of the Appalachian mountain dialect derives from Ulster (and ultimately Scotland), that features of the Otago pronunciation in New Zealand are Scottish in origin, etc. But nonstandard British speakers also influenced ESL varieties. Simo Bobda (2003) suggests that some features of African English pronunciations are actually not simplifications or innovations (as is commonly assumed) but rather retentions of such British traces – with /ɛ/ in eastern Nigerian English dialects possibly going back to Scottish and Irish missionaries, for instance, or West African /u/ or /ʊ/ representing northern English traces.

When looking at **grammar**, we find the same phenomenon – dialect patterns which are common in British and, in general, Inner Circle settler dialects. Cases in point are multiple negation (i.e. the use of more than one negative marker in a clause, e.g. *I don't have nothing to do*), the use of *never* to negate a single past time event rather than an indefinite period of time (*I never called him yesterday*), *me* for *I* in coordination (*Me and John went there*), and unmarked adverbs (*real good*). J. K. Chambers (2003) suggested that there are "**vernacular universals**," globally distributed nonstandard forms (though the notion itself and the issue of which features might belong to this class are disputed).

Whether or not they can be traced back to England, there is a wide range of grammatical patterns considered characteristic of New Englishes, many of which we have actually encountered in the text samples of the previous chapters. Some are idiosyncratic (like Singapore's *kena*-passive, or Kenya's reduplicated modal *can be able*), while others are more or less widespread. Some fairly common types include the following:

- omission of inflectional endings, e.g. the third person singular verb *-s* (*she drink milk*, Philippines), the verbal past tense marker (*I did a lot of things – I laze about, I go for movies*, Singapore), or of the plural *-s* (*both area*, Sri Lanka);
- pluralization of mass nouns, thus making them "countable." An example is found in Figure 25, from India; others include *furnitures, alphabets* 'letters', *staffs, equipments*, etc. (widespread in Africa and Asia);
- variable article usage (with respect to both omission and insertion; widespread especially in Asia);
- progressive use of stative verbs (*She is owning . . .*, Malaysia; *You must be knowing him*, India);

Figure 25 Pluralization of a mass noun: *footwears* (India)

- inversion in embedded questions but lack of inversion (or of the auxiliary altogether) in main clause interrogatives (*I asked him where is he?*, Pakistan; *What I must do?*, South African Indian English; *You been town lately?*, St. Helena);
- invariant tag questions, e.g. *You'll do the job, isn't it?* (India), *eh?* (Canada);
- omission of sentence constituents, esp. of the subject, e.g. *Can.* (Singapore), *Is nice food* (Uganda), *Here is not allowed to stop* (Hong Kong);
- reduplication, esp. to intensify adjectives, e.g. *small-small* 'very small', *different-different* (India), or *same-same* ('the same, completely identical' – which seems ubiquitous in Asia).

With respect to the central question of how such innovations emerge and spread, an interesting observation, made most explicitly in Schneider (2007a), is the fact that they tend to start at the boundary between lexis and grammar. Specific words (often verbs) and semantically coherent word groups begin to be used or to be preferred in a specific pattern, and this habit then gets more deeply entrenched, becomes regular usage, and spreads to other words, possibly to the point of becoming a generally used rule of the variety in question. A visual example was provided in Figure 5 in Chapter 5, which showed that in New Zealand the word *farewell* is used as a transitive verb with a person as its object.

Similarly, both in America and in New Zealand you can *protest something* or *appeal somebody*, in East Africa you *pick somebody*, and in India you *provide* or *present somebody something*. In fact, this last pattern, of ditransitives, has apparently been spreading to new verbs in India, as Mukherjee and Hoffmann (2006) have shown: *gift him a dream, notify us the date,* etc. The use or non-use of certain prepositions falls in the same category – compare *discuss something* with *discuss about something*, common in Asian or African Englishes; or the fact that *different* is complemented by *to, from,* or *than,* with preferences between these being strongly tied to specific varieties. Thus, using old words in slightly new ways, as it were, and then turning such spurious innovations into general habits, seems to be the entrance door for many new structures in World Englishes.

Chapter summary

In this chapter we had a closer look at where the characteristic features of World Englishes come from, and which ones they are. In language contact situations, we learned, any form or pattern uttered by anybody may or may not be picked up by other speakers, and thus become a "successful" element of a newly emerging variety. This process is commonly accounted for by the metaphor of speakers contributing their speech forms to a "pool" of available features from which some of them are then "selected" into the new variety. The reasons why certain forms win out (while others fall into disuse) are manifold (and chance certainly also quite simply plays a role in this), but they can be grouped into two distinct types. Language-internal properties (articulatory conditions, cognitive principles, etc.) may make certain forms preferable over others – more effective, perhaps, or more system-internally consistent. Language-external, sociolinguistic factors (like power, prestige, or social identity) strongly determine which language forms spread in a community because speakers employ them to symbolize social relations, real or desired group membership, and other attitudes.

All of these processes together, then, produce new varieties of global English, with each of them being a unique kaleidoscope of such features but some of them also being more widespread than others. Some features may stem from dialectal English input transmitted around the globe, others may result from transfer, or innovation and change. On the lexical plane, borrowing from indigenous languages as well as specific types of creativity (semantic shift, word-formation processes such as compounding, derivation, hybridity and calquing, and so on) generate new expressions. In the pronunciation of World Englishes we find some reductive processes and some degree of retention in addition to many other phenomena which cannot be easily accounted for. In grammar, some broader phenomena such as widespread nonstandard forms (possibly "vernacular universals") and characteristic innovations have been identified, and it has been argued that many innovations start out at the interface between lexis and grammar, with new or modified patterns starting out with certain words only and then spreading from there to others.

So, in a sense, language has a life of its own. It evolves by moving along internal laws and principles, which linguists attempt to understand. What the speakers themselves think about these processes may be a totally different story, and it is these real-life issues, the social embedding of the New Englishes, to which we turn now.

Exercises and activities

Exercise 7a Most people have some "family" or "couple" or "in-group" words commonly used in such very small social groups but not transparent to outsiders. Do you have any? If so, can you remember how they originated, and possibly why they have been retained?

Exercise 7b   Can you remember ever having deliberately picked up a word, an expression, or some other language habit from others because you found it attractive somehow? If so, how would such an experience fit into the framework outlined in this chapter?

Exercise 7c   Consider Figure 20, and discuss it more closely in the light of what you have learned in this chapter. Which phenomena possibly belong to which developmental category?

Exercise 7d   Which of the loan words listed in this chapter do you know? For the others, use dictionaries or other appropriate sources to find out what they mean. Check the *Oxford English Dictionary* (presumably to be found in your nearest University library) and your desk dictionary to see whether these words are listed in dictionaries of English.

Exercise 7e   For most new national varieties of English, dictionaries have been produced and published – there are dictionaries of South African English, Australian English, New Zealand English, Malaysian and Singaporean English, Indian English, and others. Check your library to see which ones you find. Select a few words from them and assign them to the types described above.

Exercise 7f   Consult the *Handbook of Varieties* (see the "Further reading" section below), or the interactive CD that comes with it, or other appropriate sources accessible to you, to find out

(a)   where exactly you find monophthongal realizations of the diphthongs /eɪ/ (so *face* sounds like [e:]), /oʊ/ ([o:] in *goat*), and /aɪ/ (i.e. [a:] for *time*). (Do you find anything on possible sources or causes of these processes, and their social meaning in specific communities?)

(b)   which are the main realizations of the vowel in words like *feet*, and how they are regionally distributed. (Use appropriate phonetic terms to describe the variants properly!)

Exercise 7g   If you say or hear anybody saying *I don't have no money here* – is this clear to you, and do you find it logical or effective? If you drop the plural *-s* in *I'm twenty years old*, or the past tense *-ed* in *I helped him yesterday* – would you lose any information (and if so, or if not, why?)?

Exercise 7h   Consider the following grammatical patterns, all documented in the *Handbook of Varieties*:

(a)   *enable him do it* (Nigeria)

(b)   *Didn't nobody like it* (African American English)

(c)   *They are more wiser* (Liberia)
(d)   *Eve, she go this side* (Butler English, India)
(e)   *The England is good place* (Pakistan)

Analyze them, i.e. understand how they are built and what's special about them, using appropriate descriptive terminology. Find out how widespread (or, conversely, unique) they are.

Key terms discussed in this chapter
archaisms
calques
camouflaged forms
central vowels
consonant cluster reduction (CCR)
covert prestige
demography
derivation
discourse marker
exaptation
extralinguistic (language-external)
feature pool
founder effect / principle
grammaticalization
hybrid compounds
internalized language
intralinguistic (language-internal)
isomorphism
language as a process
loans
multiple negation
overt prestige
power
prestige
reduplication
replication
Second Language Acquisition (SLA)
semantic change
simplicity
solidarity
substrate
superstrate
verb complementation
vernacular universals

Further reading

The most readable comparative survey of the linguistic properties of new varieties of English to date, with rich examples, is Mesthrie and Bhatt (2008); this book also has interesting chapters on parallels between Second Language Acquisition and new contact varieties and on the nonstandard speech of different settler groups. The earliest broader generalization of features of New Englishes can be found in Platt *et al.* (1984). For those interested in details of the phonetic or grammatical properties of any individual variety or an authoritative documentation of such properties on a global scale, the source to consult is the massive two-volume *Handbook of Varieties of English* published in 2004: Schneider *et al.* (2004) has articles on the pronunciation characteristics of more than sixty Englishes; and Kortmann *et al.* (2004) provides a survey of grammatical phenomena found in almost the same number of varieties. The *Handbook* is now also available as an affordable four-volume paperback set (Kortmann and Upton 2008, Schneider 2008, Burridge and Kortmann 2008, Mesthrie 2008). Note that it comes with a CD-ROM which offers audio samples of many varieties and interactive maps, on which each user can display the global distribution of select features and feature configurations. Chapter 4 in Schneider (2007a) surveys linguistic processes which have shaped New Englishes, as well as some of their shared features, in greater detail.

CHAPTER 8

Issues and attitudes

In this chapter . . .

The evolution of World Englishes has widely affected and modified long-standing social patterns and modes of behavior, transforming the lives of many people from one generation to another. Thus, it is a process of great cultural and political significance in many countries, and so, not surprisingly, it has been the subject of much debate. Some of the general social issues under discussion are outlined in this chapter, from a position which attempts to remain as neutral as possible. Topics will include the following:

- the association of English with "elitism" in some countries as against its uncontrolled spread also among lower-class, uneducated speakers;
- the claim that English has "killed" indigenous languages and is to be blamed for the global loss of linguistic diversity;
- the question of whether an "International English" exists or would be desirable;
- the debate about endonormativity (i.e., whether local forms of English could constitute acceptable targets) in education;
- the role of local forms of English to express local identities;
- the changing status of the notion of "native speaker of English";
- the amazingly wide spread of mixed language forms; and
- the relationship between Applied Linguistics and strategies of language teaching.

8.1 Getting ahead with English: the tension between elitism and grassroots spread

Who are the primary users of English in Outer Circle countries today? Actually, this is no longer as easy a question to answer as it may seem. The most natural and immediate response would be that these are upper class people, the leading strata in a society. It is true that in most of these countries English is primarily transmitted through the school system (frequently as the medium of instruction after the first few years), so it is associated with education, and the quality of an individual's performance tends to correlate with one's educational attainment. But in countries such as India, Nigeria, Kenya, or South Africa this is definitely no longer the whole story. There is a huge demand for English also among those with little formal education, precisely out of this instrumental motivation, because knowledge of English promises some degree of social mobility and access to better paid jobs. So English, and in practice this means indigenous forms of it, is also spreading rapidly among the less educated, often for specific purposes such as to achieve a limited communicative ability in trade or tourism.

So, while much of the public and scholarly attention is attracted by issues of education and by standard and educated usage, relatively little is known about the grassroots growth, the natural (if informal) acquisition and rapid, uncontrolled spread of English in many countries. It may happen completely naturally, through unguided natural second language acquisition in contact with speakers of English, and also, probably more regularly, in some sort of schooling context, though in comparison these tend to be schools with little funding and of limited quality. What is important here is the expansion of English into primary school education in many countries – also a problematic and controversial issue, because education in one's native language at least through the first few years of schooling is an elementary human right, but at the same time the demand for English is brought forward by many parents.

In Kenya, for example, after independence a scheme called the "New Primary Approach" brought English into elementary schools quite sweepingly. Recent statistics suggest that about three quarters of all urban and more than half of the rural workplaces are run in English, that over a third of the rural elementary school children use the language, and even among the urban poor, for instance in a slum in Nairobi, more than half of all people claim some proficiency in English (Mazrui and Mazrui 1996).

A similar situation, marked by the diffusion of English beyond the "elites," obtains in India. David Crystal confesses to have been "struck by the remarkable amount of semi-fluent or 'broken' English which is encountered in the Indian sub-continent, used by people with a limited educational background"

(2008: 4) (and he suspects that the same "smattering of English for trade and other purposes" can be found "in all parts of the world"). Viniti Vaish (2008) describes the acquisition and use of English in a lower-middle-class government school in Delhi, and she comments on English among the urban poor as follows: "this community does not speak English though members of it can listen, read and write. It is not the class that speaks Indian English. But this community uses English to improve their job prospects just as one might learn to drive a car, so as to get a job as a driver" (personal communication). An impressive recent documentation of this process, based on statistics and visits to rural schools, is Graddol (2010).

More documentation on the grassroots spread of English in many countries would be desirable – this seems a neglected subject, perhaps because of the traditional emphasis on "good usage" and the need for it. It remains to be seen where this process will lead, but it seems clear that it is a very powerful one and adds an important component to the top-centered, official views of Englishes.

These varying patterns of transmission, acquisition and use have produced an equally wide range of possible attitudes and reactions. Authorities and politicians everywhere promote the standard variety, partly for fear of loosing competitiveness in international communication, notably business. Singapore's "Speak Good English Movement," run since 2002, is a classic case in point, and a phenomenon known as the "complaint tradition," public laments about standards of English declining, can be observed in very many countries (and is characteristic of a specific developmental stage, the threat which conservative observers perceive in nativization). But governments may be able to prescribe language policies and school standards but they do not control people's minds – and I am convinced that in the long run what people really think and want to do, the "covert prestige" mentioned earlier, is much more decisive for future developments than official proclamations. The strong and stubborn defense of the use of Singlish against an official government position in Singapore, a country not really known for its grassroots democracy, is a very telling case in point. It remains to be seen whether attitudes towards English will move beyond purely utilitarian considerations on a larger scale. Only if indigenous varieties of English will grow to be the language of people's hearts, expressions of their regional identities and of community solidarity, will these varieties ultimately survive and stabilize in many Outer Circle countries. At the present moment, this is difficult to assess. There is clear evidence for the impact of the instrumental value of English on a global scale, and there is some evidence for it growing into an integrative role in some contexts, but there is little solid documentation of and also relatively little scholarly interest in this latter aspect.

In fact, there is also the opposite possibility, the perception of English as purely elitist (whether this is to be viewed as a danger is open to discussion).

If it becomes the property of an upper stratum of society only and is felt to be elitist and socially exclusive, it may be rejected by the population at large. Again, this is more a question of perception than of reality. The Philippines seem to be a country where such a process may have begun. Thompson (2003) believes that in the political struggles of the country over the last few decades, epitomized by the earlier Marcos regime on the one hand and Estrada's presidency, staged as the people coming to power, on the other, English has been instrumentalized and is increasingly seen as associated with those in power, a symbol of wealth and social segregation. The 1970s, he claims, were the golden era of English, with the language built into a national self-projection; but the hopes tied to this development have failed for many, and have led to a backlash. Even if competence in English is extremely widespread in Filipino society, it is reported that nowadays the language is met rather with resentment and is viewed as a sign of affectation by some – and in that case it seems hardly likely that it will be spreading any further. Interestingly enough, the solidarity function seems to be expressed by Taglish, the mixed code which seems immensely popular today; more on this below.

8.2 "Killer language" or denial of access?

Reactions to the globalization of English have been ambivalent. On the one hand, English has been accused of "swamping" the world, of killing indigenous languages and cultures by the hundreds, or even thousands; on the other hand, it is widely embraced also for the political and social implications tied to its use.

One of the most hotly debated recurrent topics in debates on World Englishes is the question of whether it is a "killer language." This is a position which was voiced especially by politically inclined authors labeled "radicals" by Melchers and Shaw (2003: 30), most notably Phillipson (1992). They denigrated English as a primary tool in a hidden agenda pursued by those striving to dominate the globalized world. It is true, of course, that the political dominance of English-speaking settlers has more or less completely induced a language shift on the side of indigenous peoples in many cases, beginning with Scottish and Irish Gaelic and including, to varying extents, many North American Native Indian and Australian Aboriginal languages, New Zealand's Maori (now officially promoted as a co-official national language, but in practice extremely restricted in use), and so on. Undeniably, language endangerment propelled by English is clearly one important facet of the globalization of the language. An interesting documentation of how this happens in practice, in a restricted environment, is provided by Schäfer and Egbokhare (1999), who investigated language use and the early stages of language replacement in the Emai-speaking region of Nigeria. They show that while adults retain the vernacular language and teenagers comply with this when talking to elders, peer group and school talk among adolescents is preferably in English, and children use English predominantly with their siblings and increasingly with their parents.

So, yes, it is true that many small languages around the globe are endangered today, a process comparable to the loss of biodiversity, and that this entails a deplorable loss of a community's cultural and historical roots. English is not the only or even the primary target in this, however – frequently speakers shift to major regional or national languages which are actively promoted by national language policies (Kiswahili, Filipino, Putonghua, or Bahasa Indonesia, for instance). Whether it is justified to blame the English language for devouring local languages or to view its spread as a new imperialist strategy by the economic "powers that be," with the implicit goal of dominating the world via English, is very much open to discussion, a radical position indeed.

In fact, the implicit assumption that English is being pushed and has been imposed on speakers of other languages deliberately turns out to be simply mistaken, as Brutt-Griffler (2002) has shown. During the colonial period it was not the policy of British administrators to promote the learning and spread of English to indigenous populations. Quite to the contrary, as was stated earlier – knowledge of English was recognized as a powerful tool, an instrument of learning and self-empowerment, so as far as we can tell during British colonialism and in many countries English was actually withheld from the masses and passed on to a select few of the loyal local elites only (as by Lord Lugard's "indirect rule" policy).

The local leadership, those who took power after independence, were thus largely anglicized and acculturated, frequently having been educated at British universities. As an example, consider Jomo Kenyatta, leader of Kenya's 1950s Mau Mau uprising and later the country's first president, who had studied in England and lived there for many years. Certainly this fact contributed strongly to the retention of English in the administrative running of young nations. In many countries English is, and has always potentially been, also a language of liberalization. It was the language of indigenous elites, but these elites then became the leaders of independence and liberty movements, and thus of course also national role models. The most recent extant example of this is probably South Africa's transition from apartheid to a non-racial democracy. One major reason why English has been so successful in South Africa is the fact that it was the language of the African National Congress, the organization led by Nelson Mandela which achieved the Rainbow Revolution of 1994 and since then has been the country's leading party. Its 1955 "Freedom Charter," a statement of core principles which later influenced the country's new 1996 Constitution, was written in English.

Considering the political functions of English would be incomplete, however, without referring (again) to the one property which perhaps was its most decisive advantage in its retention as an official or co-official language in many young nations: its ethnic neutrality. In a country like Nigeria the choice of English in that function was strongly motivated by the fact that it was nobody's ethnic tongue, so all ethnic groups were treated equally. The same line of thinking clearly played a role in establishing India's "Three Language Formula" or Singapore's bilingual language policy.

In a broader perspective, in all the countries under discussion here language policy is a major public issue. Deciding on which language or language variety should be chosen, promoted or tolerated for any given purpose involves identity issues, the consideration of power relationships between the groups in a society, and, typically, an immediate connection with the process of nation building. Figure 26 identifies some of the factors and developmental stages that play a role in these decision-making processes. Language policy must consider the sociolinguistic realities which it builds on at a given point in time, but it also needs to develop goals and modes of implementing the decisions taken, as well as some sort of a feedback control system to check after a while whether measures have been successful, or what should be changed. Obviously, the education system and language teaching issues play a major role in the implementation of such political decisions.

8.3 It's all about communicating: "International English," intelligibility, business English, and ELF

Another topic of current debate is the question of whether an "International English," a non-regional, common-core form of the language for use in transnational communication, e.g. in business circles, exists, or would be desirable. It has been postulated that such a language form has emerged, or should deliberately be promoted. This ties in with the general issue of "intelligibility," which has been projected as a political goal in some contexts. Obviously, there is a direct connection between the promotion of "standard" English as the target of education, the denigration of indigenous varieties, and the "complaint tradition" of deploring "falling standards" of competence, all, typically, in the interest of upholding international business connections – see Gill (2002) as a case in point, addressing these issues in Malaysia's context.

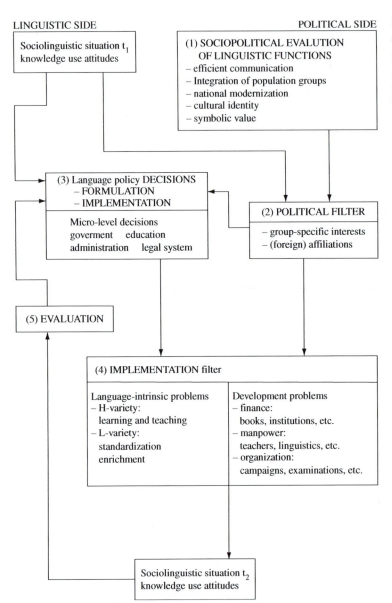

Figure 26 Flow diagram of phases and factors in language policy

(from Schmied 1991:188; reprinted by permission of Pearson Education)

In practice, this may mean little more than a strategy of avoiding overt regional markers in formal and intercultural contexts. It has been claimed that except for minor peculiarities on the levels of word choice and pronunciation, differences between national varieties of English are relatively inconspicuous, consisting mostly of subtle usage preferences which do not impede intelligibility. It is clear that there are, to use Crystal's (2004) term, "centripetal" forces in English promoting supranational homogeneity. Leaders in international interaction attempt to resort to the lexical and grammatical common core of the language and to near-standard (mostly

British or American) pronunciation norms to communicate successfully. But this is a natural and informal accommodation process. There is no "textbook" or authoritative description of "International English," and I don't think there is a need for one.

Personally, I am actually skeptical about some of these optimistic models, suggesting that our dedicated and bright leaders keep communicating impeccably in brightly lit conference centers in immaculate English. In reality, I think, a lot more muddling and struggling is going on on the ground, without anybody admitting this. Whenever I have a chance I ask friends or acquaintances in business or engineers with international contacts about how this works linguistically. I hear all kinds of interesting stories – about telephone conferences between Korean, Austrian, and American engineers in which a lot of time is spent trying to work out the others' intended meanings; about German technicians working hard to build a plant in collaboration with Chinese constructors; of questions and answers repeated and rephrased; and sometimes of failure to work out common ground. I hear no complaints – all of this is just considered natural, an unavoidable side effect, not the main point (which is getting along with one's business). Actually, it would be extremely interesting to study such situations empirically, but hardly any serious investigations of such encounters have been carried out. I suspect this is because the goal of keeping business details confidential usually keeps linguists and their microphones off-limits from such conferences and workplaces.

Ultimately, however, it's about communicating successfully, about getting one's message across. And, interestingly enough, it has been argued that second-language and learner varieties tend to be more intelligible and communicatively successful than sophisticated but possibly hard-to-follow native-like forms. Consider Figure 27, from China. Clearly this represents a learner form of English, even if it obviously comes from a rather formal, public context. Speakers from many countries would probably not use these exact compounds and use their articles differently. But the message is clear, and I suspect *working time* and *run time* are in fact more transparent and more immediately accessible than, say, *operating hours*.

A closely related topic, much better documented by linguists, is the use of "English as a Lingua Franca," or "ELF," between speakers of different languages. Vienna's VOICE project, for instance, makes transcripts of conversations between international students available on the internet (www.univie.ac.at/voice). It has been shown that in these intercultural encounters reductive processes (avoidance of complex words and structures, substitution of difficult sounds, omission of morphological endings) occur which show parallels with some features of Outer Circle Englishes. Whether ELF constitutes, or should be posited as, or is emerging to become a distinct

Figure 27 Expressive learner forms in China

language form, a norm of its own, is very much open to debate, however. The same applies to the related question of whether a "Euro English," a non-British continental European way of using English, perhaps in the corridors of the Brussels eurocracy, exists or would be desirable. I suppose these conflicts can be resolved by abstaining from viewing a language as an entity, a "secluded whole" which "exists" somehow in an abstract space (and in grammar books and dictionaries, of course), i.e. by adopting the processual view of language introduced in the previous chapter. In all these encounters English is just enacted, in whatever (variable) form, and somehow it simply works in immediate application and negotiation, in communication as a process.

8.4 **Whose norms?**

But admittedly, for certain purposes (school teaching, most importantly), some sort of a target, a set of norms, is required. A question of quite some practical importance in many countries, especially in schools, is which forms of English are accepted as "correct" or are posited as targets of language education. Typically, an exonormative tradition, upholding British English and Received Pronunciation, prevails in many postcolonial and Outer Circle countries, even if it usually clashes with internal realities, where local accents and language forms are predominant and RP is an unrealistic goal. To quote two examples: even if the West African Examinations Council and the Caribbean Examinations Council uphold the ideal of "standard English" (typically meaning "British English"), hardly any African or Caribbean speakers really produce an RP accent; and I am told that in Singapore's classrooms, despite the government's insistence on "good English," a lot of Singlish is being spoken – if only to generate understanding and rapport between teachers and students.

Thus, in the long run the forces of reality seem to be working in favor of changes towards endonormativity, the acceptance of educated local forms of English as correct (Schneider 2009). Endonormative orientations have been suggested in many countries (in Nigeria, for instance), and it has been proposed to describe the English used by educated local speakers and models (politicians, media leaders, and so on) as the forms students should also strive for. So far such suggestions have not found official approval, however – perhaps with the exception, to some extent, of India, where the Central Institute of English and Foreign Languages (CIEFL) in Hyderabad, renamed in 2007 as "English and Foreign Languages University," has contributed a lot to the description and acceptance of Indian English.

To accept new or modified norms requires some sort of a consensus, obviously, as to what they consist of. This leads to a perennial question. Given that the traditional benchmark is British or "standard" English, how should a distinction be made between an "error," deviant from some norm, and a consistent, acceptable new feature of a new variety of English? There is no easy answer to this. Basically, forms and features which are used regularly and by educated speakers of local English should ultimately qualify and be accepted as elements of a new, emerging standard variety. To successfully implement such a policy, codification will be required – the systematic and empirical analysis and description of educated indigenous forms of English in dictionaries and grammars. In addition, attitudes will have to change significantly, especially on the side of political authorities and educational gatekeepers – New Englishes would have to be endowed with overt prestige in the future. At the moment, the only region where such a change has taken place is Australia. A few decades ago British English was clearly considered the norm there, the language form required in the Australian Broadcasting Corporation's news programs, for instance. By today, however, this has changed dramatically. Australian English is nowadays accepted as an appropriate national norm, growing into the role of a regional (Pacific) lead variety. The *Macquarie Dictionary*, which at the time of its publication contributed significantly to this reorientation, codifies its lexis, and work on establishing its grammatical characteristics is making substantial progress (see Peters, Collins, and Smith 2009).

All of the other New Englishes are a few steps behind, however. They may be enjoying covert prestige right now, but they lack official recognition. Still, this positive attitude towards local Englishes, their adoption as carriers of regional identities, also marks an important step toward their ultimate acceptance. As has been pointed out, in many countries distinctive local forms of English are increasingly positively evaluated as expressions of regional identities there. Singlish is a case in point, but similar tendencies, often in opposition with official policy-makers, can be observed widely. We have reports which document that in Malaysian business training sessions, for instance, during breaks the instructors deliberately fall back to distinctively local ways of English usage (avoided during the "official" parts of the sessions) in order to establish social proximity with the participants. Structurally, what frequently happens in such cases is that individual features (words, phrases, pronunciation details, etc.) are selected and "recycled" to serve expressive symbolic purposes. Much of this operates subconsciously and automatically, though some forms then may become overt markers – New Zealanders know of their habit of centralizing the i-vowel (thus saying "fush and chups"), and Singaporeans regard the particle *la* as an indicator of their own colloquial style.

8.5 Whose language? "Native," "first," "dominant," or what?

One reason why differences between New Englishes and, say, British English are typically interpreted as deviance from a pre-existing norm is the assumption that perfect knowledge of a language comes from the status of being a native speaker. This concept thus gives Inner Circle speakers a kind of natural authority: they are assumed to acquire their language competence from the crib, as it were. This view is increasingly challenged today, however, and rightly so. It has been shown that the notion of nativeness stems very largely from nineteenth-century nationalism, construing a special relationship between an individual's "pure" national ancestry and his or her language knowledge (Hackert 2009).

In the anglicized corners of today's globalized world, things are much more complicated than that, however. In many countries there are speakers whose command of the language and exposure to it come close to those

Figure 28 Children growing up in Yaoundé, Cameroon, speaking English natively

of native speakers, or who would need to be classified as such. There are speakers who, despite having grown up for the first few years of their lives with an indigenous mother tongue, now use mostly or only English in their daily lives – some linguists would call them "dominant" or "first" language speakers of English. Accordingly, Kachru distinguished "functional nativeness" from "genetic nativeness," thus arguing that these "functionally native" speakers are entitled to claim "ownership" of the language as well.

Increasingly, however, there are also native speakers of New Englishes in a straightforward sense. In Africa and Asia many speakers acquire English (or, in some regions, Pidgin English) as their "first" language in early childhood, either exclusively or together with indigenous tongues. Figure 28 shows Daniela and Edgar as an example, children who are growing up in Yaoundé, Cameroon, speaking English only.

These children may be taken to symbolize a growing trend. Increasingly frequently, primarily in urban and educated contexts, parents choose English as a family language, and children born into such marriages are thus raised as native speakers of English. In part this may be motivated by the idea of giving their children a competitive edge later in life; in other cases English just happens to be the language which parents from different ethnic backgrounds share. In many countries this may still be a marginal phenomenon; but in some of Africa's rapidly growing cities this description is reported to apply to a few percent of the population (nobody has exact statistics), and in Singapore, as was mentioned earlier, more than a third of all children grow up with English acquired from the earliest days of childhood.

Oddly enough, the notion of "mother tongue" is frequently not applied in these instances, as it tends to be emotionally loaded and reserved for ethnic ancestral languages. This is officially the case in Singapore, for example. "Mother Tongue," in the nation's official political lingo, is reserved for the Asian ancestral languages which children have to learn in school, even if, strictly speaking, the children do not even understand these languages. For Chinese children, for example, their "mother tongue" is Mandarin by definition, while in fact they may have learned Hokkien or Cantonese, not mutually intelligible with Mandarin, from their parents. This strange political language leads to the absurd consequence that Singapore's Eurasians, a small population group of European and Asian ancestry who for generations have spoken English in their homes, do not officially have a "mother tongue" at all – as English is not permissible in that role. By implication, a similar understanding obtains in Africa. I vividly remember a narrative which a Cameroonian fellow linguist once told me. She had asked her mother what her own mother tongue was, and her mother gave her the name of her family's ancestral African tongue – to which the child's response was "But Mum, I don't speak that language at all!" This shows how deeply ideological the terms "native speaker" and "mother tongue" are.

8.6 Language mixing and cultural hybridity

It is interesting to see that one of the strongest trends to be observed in Outer Circle countries is the ubiquity of mixed language varieties. In most of the countries under discussion English is not replacing indigenous languages – it is simply added on to persistent local language habits, and it thus contributes to the growth of cultural hybridity. Indigenous cultures are westernized, and speakers move freely from local to western modes of behavior and back. Frequently, such hybrid cultures and orientations are explicitly expressed and symbolized through mixed codes, linguistic usage in which speakers switch freely between English and local languages on all levels. Words or phrases from one language are liberally embedded into discourse in the other, or there is constant switching between clauses, sentences, and longer utterances from either language into the other going on.

Figure 29 Euro-Asian cultural hybridity (Melaka, Malaysia)

Such mixed language forms are widely used in multilingual settings, especially among young people and in urban and educated contexts. There is also a momentum of playfulness here, but essentially these mixed codes are not fun products; they are deliberately chosen as appropriate expressions of the speakers' multicultural and multilingual backgrounds and personalities, their culturally hybrid identities. Notice that this applies strongly to linguistic usage, but it also manifests itself in distinctly fused "transcultural" forms of expression, such as Japanese hip hop (cf. Pennycook 2007) or the like, symbolized, if you so wish, in Figure 29.

Some of these mixed codes have been mentioned in this book, and three were actually illustrated in Chapter 6 – Malaysia's mixed variety, and Kenya's Sheng and Engsh. In northern India, "Hinglish" is reported to be spreading vigorously, also in the media and in advertising. In the Philippines, Taglish seems to be moving into the role of a socially unmarked informal mode of conversation in addition to being used in the media. Similar phenomena are found in South Africa, Hong Kong (sometimes called "mix-mix," associated primarily with students), Cameroon (with Camfranglais also incorporating a French component), and elsewhere. Gatekeepers of linguistic propriety tend to resent these mixed varieties everywhere, for fear of seeing "good," pure, standard forms of languages polluted. In reality, it's just the opposite: these are language habits which are cognitively creative and culturally appropriate.

8.7 **Pedagogical strategies and considerations**

New Englishes are mostly second languages, so obviously learning and teaching are important issues in discussing them, in particular in local contexts. Hence, World Englishes is very much an Applied Linguistics discipline, especially so in Asia and Africa, where many scholars and teachers are primarily interested in teaching strategies and pedagogical issues.

In Outer Circle countries, the conditions of acquiring and learning English vary widely. In a sense, natural language acquisition – the Nigerian market lady, the Indian rickshaw driver in contact with tourists – are part of this continuum, and there are also many speakers who acquire English quite informally, and nonetheless successfully. However, as this section focuses on pedagogical strategies let us have a closer look at formal schooling contexts. Here there is a wide range too, from an African village school with hardly any resources to top-ranking Asian universities. But it seems that economic constraints and cultural traditions, an emphasis on hierarchies and authority, have produced some similarities in early phases of teaching English which can be found in several countries.

In general, it is probably fair to say that repetitive and passive language skills tend to be given priority over productive language usage, and in many cases writing receives more attention than speaking. In many countries language teaching is characterized by a tradition of rote learning, reading out loud and chorus repetition (think of Li Yang's "Crazy English" teaching method in China, mentioned in the previous chapter!). Much energy tends to go into vocabulary learning, the teaching of "grammar rules," and also into the development of reading and translation skills. In comparison, less emphasis is given to the development of oral fluency and the goal of achieving "communicative competence," i.e. to practicing speaking and appropriate language use in situations. But knowing or learning a language is mainly about the ability to communicate, so it is clear that these oral skills need to be given more weight these days. The need for such a redirection is evident. It has been observed, for example, that government schools in India equip students with a baseline knowledge in vocabulary and grammar but that students who can afford to do so supplement this by frequenting commercial institutes which offer spoken English courses. So it doesn't come as a surprise that offers specifically for "Spoken English," as in Figure 30, are flourishing.

This observation highlights a wider aspect which cannot be neglected today. Teaching and learning English is also big business nowadays. It is a hugely profitable battleground for dictionary producers and other publishing houses, for language schools and trainers, and for institutions like

Figure 30 Teaching "Spoken English" is big business (India)

the British Council. Of course, many of the companies offering such teaching materials, tools, and services are based in Inner Circle countries, notably England, so upholding the old myth that only British English is the best and the only "correct" form of the language is in their immediate interest. The same applies to staff-recruiting strategies. In many countries it is sufficient to be a native speaker to be employed as a language teacher, without requiring any language teaching (or TESOL, "Teaching English to speakers of other languages") training and without any familiarity with indigenous cultures or languages. But this is a problem – a teacher freshly recruited from, say, Nebraska to teach English somewhere in China will face difficulties in understanding the grammatical, phonological, and cultural problems which his or her students will be faced with, and thus in giving appropriate advice.

This ties in with the central political question mentioned before, the choice of a target variety in language education. An exonormative orientation, favoring native-speaker and usually British English, is opposed to an endonormative attitude which would accept educated local forms of using English as the goal for students to strive for. Exonormativity is supported by history and tradition, and by the assumption that this is the "best," or perhaps even the only "correct," form of the language, which, thus, naturally must be offered to (and expected from) students. And of course it is also promoted by the availability of books, teaching materials, and so on, pushed by international publishing houses. But it comes with a price, and a high one at that, a permanent lie, as it were. The implied goal of "passing for a native" is bound to produce permanent frustration, while it gives a huge advantage to British speakers. An undeserved one, though – the only reasonably sounding cause for such a choice has been intelligibility, but, as was stated before, it has been shown that ESL varieties, typically marked by a syllable-timed rhythm and more careful articulation, are actually more intelligible to speakers of other Englishes than natives.

Endonormative teaching targets are much more realistic to achieve, and also more sensitive to local cultural needs. And they have the additional advantage of developing and supporting local resources. Kirkpatrick (2007) argues that indigenous teachers of English, even if they are second-language users themselves, may be much more appropriate and successful in that role because they share the students' cultural and linguistic, often multilingual, backgrounds. They are also familiar with acquisition strategies and the specific learning difficulties which are to be expected, having learned English as a second language themselves, with all the difficulties involved in this process. Currently such strategy considerations are under debate in many countries. In the long run I am convinced that the way to go is the pooling and development of local resources, the recruitment of well-trained teachers from the respective countries, and the recognition of indigenous cultural background factors and, in most cases, multilingual resources.

Chapter summary

In this chapter we have considered a number of sociocultural contexts and considerations in which the emergence and acquisition of World Englishes are embedded, and we have seen that a number of important political issues are at stake in which competing views and interests become effective. English exists both as an elitist code, disseminated by formal education and as such mainly reserved for the upper echelons in a society, and as a useful tool acquired and striven for by the less affluent in simpler schooling conditions or just naturally, in everyday encounters. It can be viewed as detrimental to indigenous languages and cultures, sacrificing them in the interest of globalization and internationalization, but in contrast it emerges increasingly frequently as a language of opportunity and of liberalization, and also as a local identity carrier in a distinctly indigenous form, no longer perceived as alien by its users. Proposals and models on the development of an "International English," of globally intelligible business English forms, or of explicit "Lingua Franca" norms were outlined but viewed with some skepticism, arguing that in reality speakers just communicate with each other somehow, working out their shared purpose in mutual interactions (and largely independent of language norm considerations). The tension between exonormative and endonormative orientations, most importantly in teaching contexts, was discussed, arguing that the move towards endo-normativity is desirable and likely to be successful in the long run. All of this was viewed against a critical view of the notion of a "native speaker," shown to have been rooted in English nationalism and to be no longer appropriate in today's multilingual and multicultural settings. We found that, when looking closely, global reality has produced "native speakers" of "ESL" varieties in surprisingly large numbers, a fact which seems contra-dictory in itself, at least in a conservative perspective. The fact that complex identities in multicultural environments find their most widespread expres-sions in rapidly growing mixed codes was briefly pointed out. Finally, pedagogical conditions and considerations resulting from the growth of World Englishes were weighed, and an argument for endonormative targets and indigenous, multicultural teachers was put forward.

Exercises and activities

Exercise 8a	Contextualize and assess your own acquisition of English in the light of the parameters addressed in this chapter. How much formal tuition did you receive on issues of lexis, pronunciation, or grammar? Has your usage ever been corrected, and if so, was this justified?
Exercise 8b	How about your experience with successful or unsuccessful international or intercultural communication in English?
Exercise 8c	Do you have any views on whether the global spread of English is "good" or "bad," useful or doing harm? Discuss.
Exercise 8d	Do you think there is a need for an "International English"? If so, which language elements should be part of it, and who would be entitled to decide such matters?
Exercise 8e	Do you think that native speakers automatically speak "better" English than non-native speakers? Do you think teachers of English should preferably be native speakers, or not? Provide arguments for your position.

Exercise 8f   As a non-native academic user of English, I remember having been told by an American dialect speaker on one occasion: "Well, you at least studied English at the University – I only learned it on the street; you speak it right, I don't." Does such an attitude sound familiar? What would you think of it?

Key terms discussed in this chapter
complaint tradition
elitism
endonormativity
English as a Lingua Franca (ELF)
Euro English
exonormativity
identity
indirect rule
intelligibility
killer language
mixed language varieties
mother tongue
native speaker
norms (of language teaching)
pedagogy
Speak Good English Movement (SGEM; Singapore)
TESOL
transcultural

Further reading
Brutt-Griffler (2002) discusses the historical expansion of English with a special eye on teaching contexts and its elitist character in former times. There is a fairly rich literature on code-switching and bilingualism (e.g. Myers-Scotton 2002, Gardner-Chloros 2009), but so far no survey of mixed codes involving World Englishes has been published. Thompson (2003) presents a very rich case study of language mixing in the Philippines. Issues of norm-setting, international English, or lingua franca uses are widely discussed in the World Englishes literature; many pertinent texts are collected in Kachru, Kachru, and Nelson (2006) and in Bolton and Kachru (2006). Seidlhofer's (2003) collection compiles and contextualizes readings with highly controversial views on the globalization of English, linguistic imperialism, language teaching strategies, and other related issues. Kirkpatrick (2007) surveys World Englishes particularly in the light of language teaching issues. His concluding chapter is very much in line with the views which I have also presented above.

CHAPTER 9

Conclusion

We have tracked down the English language in its historical diffusion, across several continents, moving into all kinds of countries and blending with all kinds of cultures. Certainly this is a most remarkable process, resulting from and at the same time enabling further degrees of globalization, the world becoming a single "global village," as Marshall McLuhan predicted in the 1960s. We have seen that this process has many forms and facets, and it can be viewed from a variety of perspectives – political, social, pedagogical, structural – you name it.

Has this been a success story? Somehow yes, certainly – but the focus on English as a language should not distract our attention from the fact that essentially all of this is about people and their desire to communicate with each other. Communication to our mutual benefit is what counts. If English serves as a useful tool in this process, fine; if other languages – indigenous ones, regional ones, other global ones – do the job, all the better. What the world needs is peaceful mutual respect; there is no need for any people or any language to dominate others. (I realize I'm being idealistic here, but ideals are important as goals, even if by their very nature they do not conform to reality.) There have been speculations on the future of English (Graddol 1997), and one view is that English will actually be declining again, with other national and regional languages like Chinese, Bahasa Indonesia, Hindi, or Spanish growing, together with their native speaker numbers. At the moment, however, no severe break in the further expansion of English is foreseeable. Given frequent pedagogical, political, and prescriptive interference, or at least attempts at it, one question is whether, and to what extent and in which direction this process of the global spread and local adoption of English can be, and should be, steered. At this point, it seems clear that the process is simply continuing on its own, in many ways and directions, and it will be worth observing.

English itself has been significantly transformed in this process, however. The term increasingly used for this process is "glocalization." The English language has been globalized, has become the world's leading language, but at the same time, as we have seen in many instances and case studies, it is being localized, fusing with indigenous language input to yield new dialects suitable for the expression of local people's hearts and minds. This, I think, is not only a most fascinating process but also an encouraging perspective.

In the presence of strongly prescriptive traditions, this is a piece of reality which needs wider recognition. English is not just the codified standard that we tend to associate with it and that our school teachers talk about – it is also any utterance produced by any indigenous speaker around the globe. We need mutual respect between different ethnolinguistic groups, which in many societies must include the promotion of bi- and multilingualism, depending on peoples' needs and desires, but should also entail the acceptance of different, localized forms of English.

One last word – a word of reflection and encouragement, if I may. It's simple. If you have a chance to go to other places and to see, or listen, for yourself, do so. I hope you've found this book interesting; but it doesn't compare to the richness and versatility and creativity of real life, and of all the linguistic and cultural diversity out there. As an academic from a rather wealthy country I have been privileged and lucky. I've had a chance to visit many of the countries I have written about, to talk to people there, and to tune in to many of these Englishes. Many speakers have offered their accents and their world views to me, and many colleagues, in many conversations and activities, have shared their more intense familiarity with local situations and customs with me. I have always treasured these experiences, I am immensely grateful for them, and I would like to share them. I am not blind to the fact that being able to travel is a huge privilege in itself, of course. Those of us who happen to be among the lucky few, in global terms, who get this opportunity shouldn't forget we are privileged, and we should do your best to develop the respect for other cultures that results as an obligation from that privilege. It also entails an obligation to contribute to the empowerment of those who are less fortunate. In my view, both improving access to English for anybody wishing to get access to it and strengthening the respect of indigenous cultures and languages contribute to such empowerment.

But we need to appreciate diversity, in language behavior and patterns of life, and to contribute to the knowledge about each other. Local people are typically as interested in visitors as the latter are the other way round. As the speaker I quoted in my first chapter said, in a slightly different context: "knowledge is generator." True. Let us generate mutual respect by learning and knowing more about each other, and by appreciating the diversity of life and language patterns. Variability is a core property of both languages and cultures, a property which generates novelty, socially successful communication, and joint development – things we all need in a globalized and glocalized world.

Key terms discussed in this chapter
empowerment
global village
glocalization

Appendix 1: Phonetic characters (IPA symbols) employed

Unlike letters, IPA characters represent individual sounds. This Appendix cannot replace a course or book in phonetics, but for the benefit of readers with little or no training in phonetics (or those who need a reminder) here is an attempt at defining the sound symbols by explaining what happens in the mouth in the articulation of the respective sounds. (Further phonetic terms are explained in the Glossary.)

Fundamentally and also in terms of articulatory processes, it makes sense to distinguish vowels from consonants.

Vowels

The difference between how individual vowels sound (their "quality") is achieved by

- different degrees of opening the mouth, which correlate with a higher or lower position of the hump which the tongue forms, and
- by moving this hump (the "back" of the tongue) back and forth.

So it is defined best by indicating the position of the back of the tongue on a two-dimensional plane insider the oral cavity, with the two dimensions being defined as

- "high–low" and
- "front–back."

(For the "high–low" dimension the terms "close–open" are also used.)

The shape of this two-dimensional space, within which the hump of the tongue can move, roughly has the shape of a trapezium, so the quality of any individual vowel (symbol) is conventionally indicated by showing its position in this "vowel trapezium."

Incidentally, how a vowel sounds is also determined by whether or not, or how far, the lips are protruded ("rounded"), but in English this tends to be less important because back vowels are usually rounded and front vowels are not, so let's ignore this for the time being.

It is also customary to distinguish "short" and "long" vowels (with length indicated by a colon /ː/ after the respective vowel symbol), although in reality and in many varieties this is actually more complicated – length and temporal duration do not always go together, and "long" and "short" vowels just tend to sound slightly differently.

On that basis, the vowels of English (based on British English RP as a reference variety) in the vowel trapezium and their respective symbols are roughly as follows:

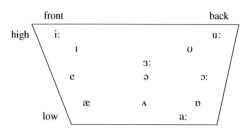

/iː/ as in *beat*

/ɪ/ as in *bit*

/e/ as in *bed*

/æ/ as in *bad*

/ɜː/ as in *bird*

/ə/ as in *a(bout)*

/ʌ/ as in *but*

/aː/ as in *part*

/uː/ as in *fool*

/ʊ/ as in *full*

/ɔː/ as in *Paul*

/ɒ/ as in *pot*

The symbol /ɛ/ is sometimes used to represent a slightly more open variant of /e/.

In the case of the diphthongs, roughly the starting and finishing point of a gliding movement are indicated:

/eɪ/ as in *day*

/aʊ/ as in *house*

/eə/ as in *there*

/aɪ/ as in *time*

/əʊ/ as in *show*

/ɪə/ as in *here*

/ɔɪ/ as in *boy*

/ʊə/ as in *cure*

Consonants

Consonants result from some sort of major impediment of the air stream in the oral cavity. They are defined by where ("place of articulation") and how ("manner of articulation") this impediment is produced.

Typically, consonants come in pairs of voiceless (vocal cords not vibrating) vs. voiced (vocal cords vibrating). However, nasals and approximants are always voiced.

Simplifying the scheme somewhat, the following can be distinguished:

Places of articulation

- *bilabial* (both lips)
- *labiodental* (lower lips and upper teeth)
- *dental* (between the teeth)
- *alveolar* (at the ridge behind the upper teeth inside the mouth)
- *palatal* (at the front, bone part of the roof of the mouth)
- *velar* (at the back, tissue part of the roof of the mouth)

Manners of articulation

- *stops* (also called plosives): momentary closure of oral cavity, behind which the air pressure increases and is then suddenly released
- *fricatives*: strong, audible friction produced by two articulators close to each other

- *affricates*: intrinsic combination of a stop and friction movement at the same place
- *nasals*: sounds produced with the mouth closed at some point, and the air stream escaping through the nose

In addition there are the *approximants*, which have special properties which make them "approximate" vowels in some respects – in being always voiced, for instance (and are not charted below):

- the *semi-vowels* /j/ and /w/ (close to the vowels /i/ and /u/ but with more friction);
- the lateral /l/ (with a groove-shaped tongue formation in the palatal region), and
- /r/ (which can be realized in a number of ways, varying from one region to another).

Finally, there is /h/, essentially unmodulated air stream.

This yields the following consonants:

	bilabial	labio-dental	dental	alveolar	palatal	velar
stops	p b			t d		k g
fricatives		f v	θ ð	s z	ʃ ʒ	
affricates				tʃ dʒ		
nasals	m			n		ŋ

/p/ as in *pit*, /b/ as in *bit* /t/ as in *tip*, /d/ as in *dig*   /k/ as in *kit*, /g/ as in *get*
/f/ as in *fit*, /v/ as in *live* /θ/ as in *thing*, /ð/ as in *this* /s/ as in *sing*, /z/ as in *zeal*
                                                 /ʃ/ as in *ship*, /ʒ/ as in *pleasure*

/tʃ/ as in *chip*   /dʒ/ as in *job*
/m/ as in *map*   /n/ as in *net*   /ŋ/ as in *sing*
/j/ as in *young*   /w/ as in *what*
/l/ as in *long*   /r/ as in *ring*   /h/ as in *hit*

Appendix 2: A list of guiding questions on English in any specific region

Let us assume you wish or need to get more specific and to work out more detailed information on English as used Anywhere-in-the-World – perhaps for a paper, a class presentation, or the like. It may be tempting to replicate what you find in any source, but it is more interesting and more challenging to ask a few principled questions and to see whether it is possible to find responses. Here are a few guiding questions which you can ask and apply practically anywhere, and which will help you to structure your work:

1 History

- When did English arrive in your area, who brought it there, and why?
- When and how did it spread and develop? What was the sociolinguistic and cultural background of its early uses and developments? Was it used only by native-speaking in-migrants, or also by the indigenous population (and if so, [since] when, why, by whom)?
- Were there later settler groups or immigrant streams or other developments that modified or influenced its character?
- Which other languages and cultures did it get into contact with? What were the consequences of such contact?

2 Current political and sociocultural background; language attitudes; users and usage conditions

- Characterize your country with respect to its character, population structure, and political situation (especially insofar as these have consequences for the language situation).
- Are there any other languages spoken in your area? If so, which? What is the mutual relationship and role distribution between these languages like?
- Which are the major varieties (regional and social dialects), if any, of English in your area?
- What is the role of English in the educational system? In which school types / stages of education is it taught (subject of instruction) or used (medium of instruction)?

- Is there a prevailing attitude towards English or its varieties?
- If English is not the only language used in your country: Who uses it characteristically (regionally, socially), in which typical domains/situations/styles? Similarly, if different forms of English are used in your area: what is the functional distribution of its varieties?

3 Structural characteristics, norms, and varieties

- Which forms (words, sounds, word forms, constructions) are characteristic of English as used in your area on the levels of vocabulary, pronunciation, and grammar? Define and exemplify these! (Note: you have to be selective and exemplary in dealing with this question!)
- Are speakers aware of these characteristics, and any peculiarities of the way they speak English? Do others recognize the origin of a speaker from your area, and if so, by means of which characteristics?
- Are there several varieties of English found in your area? If so, how do they differ from each other in their linguistic properties, in their sociolinguistic assignments, and in their conditions of use?
- Which kind of English counts as the locally correct "norm," to be aimed at and used in education, in formal situations, etc.? British / American / local?

4 Documentation and research coverage; codification (grammars, dictionaries)

- Characterize the amount and kind of documentation that we have on English in your area in general terms. Are there any introductory descriptive surveys which cover this form of English specifically?
- How much research has been carried out, or writing been done, on your variety of English in recent years? Which have been major topics of investigation, and local concerns (descriptive, sociolinguistic, political, pedagogical)?
- Has English in your area achieved any kind of codification? For instance, is there a special dictionary on English in your area available? If so, how comprehensive is it, and what is its goal? Have any grammatical characteristics been described, or accepted as a local norm?

5 Global assessment and possible future perspectives

- Is English as used in your area highly distinctive, or, conversely, quite similar to or closely related with other (neighboring?) Englishes? To which other varieties can it reasonably be compared?
- On the basis of all the facts that you have assembled – can you make an educated guess as to its possible future fate and development?

Note that these are guiding questions that we can use to assess, compare, and relate individual varieties, and that might lead you in your search for relevant information, but this listing of topics and questions is meant to be suggestive and helpful; there is no need to adhere to it slavishly! Several questions will not apply to certain varieties/areas, and others will be relatively more or less important, or more or less well covered. On some questions it may be difficult, or even impossible, to find answers, or the answers that we have may necessarily remain fuzzy or speculative.

Glossary

adjective   a major grammatical word class, e.g. *old, happy, beautiful, diligent.* Adjectives usually allow comparative and superlative forms (e.g. *happier, most attractive*); they typically premodify a ⇒ noun in a ⇒ noun phrase (e.g. *a sad story*) or build a predicate with a ⇒ copula verb (e.g. *she is nice*); they are assumed to express "qualities" or "properties."

adverb   a major grammatical word class, frequently derived from an ⇒ adjective by a suffix *-ly* and typically realizing an ⇒ adverbial, e.g. *highly, rapidly*, but also premodifying adjectives, e.g. *very*

adverbial   a major, typically non-obligatory, syntactic function which modifies the verb or clause and gives temporal, local, causal, or modal information, typically realized by an adverb, a prepositional phrase, or a clause, e.g. *then, behind the wall, because they didn't know*

affix   a ⇒ morpheme attached to a word, typically either a ⇒ prefix or a ⇒ suffix

affricate   a consonantal sound type which inherently combines a stop and a friction movement. In English these are voiceless /tʃ/ (in *chip*) and voiced /dʒ/ (in *job*)

alveolar   a place of articulation for consonants in the mouth; the ridge of bone immediately behind the teeth. Alveolar sounds are /t/, /d/, and /n/.

article   a word class, a sub-class of ⇒ determiners, coming as definite article (*the*) or indefinite article (*a/an*)

aspiration   a strongly audible breath-like sound component, esp. in association with voiceless stops, e.g. *tip* sounds like *tʰip*

auxiliary   a class of verbs which mainly perform syntactic functions (and mostly need to be complemented by a full verb in the predicate), e.g. *is, are, had, will, might*

bilabial   a place of articulation for consonants, involving both lips

bilingual(ism)   regular use (and full command) of two languages, by individuals or speech communities

borrowing   use of ⇒ loan words

calque   item-by-item replacement of words or morphemes of one language in another, thus rendering a phrase or idiom; e.g. the compound *eye water* 'tears' in the Caribbean, reflecting a combination of the equivalents of *eye + water* meaning 'tears' in an African substrate language

clause   a simple sentence; a minimally complete syntactic unit, consisting of at least a subject and a predicate (plus, possibly, objects, adverbials, etc.). Clauses can constitute functional parts of (complex) sentences ("be embedded in them"), e.g. the underlined units in *After he entered she left* or *What he said is not true.*

complementation   the property of verbs to require or allow certain grammatical constituents only (like noun phrases or certain clauses) to build a complete sentence

complementizer   a function word introducing and connecting a clausal complement, e.g. *that* introducing an object clause in *I knew that he'd come*

consonants   a major class of sounds, characterized by the fact that the air stream from the lungs is strongly hindered or even temporarily interrupted somewhere in the mouth, yielding different consonants like /p/, /g/, /v/, or /s/

consonant cluster   a sequence of two or more consonants in a row, e.g. in *stripped* /strɪpt/

consonant cluster reduction ("CCR")   a tendency to omit one consonant (typically the last one) in a consonant cluster, e.g. *and > an'*, *test > tes'*

constituent   functional unit of a sentence; a group of words (phrase or clause) which together fulfill a syntactic function, e.g. subject or adverbial

conversion   a process of forming a new word of a different word class without changing its form, e.g. *bridge > to bridge*, *up/down > the ups and downs*

copula   a verbal function which connects a ⇒ subject and a predicative ⇒ adjective, typically realized by a form of the verb *be*, e.g. *they were wrong*

count nouns   nouns perceived as denoting distinct, countable entities, thus having the grammatical properties of allowing pluralization and of following numerals or indefinite articles

creole   a class of languages resulting from heavy language contact and restructuring, typically amongst slaves in European plantation colonies; characterized by a mixture of substrate (especially in the grammar) and superstrate (especially in lexis) influences

deictic   the function of identifying an entity by "pointing" to it in the immediate environment, usually expressed by words such as *this*, *here*, or (referring to a point in time) *now*

dental   a place of articulation for consonants, involving the teeth

dialect   a language form associated with a particular region (regional dialect) or a social group (social dialect)

dialect mixing   a process in which speakers or speaker groups of different but related dialects come to communicate with each other on a regular basis and thereby pick up each others' dialect characteristics, thus possibly creating a new "mixed" dialect

determiner   a class of function words which typically introduce a noun phrase and determine the reference of the noun, e.g. *the, those, an, some*

diphthong   a type of ⇒ vowel characterized by a gliding movement of the tongue from one position to another and thus sounding like a sequence of two vowels, as in /eɪ/ in *day* or *rate*, or /aɪ/ in *time* or *high*

direct object   an ⇒ object after a ⇒ monotransitive verb, typically understood as the entity affected by the activity expressed by the verb, e.g. *They beat their opponents*, *Mary wanted you to come*, typically asked for by "Who" [did they beat?] or "What" [did she want?]

discourse particles   words or (usually short) word groups which primarily serve to structure conversations, e.g. by signaling the start of a turn or a speaker's attitude to what is said, e.g. *Well, you know, really*

ditransitive   the grammatical property of certain verbs to require or imply two objects, a direct and an indirect one, e.g. *find me*[indirO] *a partner*[dirO]; a kind of verb ⇒ complementation

do-**support**   the fact that English full verbs require an auxiliary *do* in certain constructions, most notably negation and interrogatives; cf. *they know* but *they do not know* and *do they know?*

Early Modern English   the period of the English language roughly from the fifteenth century to *c.* 1700, including the earliest stages of colonial expansion

endonormative   an attitude which promotes forms of behavior (e.g. language forms) used within a community as norm

epenthesis   insertion of a sound in a word, typically of a vowel to break up a consonant cluster, e.g. *film > filim*

exonormative   an attitude which promotes forms of behavior (e.g. language forms) used within another community (but not one's own) as norm

first person   a grammatical category referring to or including the speaker, typically expressed by the pronouns *I* and *we*

founder effect / principle   the idea that in a newly formed community (e.g. a colonial settlement) the earliest, "founder" members / generations had a disproportionally large impact upon an emerging norm

fricative   a class of ⇒ consonants, characterized by the air stream from the lungs being strongly impeded by a narrowing of the mouth somewhere so that audible friction is produced, as in /s/ or /f/

function words   word classes whose job it is mainly to express grammatical functions, i.e. relations between other words, such as prepositions (e.g. *to, for, with*), conjunctions (e.g. *and, because, when*), pronouns (*it, they*), etc.

glocal   a mixture of global and local; local adaptations of objects (including language forms) which have spread globally

glottal stop   a consonant-like sound produced by a sudden opening of the vocal folds, occasionally rendered in writing by *uh-uh*

grammar   the set or rules which regulate how a language "works," i.e. how a sentence is composed out of relatively simple units such as words; typically assumed to subsume ⇒ syntax and ⇒ morphology

grammaticalization   a long-term recategorization process in which a formerly lexical word loses some of its meaning and becomes a grammatical item, a function word, e.g. *(a) front > in front of; (by the) cause (of) > because*

Great Vowel Shift   a systematic series of changes of long vowels in English which essentially modified all pronunciations of long vowels and diphthongs, roughly between the fourteenth and seventeenth centuries

head   the most important word in a syntactic ⇒ phrase, which also defines the category of the phrase, e.g. the core noun in a noun phrase: *the old man in the garden*

hybridity   a fusion of two entities from culturally different sources – in the present context mostly a mixture of components from two different languages

identity   a sociological concept which states that speakers establish and symbolize subjectively important group coherence, distinguishing "us" from "them," amongst other things by symbolic means such as dress, hairdo, and conventions of behavior including dialect usage

idiom   an expression which consists of several words but is non-transparent, i.e. knowing the words does not help in knowing the meaning of the idiom; e.g. *kick the bucket, spill the beans*; thus, a kind of multi-word lexeme

indirect object   an ⇒ object after a ⇒ ditransitive verb, typically nominal with a human referent and understood as the "beneficiary," a person benefiting from an activity or receiving something (the direct object), e.g. *I gave my friend that money, They told me the truth*

indirect rule   a principle of governance, employed in British colonies, in which indigenous rulers are formally in power but in fact serve the interests of the colonial power

inflection   appending a grammatical suffix to a word (e.g. plural -*s* to a noun, past tense -*ed* to a verb)

intelligibility   the property of a linguistic expression of being easily understood

International Phonetics Association   a scholarly organization, founded in 1886, the goal of which is to promote and to provide a consistent framework for the study and description of speech sounds in any human language

intransitive   the grammatical property of certain verbs to be able to stand alone, i.e. not to require an object, as in *she was smiling*; a kind of verb ⇒ complementation

interrogative   question structure, syntactically typically marked by ⇒ inversion

invariant   not changing its form in different grammatical functions and contexts

inversion   the movement of an auxiliary verb in front of its subject, usually to mark a question; cf. affirmative *he is right* vs. interrogative *is he right?*

isomorphism   a cognitive principle of language structure claiming a one-to-one relationship between a minimum "concept" and a linguistic form, i.e. each "idea" has and is realized by a form of its own; e.g. *wanted* = *want* 'want' + -*ed* 'past'

koinéization   a process of contact between speakers of different but related dialects which leads to the emergence of a *koiné*, a fairly neutral compromise dialect devoid of strongly dialectal forms (because these, not being shared by and understandable to many other speakers, tend to be communicatively unsuccessful and thus lost)

labial   a place of articulation for consonants in the mouth, involving lips

labiodental   a place of articulation for consonants in the mouth, involving the lower lips and upper teeth

language shift   the case that a (typically socially inferior) group gives up their ancestral language altogether and adopts another language (typically the dominant one) as their own

lexifier   a language which in a language contact situation provides most of the vocabulary to a newly emerging mixed or contact language variety

lexis   the word stock of a language, its vocabulary (viewed as a level of language organization equivalent to phonology and grammar)

lingua franca   a language used to communicate between speakers who speak different languages as their mother tongues

loan (words)   elements of one language (usually words) which come to be regularly used in another, typically with some phonetic adjustment

marker   a form (typically a ⇒ morpheme) expressing some grammatical category

mass nouns   nouns which have the property of being ⇒ uncountable, e.g. *butter*

Middle English   the period of the English language in the Middle Ages, roughly from the Norman Conquest of 1066 to the fifteenth century

modifier/-fy   a (group of) word(s) embedded in a phrase which is syntactically not obligatory and provides additional (but not necessary) information; ⇒ premodifier, postmodifier, for examples

monophthong   a single, pure vowel (as opposed to a ⇒ diphthong), e.g. /ɪ/ in *hit* or /iː/ in *heat*

monotransitive   the grammatical property of certain verbs to require or allow a single, direct object, mostly directly following the verb, as in *watching this movie*; a kind of verb ⇒ complementation

morpheme   smallest meaningful entity in any language, such that it can be identified by combining (largely) the same form (sound sequence) and (largely) the same meaning in all of its occurrences (e.g. *wife/wive-* 'married female', *-ed* '(referring to a state or activity) occurred at a past point in time')

morphology   the study of how complex words are build of smaller, meaningful entities (⇒ morphemes), typically subdivided into grammatical morphology or inflection (e.g. *want-ed*, *girl-s*) and lexical morphology or word-formation (e.g. *un-happy*, *text-book*)

mother tongue   the language first and naturally acquired by an infant at an early age

multilingual(ism)   regular use (and full command) of more than two languages, by individuals or speech communities

multiple negation   a grammatical construction marked by two or more negatives in a single clause, e.g. *I don't have no money*; considered nonstandard in English

nasal   a group of consonantal sounds articulated with a complete closure of the mouth and the airstream fully escaping through the nose; in English, /m/ (with a bilabial closure), /n/ (alveolar), and /ŋ/ (velar)

nativization   the process of a language variety developing local characteristics; the central stage in the evolutionary "Dynamic Model" shifting from exonormativity to endonormativity

native speaker   a speaker who has acquired a given language as his or her mother tongue, in earliest childhood

neutralization   a tendency for distinct sounds (phonemes) to be articulated identically in certain contexts

non-rhotic   an accent in which a ⇒ "postvocalic r" is not pronounced at all

norm   a form of a language established as the target of language education and correctness of usage

noun   a major grammatical class of words, e.g. *cat, computer, mountain, peace*. Most nouns have (unmarked) singular and plural (typically marked with a suffix *-s*) forms; they function as heads of noun phrases (and thus in a sentence typically as subject or object); concrete nouns are said to denote "things" (though many abstract ones do not).

noun phrase   a ⇒ phrase with a noun as head and performing a nominal function (typically, subject, object, or complement to a preposition) in a clause, e.g. *The old man was crying*, *With a little effort you can climb this mountain*

object   a core constituent of a sentence, obligatorily required by certain ("transitive") verbs, mostly following the predicate and typically nominal or clausal, e.g. *I'm reading a book*, *I know that it is raining*, with the sub-types of ⇒ direct and ⇒ indirect object

Old English   the earliest period of the English language (also called Anglo-Saxon), roughly from the earliest Germanic settlement in 449 to the Norman Conquest of 1066

palatal   a place of articulation for consonants in the mouth; articulated at the palate, the hard bone in the middle of the roof of the oral cavity

peripheral (vowels)   articulated at the margins (the periphery) of the oral space, as against relatively more central articulation positions of the tongue; e.g. [i] vs. [ɪ], and [u] vs. [ʊ]

phoneme   a sound which in any given language is systematically important, an element of the sound ⇒ system of that language with which it builds its words

phonetic   having to do with ⇒ phonetics

phonetic characters (symbols)   special symbols devised to represent individual sounds (⇒ phonemes) on paper. Do not confuse them with letters: Letters do this as well but highly imperfectly because there is no one-to-one relationship between letters and sounds. The same sound may be represented by different letters (e.g. /f/ by "f" in *fill* but by "gh" in *laugh*), and the same letter may represent different sounds ("o" may mean /ʊ/ in *wolf*, /ʌ/ in *son*, and /ɪ/ in *women*). See Appendix 1 for the phonetic characters employed in this book.

phonetics   the description of human speech sounds, by working out the movements made in producing them inside one's mouth, usually with attention to articulatory detail

phonological   having to do with ⇒ phonology

phonology   the study of the sound ⇒ system of any given language, which assumes that out of the infinite set of sound productions every human language builds upon a limited number of recognizable sounds which it uses to build its words (the ⇒ phonemes)

phonotactics   rules of any specific language as to how sounds can be combined to form words, e.g. on how many consonants in a row are permissible

phrase   a group of words (without a clausal structure) which together fulfill a syntactic function, with a head word which defines the phrase status; ⇒ noun phrase for an example

plosive   ⇒ stop

plural   a grammatical category of (primarily) nouns, indicating that more than one entity is referred to, as against the singular, typically expressed in English by means of an *-s* ending on nouns, e.g. *one cat* (singular) vs. *many cat-s* (plural)

postmodifier   a ⇒ modifier following its head word, e.g. *the man in the garden*

postvocalic r   the sound /r/ when occurring after a vowel and either at the end of words or syllables (as in *car* or *energy*) or before a consonant (as in *card* or *fourth*), but not between vowels (as in *borrow*)

pragmatic(s)   sub-discipline of linguistics; the study of language use in context, including aspects such as situational reference, politeness, conversational conventions, etc.

predicate   a core constituent of a sentence and obligatory syntactic function, typically verbal, following the subject (in affirmative sentences), and expressing an activity or state, as in *The dogs were barking* (though all of these properties can be altered)

prefix ⇒ morpheme appended in front of a word, typically to coin a new word (e.g. *dis+appear*)

premodifier a ⇒ modifier preceding its head word, e.g. *an old man*

prenominal standing before a ⇒ noun

preposition a word class, e.g. *with, in, after, for*; typically introducing (and together with a following noun phrase building) a ⇒ preposition phrase and expressing a relational (temporal, local, …) meaning

preposition phrase a ⇒ phrase which typically consists of a ⇒ preposition and a following ⇒ noun phrase and fills an ⇒ adverbial function in a clause or sentence, e.g. *after this incident, on the road, with a knife*

preverbal standing before a ⇒ verb

pro-drop syntactic property (rule) of some languages and dialects of allowing sentences without a subject (assumed as resulting from a pronoun which was dropped), e.g. Singaporean *Can.*

proposition the meaning of a ⇒ clause (or sentence), typically consisting of a (verbal) predication and one or more (nominal) arguments (subject, object, etc.)

question tag ⇒ tag question

quotative expression introducing the exact rendition of direct speech, e.g. *He said* "…"; typically verbs of speaking

reduplication doubling a form, typically to intensify its meaning, e.g. *small small* 'very small'

relative clause a ⇒ clause which is embedded in a ⇒ noun phrase and ⇒ postmodifies the ⇒ head noun, e.g. *the man who collected the bill*

relative pronoun in a ⇒ relative clause the word (a pronoun, typically *who, which,* or *that*) which connects the clause to its head noun (and represents it semantically in the clause), e.g. *the man who collected the bill*

relativizer a function word introducing and connecting a relative clause, typically a relative pronoun, as in *my friend who helped me*

rhotic an accent in which a ⇒ postvocalic r is audibly pronounced

schwa a central vowel (the first one in *about* or the last one in *father*), transcribed as /ə/, which is always unstressed in English

second person a grammatical category referring to or including the addressee, typically expressed by the pronoun *you*

semi-vowel a class of sounds which are basically consonants but resemble vowels in some respects; in English, /j/ as in *you* and /w/ as in *water*

shift ⇒ language shift

singular a grammatical category of (primarily) nouns, indicating that precisely one entity is referred to; opposite of ⇒ plural

sociolinguistics a sub-discipline of linguistics which emphasizes the social conditions of language usage, e.g. the real-life preferred usage of certain forms by specific speaker groups defined by parameters such as gender, age, or class, but also social issues such as language policy

standard a form of a language which is conventionally considered "correct" or "proper," appropriate for formal and public usage, in a community

stop a class of ⇒ consonants, characterized by the air stream from the lungs being very briefly interrupted by a momentary closure somewhere in the oral cavity, as in /t/ or /b/

stress-timing a rhythmic articulation pattern such that, irrespective of the number of syllables in between, the amount of time between two stresses is roughly equal, so that unstressed syllables tend to be strongly reduced. Typical of native varieties such as British English.

subject a core constituent of a sentence and obligatory syntactic function, typically nominal, preceding a predicate (in affirmative sentences) and referring to an agent, as in *The dogs were barking* (though all of these properties can be altered)

substrate in language contact, creolization and ⇒ language shift, the language of the socially inferior group which is gradually given up but in this process is assumed to exert some influence on the newly adopted language through the transfer of some of its properties

suffix ⇒ morpheme added to a word at the end, e.g. *-dom* in *kingdom*, *-s* in *cats*

superstrate in language contact, creolization and ⇒ language shift, the language of the socially superior group, assumed to be the target of language acquisition and shift

SVO order word order rule which states that in an affirmative sentence with a subject, a predicate, and a direct object, the constituent order subject–verb–object is fixed, e.g. *The dog*[S] *chases*[V] *the cat*[O].

syllable-timing a rhythmic articulation pattern such that each syllable takes an approximately equal amount of time; considered typical of New Englishes

syntax the set of rules which regulate how words combine to form well-formed sentences (e.g. which word classes there are, which sequences of words are permitted, or how one pattern can be transformed into another)

system the idea that a language consists of units of whatever kind (sounds, words, phrases, sentences, etc.) which work together to build higher-order units (with sounds building words, words building phrases, etc.) and thus a structured relationship between these units

tabula rasa Latin for 'blank slate', a state without any pre-existing input; in the present context, typically the assumption that a migrant community coming to a new (uninhabited, or assumed to be so) territory builds upon their own resources only to develop a new (linguistic) norm

tag question a short interrogative word sequence (typically consisting of an auxiliary and a pronoun subject) appended to a main clause, usually to seek confirmation, e.g. *You are coming, aren't you?*

third person a grammatical category referring to an entity under discussion, typically expressed by a pronoun (*she, it, they*) or (as a subject) a noun phrase (*my friend, many people*)

transcript the fixing of sounds (pronunciation) in a text or utterance on paper by means of ⇒ phonetic characters

transfer a process in which properties (structures, sound patterns, also words) of one language (typically a substrate language in a process of language shift) are inadvertently retained when acquiring another language, so that the adopted language is slightly modified, acquiring features derived from the original language

transitive the grammatical property of certain verbs to require or allow an object, mostly directly following the verb, as in *to ask a question*; a kind of verb ⇒ complementation

uncountable   a grammatical property of some nouns which do not accept plurals, numerals, and indefinite articles because they denote entities which are "masses" and cannot be counted individually

variability   the fact that the realization of language forms is always slightly different from one instance to another, depending upon social, situational, and other factors; i.e., that there are "different ways of saying (encoding) the same thing"

variation   variability as a fundamental property of and approach to studying language

variety   any specific, complete type of a language with distinctive properties on the levels of vocabulary, pronunciation, and grammar; similar to "dialect" but more neutral, avoiding evaluative connotations

velar   a place of articulation for consonants in the mouth; articulated at the velum, the soft tissue in the back of the roof of the oral cavity

verb   a major grammatical word class, subdivided into ⇒ auxiliaries and full verbs, e.g. *run, cry, talk, think*. Full verbs have a past tense form, take a third person singular *-s* ending, and form the predicate of a clause or sentence; they are said to denote actions, events, or states.

vocalization   a consonant (typically /r/ or /l/) is not articulated as such but "as a vowel," having merged with the previous vowel, e.g. *card* /ka:d/, *old* /ɔʊd/

voiceless   property of some consonants of being articulated without vibrating vocal chords, as opposed to ⇒ voicing / voiced sounds

voicing   the articulatory movement of vibration in the vocal chords, producing voiced sounds (i.e. all vowels and some consonants, e.g. /v/, /z/, /g/ as against unvoiced /f/, /s/, /k/)

vowels   a major class of sounds, characterized by the fact that the air stream from the lungs comes out freely through the open mouth (though it is modulated by the degree of opening and by how the tongue is shaped, yielding different vowels like /i/, /e/, /a/ or /u/).

word class   a set of words which share important grammatical properties, i.e. behave (largely) identically in building sentences and accept the same endings (e.g. nouns, verbs, prepositions, etc.)

word formation   the process of building new complex words (thus enriching the vocabulary of a language) by various systematic processes, e.g. combining simple words (*text+book*) or prefixes and simple words (*un+happy*); usually considered a branch of ⇒ morphology

References

Adamson, Bob. 2004. *China's English: A History of English in Chinese Education.* Hong Kong: Hong Kong University Press.

Aitchison, Jean. 2001. *Language Change: Progress or Decay?* 3rd edn. Cambridge: Cambridge University Press.

Algeo, John, ed. 2001. *The Cambridge History of the English Language.* Vol. VI: *English in North America.* Cambridge: Cambridge University Press.

2006. *British or American English? A Handbook of Word and Grammar Patterns.* Cambridge: Cambridge University Press.

Bailey, Guy. 1997. "When did Southern English begin?" In Edgar W. Schneider, ed. 1997. *Englishes Around the World.* Vol. I: *General Studies, British Isles, North America. Studies in Honour of Manfred Görlach.* Amsterdam, Philadelphia, PA: Benjamins, 255–75.

Barber, Charles. 2000. *The English Language: A Historical Introduction.* Cambridge: Cambridge University Press.

Bao, Zhiming. 2005. "The aspectual system of Singapore English and the systemic substratist explanation." *Journal of Linguistics* 41: 237–67.

Baugh, Albert C., and Thomas Cable. 2002. *A History of the English Language.* 5th edn. London: Routledge.

Bautista, Maria Lourdes S., ed. 1997. *English Is an Asian Language: The Philippine Context. Proceedings of the Conference Held in Manila on August 2–3, 1996.* Sydney: Macquarie Library Ltd.

Bell, Allan, and Koenraad Kuiper, eds. 2000. *New Zealand English.* Amsterdam, Philadelphia, PA: Benjamins.

Biermeier, Thomas. 2008. *Word-Formation in New Englishes: A Corpus-based Analysis.* Berlin: Lit Verlag.

Blair, David, and Peter Collins, eds. 2001. *English in Australia.* Amsterdam, Philadelphia, PA: Benjamins.

Bolton, Kingsley, ed. 2002. *Hong Kong English: Autonomy and Creativity.* Hong Kong: Hong Kong University Press.

2003. *Chinese Englishes: A Sociolinguistic History.* Cambridge: Cambridge University Press.

Bolton, Kingsley, and Braj B. Kachru, eds. 2006. *World Englishes: Critical Concepts in Linguistics.* 6 vols. London: Routledge.

Brutt-Griffler, Janina. 2002. *World English: A Study of its Development.* Clevedon: Multilingual Matters.

Burridge, Kate, and Bernd Kortmann, eds. 2008. *Varieties of English.* Vol. III: *The Pacific and Australasia.* Berlin, New York: Mouton de Gruyter.

Carver, Craig. 1987. *American Regional Dialects: A Word Geography*. Ann Arbor: University of Michigan Press.

Cassidy, Frederic G., Joan Hall, *et al.* 1986–2002. *Dictionary of American Regional English*. Vol. I (A–C); Vol. II (D–H); Vol. III (I–O); Vol. IV (P–Sk). Cambridge, MA: Belknap Press of Harvard University Press.

Chambers, J. K. 2003. *Sociolinguistic Theory*. 2nd edn. Malden, MA, Oxford: Blackwell.

Chambers, J. K., and Peter Trudgill. 1998. *Dialectology*. 2nd edn. Cambridge: Cambridge University Press.

Christie, Pauline. 2003. *Language in Jamaica*. Kinston: Arawak.

Crystal, David. 1988. *The English Language*. London: Penguin Books.

2003. *English as a Global Language*. 2nd edn. Cambridge: Cambridge University Press.

2004. *The Language Revolution*. Cambridge, Malden, MA: Polity Press.

2008. "Two thousand million? Updates on the statistics of English." *English Today 93* 24: 3–6.

Dalziel, Nigel. 2006. *The Penguin Historical Atlas of the British Empire*. London: Penguin Books.

D'Costa, Jean, and Barbara Lalla, eds. 1989. *Voices in Exile: Jamaican Texts of the 18th and 19th Centuries*. Tuscaloosa: University of Alabama Press.

de Klerk, Vivian, ed. 1996. *Focus on South Africa*. Amsterdam, Philadelphia, PA: Benjamins.

Delbridge, Arthur, *et al.* 1981. *The Macquarie Dictionary*. Sydney: Macquarie Library.

Deterding, David. 2007. *Singapore English*. Edinburgh: Edinburgh University Press.

Deuber, Dagmar. 2005. *Nigerian Pidgin in Lagos: Language Contact, Variation and Change in an African Urban Setting*. London: Battlebridge.

Fennell, Barbara A. 2001. *A History of English: A Sociolinguistic Approach*. Oxford, Malden, MA: Blackwell.

Fishman, Joshua A., Andrew W. Conrad, and Alma Rubal-Lopez, eds. 1996. *Post-Imperial English: Status Change in Former British and American Colonies 1940–1990*. Berlin, New York: Mouton de Gruyter.

Folkes, Paul, and Gerard Docherty, eds. 1999. *Urban Voices: Accent Studies in the British Isles*. London: Arnold.

Francis, W. Nelson. 1983. *Dialectology: An Introduction*. New York: Longman.

Gardner-Chloros, Penelope. 2009. *Code-switching*. Cambridge: Cambridge University Press.

Gill, Saran Kaur. 2002. *International Communication: English Language Challenges for Malaysia*. Serdang: Universiti Putra Malaysia.

Gordon, Elizabeth, Lyle Campbell, Jennifer Hay, Margaret Maclagan, Andrea Sudbury, and Peter Trudgill. 2004. *New Zealand English: Its Origins and Evolution*. Cambridge: Cambridge University Press.

Gordon, Elizabeth, and Tony Deverson. 1998. *New Zealand English and English in New Zealand*. Auckland: New House.

Graddol, David. 1997. *The Future of English: A Guide to Forecasting the Popularity of English in the 21st Century*. London: British Council.

2010. *English Next India*. London: British Council.

Green, Lisa J. 2002. *African American English: A Linguistic Introduction*. Cambridge: Cambridge University Press.

Gupta, Anthea Fraser. 1997. "Colonisation, migration, and functions of English." In Edgar W. Schneider, ed. *Englishes Around the World*. Vol. I: *General Studies, British Isles, North America. Studies in Honour of Manfred Görlach*. Amsterdam, Philadelphia: Benjamins, 47–58.

Hackert, Stephanie. 2009. "The native speaker in World Englishes: A chapter in nineteenth-century linguistic thought." University of Regensburg Habilitationsschrift.

Hay, Jennifer, Margaret Maclagan, and Elizabeth Gordon. 2008. *New Zealand English*. Edinburgh: Edinburgh University Press.

Hickey, Raymond, ed. 2004. *Legacies of Colonial English: Studies in Transported Dialects*. Cambridge: Cambridge University Press.

Jowitt, David. 1991. *Nigerian English Usage: An Introduction*. Ikeja: Longman Nigeria.

Kachru, Braj B., ed. 1992. *The Other Tongue: English across Cultures*. 2nd edn. Urbana, Chicago: University of Illinois Press.

2005. *Asian Englishes: Beyond the Canon*. Hong Kong: Hong Kong University Press.

Kachru, Braj, Yamuna Kachru, and Cecil Nelson, eds. 2006. *The Handbook of World Englishes*. Malden, MA: Blackwell.

Kachru, Yamuna, and Cecil L. Nelson. 2006. *World Englishes in Asian Contexts*. Hong Kong: Hong Kong University Press.

Kirkpatrick, Andy. 2007. *World Englishes: Implications for International Communication and English Language Teaching*. Cambridge: Cambridge University Press.

Kortmann, Bernd, Kate Burridge, Rajend Mesthrie, Edgar W. Schneider, and Clive Upton, eds. 2004. *A Handbook of Varieties of English*. Vol. II: *Morphology and Syntax*. Berlin, New York: Mouton de Gruyter.

Kortmann, Bernd, and Clive Upton, eds. 2008. *Varieties of English*. Vol. I: *The British Isles*. Berlin, New York: Mouton de Gruyter.

Kretzschmar, William R., Jr. 2009. *The Linguistics of Speech*. Cambridge: Cambridge University Press.

Kurath, Hans. 1949. *A Word Geography of the Eastern United States*. Ann Arbor: University of Michigan Press.

Labov, William. 1972. *Sociolinguistic Patterns*. Philadelphia: University of Pennsylvania Press.

Labov, William, Sharon Ash, and Charles Boberg. 2006. *The Atlas of North American English: Phonetics, Phonology and Sound Change*. Berlin, New York: Mouton de Gruyter.

Lalla, Barbara, and Jean D'Costa. 1990. *Language in Exile: Three Hundred Years of Jamaican Creole*. Tuscaloosa, London: University of Alabama Press.

Leitner, Gerhard. 2004. *Australia's Many Voices*. Vol. I: *Australian English – The National Language*. Vol. II: *Ethnic Englishes, Indigenous and Migrant Languages: Policy and Education*. Berlin, New York: Mouton de Gruyter.

Lim, Lisa, ed. 2004. *Singapore English: A Grammatical Description*. Amsterdam, Philadelphia: Benjamins.

Low Ee Ling and Adam Brown. 2005. *English in Singapore: An Introduction*. Singapore: McGraw-Hill Asia.

Mazrui, Alamin M., and Ali A. Mazrui. 1996. "A tale of two Englishes: The imperial language in post-colonial Kenya and Uganda." In Fishman, Joshua A., *et al.*, eds. 1996. *Post-Imperial English: Status Change in Former British and American Colonies 1940–1990*. Berlin, New York: Mouton de Gruyter, 271–302.

McArthur, Tom. 1998. *The English Languages*. Cambridge: Cambridge University Press.
　　2002. *Oxford Guide to World English*. Oxford: Oxford University Press.

McCully, Chris. 2009. *The Sound Structure of English: An Introduction*. Cambridge: Cambridge University Press.

McMahon, April M. S. 1994. *Understanding Language Change*. Cambridge: Cambridge University Press.

Mehrotra, Raja Ram. 1998. *Indian English: Texts and Interpretation*. Amsterdam, Philadelphia: Benjamins.

Melchers, Gunnel, and Philip Shaw. 2003. *World Englishes: An Introduction*. London: Arnold.

Mencken, H. L. 1963 [1919]. *The American Language: An Inquiry into the Development of English in the United States*. One-volume abridged edn. by Raven I. McDavid, Jr. New York: Alfred Knopf. Repr. 1982.

Mesthrie, Rajend, ed. 2002. *Language in South Africa*. Cambridge: Cambridge University Press.
　　2006. "Anti-deletions in an L2 grammar: A study of Black South African English mesolect." *English World-Wide* 27: 111–45.
　　ed. 2008. *Varieties of English*. Vol. IV: *Africa, South and Southeast Asia*. Berlin, New York: Mouton de Gruyter.

Mesthrie, Rajend, and Rakesh Bhatt. 2008. *World Englishes*. Cambridge: Cambridge University Press.

Mitchell, Alexander G., and Arthur Delbridge. 1965. *The Speech of Australian Adolescents: A Survey*. Sydney: Angus & Robertson.

Moore, Bruce. 2001. "Australian English: Australian identity." In Bruce Moore, ed., *"Who's Centric Now?" The Present State of Post-Colonial Englishes*. South Melbourne: Oxford University Press, 44–58.
　　2008. *Speaking Our Language: The Story of Australian English*. Melbourne, Oxford: Oxford University Press.

Mufwene, Salikoko S. 2001. *The Ecology of Language Evolution*. Cambridge: Cambridge University Press.

Mühlhäusler, Peter, Thomas E. Dutton, and Suzanne Romaine. 2003. *Tok Pisin Texts: From the Beginning to the Present*. Amsterdam, Philadelphia: Benjamins.

Mukherjee, Joybrato, and Sebastian Hoffmann. 2006. "Describing verb-complementational profiles of New Englishes: A pilot study of Indian English." *English World-Wide* 27: 147–73.

Myers-Scotton, Carol. 2002. *Contact Linguistics. Bilingual Encounters and Grammatical Outcomes*. Oxford: Oxford University Press.

Nagle, Stephen J., and Sara L. Sanders, eds. 2003. *English in the Southern United States*. Cambridge: Cambridge University Press.

Obiechina, Emmanuel N., ed. 1972. *Onitsha Market Literature* (African Writers Series). London: Heinemann.

Orsman, Elizabeth, and Harry Orsman. 1994. *The New Zealand Dictionary*. Educational Edition. Takapuna: New House.

Orton, Harold, *et al.* 1962–71. *The Survey of English Dialects: The Basic Material.* Introduction and 4 volumes in 12 parts. Leeds: E. J. Arnold.

Orton, Harold, Stewart Sanderson, and John Widdowson, eds. 1978. *The Linguistic Atlas of England.* London: Croom Helm.

Pederson, Lee, *et al.* 1986–91. *Linguistic Atlas of the Gulf States.* 7 vols. Athens, GA: University of Georgia Press.

Pennycook, Alastair. 2007. *Global Englishes and Transcultural Flows.* London, New York: Routledge.

Peters, Pam, Peter Collins, and Adam Smith, eds. 2009. *Comparative Studies in Australian and New Zealand English: Grammar and Beyond.* Amsterdam, Philadelphia: Benjamins.

Phillipson, Robert. 1992. *Linguistic Imperialism.* Oxford: Oxford University Press.

Platt, John, Heidi Weber, and Mian Lian Ho. 1984. *The New Englishes.* London: Routledge & Kegan Paul.

Quirk, Randolph, Sidney Greenbaum, Geoffrey Leech, and Jan Svartvik. 1985. *A Comprehensive Grammar of the English Language.* London, New York: Longman.

Roberts, Peter A. 1988. *West Indians and Their Language.* Cambridge: Cambridge University Press.

Rohdenburg, Günter, and Julia Schlüter. 2009. *One Language, Two Grammars? Differences between British and American English.* Cambridge: Cambridge University Press.

Sailaja, Pingali. 2009. *Indian English.* Edinburgh: Edinburgh University Press.

Sakoda, Kent, and Jeff Siegel. 2003. *Pidgin Grammar: An Introduction to the Creole Language of Hawai'i.* Honolulu: Bess Press.

Schäfer, Ronald P., and Francis O. Egbokhare. 1999. "English and the pace of endangerment in Nigeria." *World Englishes* 18: 381–91.

Schmied, Josef J. 1991. *English in Africa: An Introduction.* London, New York: Longman.

Schneider, Edgar W. 1990. "The cline of creoleness in English-oriented creoles and semi-creoles of the Caribbean." *English World-Wide* 11: 79–113.

    ed. 1997. *Englishes Around the World.* Vol. I: *General Studies, British Isles, North America.* Vol. II: *Caribbean, Africa, Asia, Australasia. Studies in Honour of Manfred Görlach.* Amsterdam, Philadelphia, PA: Benjamins.

    2003. "The dynamics of New Englishes: From identity construction to dialect birth." *Language* 79: 233–81.

    2004. "The English dialect heritage of the Southern United States." In Raymond Hickey, ed., *Legacies of Colonial English.* Cambridge: Cambridge University Press, 262–309.

    2007a. *Postcolonial English: Varieties Around the World.* Cambridge: Cambridge University Press.

    2007b. "Language, humour and gender in Ali G's *Innit.*" In Helge Nowak, ed., *Comedy and Gender: Essays in Honour of Dieter A. Berger.* Heidelberg: Winter, 217–32.

    ed. 2008. *Varieties of English.* Vol. II: *The Americas and the Caribbean.* Berlin, New York: Mouton de Gruyter.

2009. "New Englishes, new norms: Growth and maturity in languages." In Christopher Ward, ed. *Language Teaching in a Multilingual World: Challenges and Opportunities*. Singapore: SEAMEO Regional Language Centre, 191–214.

Schneider, Edgar W., Kate Burridge, Bernd Kortmann, Rajend Mesthrie, and Clive Upton, eds. 2004. *A Handbook of Varieties of English*. Vol. I: *Phonology*. Berlin, New York: Mouton de Gruyter.

Schneider, Edgar W., and Christian Wagner. 2006. "The variability of literary dialect in Jamaican Creole: Thelwell's *The Harder They Come*." *Journal of Pidgin and Creole Languages* 21: 45–95.

Schreier, Daniel. 2003. *Isolation and Language Change: Contemporary and Sociohistorical Evidence from Tristan da Cunha English*. Houndmills: Palgrave Macmillan.

2005. *Consonant Change in English Worldwide: Synchrony Meets Diachrony*. Houndmills, New York: Palgrave Macmillan.

2008. *St Helenian English: Origins, Evolution and Variation*. Amsterdam, Philadelpia: Benjamins.

Schreier, Daniel, and Karen Lavarello-Schreier. 2003. *Tristan da Cunha: History, People, Language*. London: Battlebridge.

Sedlatschek, Andreas. 2009. *Contemporary Indian English: Change and Variation*. Amsterdam, Philadelphia, PA: Benjamins.

Seidlhofer, Barbara, ed. 2003. *Controversies in Applied Linguistics*. Oxford: Oxford University Press.

Simo Bobda, Augustin. 2003. "The formation of regional and national features in African English pronunciation: An exploration of some non-interference factors." *English World-Wide* 24: 17–42.

Simonson, Douglas. 1981. *Pidgin To Da Max*. Honolulu: Beppovision/Bess Press.

Smith, Geoff. 2002. *Growing Up with Tok Pisin: Contact, Creolization and Change in Papua New Guinea's National Language*. London: Battlebridge.

Stanlaw, James. 2004. *Japanese English: Language and Culture Contact*. Hong Kong: Hong Kong University Press.

Thomason, Sarah G. 2001. *Language Contact: An Introduction*. Washington, DC: Georgetown University Press.

Thomason, Sarah Grey, and Terrence Kaufman. 1988. *Language Contact, Creolization and Genetic Linguistics*. Berkeley, Los Angeles: University of California Press.

Thompson, Roger M. 2003. *Filipino English and Taglish: Language Switching from Multiple Perspectives*. Amsterdam, Philadelphia, PA: Benjamins.

Tottie, Gunnel. 2002. *An Introduction to American English*. Malden, MA, Oxford: Blackwell.

Tristram, Hildegard, ed. 1997–2006. *The Celtic Englishes I – IV*. Heidelberg: Winter; Potsdam: Universitätsverlag.

Trudgill, Peter. 1990. *The Dialects of England*. Cambridge, MA: Blackwell.

2004. *New-Dialect Formation: The Inevitability of Colonial Englishes*. Edinburgh: Edinburgh University Press.

Tryon, Darrell T., and Jean Michel Charpentier. 2004. *Pacific Pidgins and Creoles: Origins, Growth, and Development*. Berlin, New York: Mouton de Gruyter.

Turner, George W. 1966. *The English Language in Australia and New Zealand*. London: Longmans.

Upton, Clive, and J. D. A. Widdowson. 2006. *An Atlas of English Dialects*. London: Taylor & Francis.

Vaish, Viniti. 2008. *Biliteracy and Globalization: English Language Education in India*. Clevedon: Multilingual Matters.

Wales, Katie. 2006. *Northern English: A Social and Cultural History*. Cambridge: Cambridge University Press.

Wee, Lionel. 2003. "The birth of a particle: *know* in Singapore English." *World Englishes* 22: 5–13.

Williams, Jessica. 1987. "Non-native varieties of English: A special case of language acquisition." *English World-Wide* 8: 161–99.

Wiltshire, Caroline. 2005. "The 'Indian English' of Tibeto-Burman language speakers." *English World-Wide* 26: 275–300.

Winford, Donald. 2003. *An Introduction to Contact Linguistics*. Malden, MA, Oxford: Blackwell.

Wolfram, Walt, and Natalie Schilling-Estes. 2005. *American English: Dialects and Variation*. 2nd edn. Malden, MA, Oxford: Blackwell.

Wolfram, Walt, and Ben Ward, eds. 2006. *American Voices: How Dialects Differ from Coast to Coast*. Malden, MA: Blackwell.

Index

Made in the USA
Lexington, KY
01 September 2017